Sidney to Milton, 1580-1660

transitions

General Editor: Julian Wolfreys

---

transitions Series
Series Standing Order ISBN 0–333–73684–6
(*outside North America only*)

You can receive future titles in this series as they are published by
placing a standing order. Please contact your bookseller or, in case of
difficulty, write to us at the address below with your name and address,
the title of the series and the ISBN quoted above.

Customer Services Department, Macmillan Distribution Ltd
Houndmills, Basingstoke, Hampshire RG21 6XS, England

---

transitions

Sidney to Milton, 1580–1660

Marion Wynne-Davies

First published 2003 by
PALGRAVE MACMILLAN
Houndmills, Basingstoke, Hampshire RG21 6XS and
175 Fifth Avenue, New York, N.Y. 10010
Companies and representatives throughout the world

PALGRAVE MACMILLAN is the global academic imprint of the Palgrave Macmillan division of St. Martin's Press, LLC and of Palgrave Macmillan Ltd. Macmillan® is a registered trademark in the United States, United Kingdom and other countries. Palgrave is a registered trademark in the European Union and other countries.

ISBN 0–333–69618–2 hardback
ISBN 0–333–69619–0 paperback

This book is printed on paper suitable for recycling and made from fully managed and sustained forest sources.

A catalogue record for this book is available from the British Library.

Library of Congress Cataloging-in-Publication Data
Wynne-Davies, Marion.
    Sidney to Milton, 1580–1660 / Marion Wynne-Davies.
        p. cm. — (Transitions)
    Includes bibliographical references and index.
    ISBN 0-333-69618-2
        1. English literature—Early modern, 1500–1700—History and criticism.
2. Sidney, Philip, Sir, 1554–1586—Criticism and interpretation. 3. Milton,
John, 1608–1674—Criticism and interpretation. I. Title. II. Transitions
(Palgrave Macmillan (Firm))

PR435 .W96 2002
821'.0309–dc21   2002026766

10 9 8 7 6 5 4 3 2 1
12 11 10 09 08 07 06 05 04 03

Printed in China

Contents

General Editor's Preface

Transitions: *transition*-, n. of action. 1. A passing or passage from one condition, action or (rarely) place, to another. 2. Passage in thought, speech, or writing, from one subject to another. 3. **a.** The passing from one note to another. **b.** The passing from one key to another, modulation. 4. The passage from an earlier to a later stage of development or formation . . . change from an earlier style to a later; a style of intermediate or mixed character . . . the historical passage of language from one well-defined stage to another.

The aim of *Transitions* is to explore passages and movements in language, literature and culture from Chaucer to the present day. The series also seeks to examine the ways in which the very idea of transition affects the reader's sense of period so as to address anew questions of literary history and periodisation. The writers in this series unfold the cultural and historical mediations of literature during what are commonly recognised as crucial moments in the development of English literature, addressing, as the OED puts it, the 'historical passage of language from one well-defined stage to another'.

Recognising the need to contextualise literary study, the authors offer close readings of canonical and now marginalised or overlooked literary texts from all genres, bringing to this study the rigour of historical knowledge and the sophistication of theoretically informed evaluations of writers and movements from the last 700 years. At the same time as each writer, whether Chaucer or Shakespeare, Milton or Pope, Byron, Dickens, George Eliot, Virginia Woolf or Salman Rushdie, is shown to produce his or her texts within a discernible historical, cultural, ideological and philosophical milieu, the text is read from the vantage point of recent theoretical interests and concerns. The purpose in bringing theoretical knowledge to the reading of a wide range of works is to demonstrate how the literature is always open to transition, whether in the instance of its production or in succeeding moments of its critical reception.

The series desires to enable the reader to transform her/his own reading and writing transactions by comprehending past developments. Each book in the second tranche of the series offers a pedagogical guide to the poetics and politics of particular eras, as well as to the subsequent critical comprehension of periods and periodisation. As well as transforming the cultural and literary past by interpreting its transition from the perspective of the critical and theoretical present, each study enacts transitional readings of a number of literary texts, all of which are themselves conceivable as having effected transition at the moments of their first appearance. The readings offered in these books seek, through close critical reading, historical contextualisation and theoretical engagement, to demonstrate certain possibilities in reading to the student reader.

It is hoped that the student will find this series liberating because the series seeks to move beyond rigid definitions of period. What is important is the sense of passage, of motion. Rather than providing a definitive model of literature's past, *Transitions* aims to place you in an active dialogue with the writing and culture of other eras, so as to comprehend not only how the present reads the past, but how the past can read the present.

Julian Wolfreys

Acknowledgements

This book is the product of many years of accumulated teaching, research and discussions with colleagues. As such, my thanks are due to those students, fellow departmental and library staff I worked with from the University of Liverpool, Lancaster University, Keele University, and the University of Dundee. Of these there are a few to whom I am particularly grateful for their advice on the authors discussed in this book: Brean Hammond who generously shared his ideas on Thomas Middleton; Ann Thompson whose edition of *The Taming of the Shrew* brought about a re-evaluation of my understanding of that play; Helen Wilcox who first interested me in autobiographical works; Roger Pooley who helped me appreciate the power of Early Modern prose; Alison Easton who focused my work on Early Modern women writers; Richard Dutton who encouraged my work on Shakespeare; and David Robb for his tenacious belief in the project.

Beyond my colleagues I owe thanks to all those who as fellow researchers have enlightened my own work with their enthusiasm and erudition. Again those to whom a special debt in relation to the material discussed in this volume are: S. P. Cerasano, Fran Teague, Georgianna Ziegler, Alison Findlay, Stephanie Hodgson Wright, Gweno Williams, Douglas Brooks-Davies, Jim Stewart, Elizabeth Foyster and Rachel Jones. Above all I wish to thank those students past and present who have produced imaginative readings, responded enthusiastically to a range of obscure texts and, perhaps above all, told me when I was wrong.

Writing a book is often a long process and this one has assuredly been more delayed than either I or my series editor, Julian Wolfreys, would have wished. But Julian's support and his intelligent and erudite comments have been unflagging; my thanks to him and to my editor at Palgrave Macmillan, Anna Sandeman.

Finally, my thanks are due to my family. The selfless support of my husband, Geoff Ward, and the uncomprehending enthusiasm of my sons, Richard and Robbie, have provided invaluable sustenance. As always, this book is for them.

Marion Wynne-Davies
University of Dundee

Introduction

'The great movement which goes by the name of the Renascence'
(Matthew Arnold)

It was Matthew Arnold who first categorised English sixteenth- and seventeenth-century culture as the 'Renascence' (or 'Renaissance'), defining the period in terms of both 'great[ness]' and a unified artistic 'movement' (Arnold 1965, 172). Before Arnold's description, in his essay 'Herbraism and Hellenism', scholars would have recognised a certain commonality amongst writers and artists of the period, but there was no precise and mutually agreed definition. Certainly the term 'Renaissance' was known and used by writers of the time to signify the 'rebirth' of knowledge, the recovery of classical material made accessible to all through the advent of the printing press. Yet, the categorisation implied by Arnold's depiction of a rough parameter encompassing the period's literary production would have necessarily been unrecognised by those living and writing at that time. For example he decribes the period as:

> The Renascence, that great re-awakening of Hellenism, that irresistible return of humanity to nature and to seeing things as they are . . . in art [and] in literature. (Arnold 1965, 173)

Of course, the past is always organised and ordered by the present in order to make it more comprehensible, and present-day critics are equally as prone to such compartmentalising as Arnold. So that, as Arnold classified Shakespeare and his contemporaries as 'Renaissance' authors, so we in turn, refer to him as a 'Victorian' writer. Any representation of knowledge and analysis of historical material require a certain degree of such formulisation, yet at the same time it is important to read texts not only for conformity to periodisation, but for resistance to those defining boundaries. By rereading works within their historical contexts it is possible to identify traces of the cultural struggle that define a period, not as a static and harmonious whole, but as a series of changing discourses. This book sets out, therefore, not to define a 'great movement', but to illuminate a time of transformation and a culture in transition.

The chronological focus for this study begins in 1587 with the death of Philip Sidney and concludes in 1660, the year in which a common hangman publicly burned John Milton's books. At the same time, it examines the transition of literary genres, so that poetic discourses are traced from Thomas Wyatt's Petrarchan sonnets of the 1540s, through to Anne Bradstreet's New World reworking of the form in the 1660s and 70s. The period of dramatic production considered here is more curtailed, tracing the movement from the open-air theatres in the 1590s, to the development of small covered theatres in the 1620s. Finally, the prose works excavated provide parallels and changes from the Elizabethan texts of John Lyly and Thomas Nashe, and the post-Restoration pieces of Margaret Cavendish and John Bunyan. In this manner the boundaries of period are exposed as inadequate definitions of the very genres they attempt to explain. Yet there are mutualities of discourse that stretch across genre, location and time, which are acknowledged, utilised, altered and rejected, and it is the purpose of this book to elucidate these concerns and the relationships between them.

Chapter 1 examines the overall context of the period in relation to two writers, Elizabeth I and Philip Sidney. By analysing Elizabeth's own verse it becomes possible to highlight a number of the key political discourses of the day, looking at the role of the court and monarch, questions of authority and religious schism. Similar themes emerge through a reading of Philip Sidney's sonnet sequence, *Astrophil and Stella* and *An Apologie for Poetrie*. Indeed, the combination of the idea of Sidney as a courtly and refined writer together with texts that ostensibly set out to elevate moral and spiritual values, became a model for emulation and divergence over the subsequent century. The dialogic formulations suggested by Sidney's writings were far reaching, most notably evaluating pleasure and virtue, as well as tracing the development of poetic individualism against publicly accepted discourses. Yet Sidney's work, like that of Elizabeth I, also betrays a subtextual current that moves beyond cultural paradigms into the sphere of politics. It is, therefore, impossible to ignore the discourses of patronage, economic power and gender within works that proclaim themselves as solely concerned with literature. These are precisely the issues that this volume traces through the authors of the ensuing century, from the courtly discourse of the sonnet (Chapter 2), through the dynamics of the Renaissance stage (Chapter 3), to the upheavals of Early Modern prose fiction (Chapter 4).

In addition to the important cultural innovations during the period itself, over the last twenty years the 'Renaissance' has also been the focus for some of the most innovative and exciting theoretical developments in Western literary criticism. In 1980 Stephen Greenblatt published *Renaissance Self-Fashioning: From More to Shakespeare* and, although an interest in historicism had been increasing up to this point, it was this work that irrevocably changed critical approaches to Renaissance texts. Even the name of the period was to alter, as 'Early Modern' replaced 'Renaissance' in all the most up-to-date criticisms, ironically leaving Greenblatt's own innovative text looking slightly old fashioned in terms of its title. In the United States this theoretical trend identified itself as New Historicism, while in Britain a more politicised version was produced, called Cultural Materialism, from Jonathan Dollimore and Alan Sinfield's influential foreword to *Political Shakespeare*, where they emphasise a commitment to 'the transformation of a social order which exploits people on grounds of race, gender and class' (Dollimore and Sinfield 1985, viii). In terms of criticism, therefore, the Early Modern period has most recently become pre-eminent in the field of historical emphasis. This overwhelming trend has, of course, not gone unquestioned, with many critics asking what was so 'new' about New Historicism, and others questioning the very validity of such an exclusively historicist approach. As such, the present volume engages with certain aspects of a historicist and/or materialist approach, but it simultaneously questions the parameters of the new orthodoxy of historicism. For example, while Chapter 2 explores the idea of self-fashioning in relation to an analysis of Walter Ralegh's poetry, various theories are utilised in reading the works of other poets, such as feminism for Rachel Speght, Marxism for Michael Drayton and Postcolonial theory for Anne Bradstreet. In each case the theoretical interpretations are integrated into the overall analysis of the poet's contribution to a particular generic discourse alongside a close reading of particular texts.

From both a textual and a theoretical perspective it will now be apparent that the issue of periodisation will be a key area for discussion and exploration in this book. While areas of study are commonly delimited with historical events, the volume here focuses upon cultural issues, thereby creating an alternative 'history' of literature, which is bound to material concerns, but which also extends beyond a simple reflection of current circumstance. This awareness of the interplay between text and materiality also suggests a more fluid relationship between the past and our own time, for while we may excavate and uncover various historical details, we must simultaneously be aware that we can never escape our own periodisation. While historicists often suggest the need to retain this crucial self-awareness of temporal distance, in practice criticisms often become submerged in detail and fail to signpost sufficiently the difficulties encountered by present-day readers. This book calls attention to these slippages and to the deep recalcitrance of many Early Modern ideologies and literary devices for a postmodern reader. For example, although many women of the seventeenth century (e.g. Rachel Speght and Margaret Cavendish) published literary texts which demonstrated that they were aware of liberating a female voice, it would be wrong to interpret their writings as 'feminist' since such a political programme would have been deeply antithetical to their belief in a preordained hierarchy. Moreover, although today we often imagine these women as marginal writers because they have, until very recently, been excluded from our canon, this categorisation hardly corresponds with their actual status. By far the majority of Early Modern women writers (all in this volume) were from the noble or middle classes and their works often came out in several editions during their own lifetimes, mainly because of the social and economic influence their families were able to exert. In light of these challenges to conventional judgements on the period's literary productivity, this book includes rereadings of traditional material, alongside the uncovering of less well-known works. So that the poems of Philip Sidney are compared with those of Elizabeth I, and the sonnets of Spenser, Donne and Milton are read together with the verses of Drayton, Speght and James VI of Scotland. As such, each chapter focuses upon a specific genre in order to trace the way in which discourses shifted within their material location, but simultaneously notes the manner in which our own perceptions of texts have developed through a recognition of historical position and theoretical self-awareness.

While this volume focuses upon the immensity of change that occurred during the period we now commonly categorise as the Renaissance or Early Modern age, it would be reductive to assume that Matthew Arnold failed to note such radical cultural transitions. Indeed, Arnold annotates his use of the word 'Renascence' explaining that:

> I have ventured to give to the foreign word *Renaissance*, – destined to become of more common usage amongst us as the movement, which it denotes comes, as it will come, increasingly to interest us – an English form. (Arnold 1965, 172)

Even as Arnold specifies the literary term and its particular spelling, he simultaneously undercuts the stillness of static definition, by including at the centre of the sentence a phrase amplifying change and movement. To begin Arnold 'venture[s]', he refers to destiny and the future of our 'interest', and the movement, itself a bifurcating word implying both action and stasis, is denoted as com[ing]'. This seemingly contradictory emphasis, between content with its location of clear and defined meanings, and the vocabulary with its evocation of perpetual movement and lack of stability, may be explained in the context of the whole essay, 'Herbraism and Hellenism'.

At the beginning of this piece Arnold offers one of several definitions of the differences between 'these two points of influence [that] move . . . our world' (Arnold 1965, 163–4):

> Herbraism seizes upon certain plain, capital intimations of the Universal order, and rivets itself, one may say, with unequalled grandeur of earnestness and intensity on the study and observance of them, the best of Hellenism is to follow, with flexible activity, the whole play of the universal order, to be apprehensive of missing any part of it, of sacrificing one part to another, to slip away from resting in this or that intimation of it, however capital . . . the governing idea of Hellenism is *spontaneity of conscience*; that of Herbraism, *strictness of conscience*. (Arnold 1965, 165)

While there are, therefore, some parallels, the dominant argument of the essay distinguishes the differences between the two terms and what they represent. As we have seen, Arnold classifies the 'Renascence' as Hellenist, and he depicts the close of this period as a triumph of the Herbraist forces of Puritanism. In addition, however, he depicts these alternating forces as 'central current[s]' and 'side stream[s]' (Arnold 1965, 175) influencing our world, so that, at one time it feels more powerfully the attraction of one of them, at another time of the other; and it ought to be, though it never is, evenly and happily balanced between them. (Arnold 1965, 164)

Mathew Arnold might well have been interested in offering his own age definitions of their cultural heritage that enabled them to make sense of the radical changes which were occurring in their own age. But he simultaneously demanded that such categories – 'Hellenism', 'Herbraism', and 'Renascence' – be recognised as in perpetual flux. It is precisely this lack of balance, these radical transitions in cultural discourses that the present volume addresses.

1 Contexts

Elizabeth I

'The daughter of debate'
(Elizabeth I)

In many ways Queen Elizabeth I (1533–1603) could have been referring to herself when she spoke of the 'daughter of debate' in her short
poem, 'The Doubt of Future Foes' (Wynne-Davies 1998, 12). Indeed,
of all the political, religious and cultural debates to shake the country
during the sixteenth century it was surely the convoluted events that
surrounded Elizabeth's parentage that had the most resounding
impact and far-reaching repercussions. When Henry VIII finally
affirmed his determination to divorce his first wife, the Catholic
Queen Catherine, in order to marry Anne Boleyn with a view to
producing a male heir to the throne, the result was to be more schis-
matic than he could possibly have predicted. For Henry's marriage to
his new Protestant queen was to produce more than the swaddled
form of the young Princess Elizabeth. The English Protestant reformation, the successive violent purges affecting both faiths, internal political schism, and subsequent international allegiances were to a
certain extent catalysed by and facilitated through Henry's divorce.
Elizabeth was, therefore, in very real terms the 'daughter' of a king
and queen whose wedlock shifted the course of European politics and
the English church. And as the unexpected, and unwanted, female
heir to the English throne, Elizabeth was to overturn further expectations of gendered rulership and religious authority.

Indeed, it is still possible to perceive the debates, which had been
brought struggling into the sixteenth-century world, in our own age;
they seem to remain with us, through a process of ideological as well
as monarchic inheritance. In this sense, the Protestant queen of the
Early Modern period may be seen as a far-distant ancestor of our
second Elizabethan age. And as we proceed into the new millennium
the present British queen, who carries in her train all the attendant

value-systems of the previous century, sometimes appears as anti-quated as the aged monarch of that first Elizabethan court. This panoply of genealogical continuity is attractive, lending a sense of stability and oneness to what might appear the random shifts of power and authority. Yet such patterning is as decked in rhetorical artifice as the idealised portraits of the successive Elizabeths, for a necessary piece of information has been omitted from the argument – when Elizabeth I spoke of the 'daughter of debate' she was not refer-ring to herself at all.

Let's go back to the poem, which begins with Elizabeth's concern that 'future foes' will threaten her 'present joy' through a series of falsehoods, deceits and political subterfuge. The poem then shifts at its centre to two well-tried Early Modern political metaphors: the state as garden, and the ambitious courtier as a falcon. The first trope depicts the dissidents as encouraged by the 'changed course of [politi-cal] winds' into believing that 'the root upreared shall be', in other words, the rebels hope that Elizabeth's rule and her rightful inheri-tance of the 'family tree' will be overturned. But the Queen immedi-ately denies the success of any rebellion since, 'fruitless all their grafted guile [shall be], as shortly ye shall see'. That is, the rebels cannot lay claim to the true descent of the Tudor tree, but are 'grafted' and therefore in this instance, 'fruitless'. The poem subsequently concentrates on an astringent attack against the forces of revolt, which shifts skilfully between metaphoric allusion and political veracity. The last eight lines of the poem need therefore to be quoted in full:

> The dazzled eyes with pride, which great ambition blinds,
> Shall be unsealed by worthy wights whose foresight falsehood finds.
> The daughter of debate that discord aye doth sow
> Shall reap no gain where former rule still peace hath taught to know.
> No foreign banished wight shall anchor in this port;
> Our realm brooks not seditious sects, let them elsewhere resort.
> My rusty sword through rest shall first his edge employ
> To poll their tops that seek such change or gape for future joy.
> (Wynne-Davies 1998, 12)

The shift in metaphor from horticulture to the noble sport of falconry seems at first inappropriate, suggesting perhaps a poet who lacks maturity and skill. The allusive gaze, however, remains directed upwards, the top of the tree being succeeded by the dazzling vision of the sun. But in addition to this visual tie, the movement in trope is necessary, for these rebels are not common-garden folk but the peers of the realm. Thus, right at the heart of her 16-line poem Elizabeth uncovers the political meaning central to her text, which in turn discloses the rebellion at the heart of her realm.

The Queen's text proves to extend beyond the rhetorical bounds of poetic form and metaphoric tradition, projecting out from its inner-most lines into the actuality of Elizabethan politics. For those eyes dazzled by 'great ambition' belonged to real people, to the Earl of Arundel, the Earl of Norfolk and other Catholic lords. And it is perfectly probable that they had been plotting or preparing to plot against Elizabeth in an attempt to 'uprear' her since she had ascended the throne in 1558. At first their machinations had been unfocused, but in 1568 a specific impetus was provided in the figure of Mary Queen of Scotland. Here was a Catholic queen to supplant the Protestant Elizabeth and, moreover, a queen whose descent neatly evaded the taint of bastardy (as they would see it, 'grafting') that Henry VIII's divorce signalled to the Catholic world. Mary's claim to the English throne came from her father, James V of Scotland, whose mother, Mary Tudor, was the daughter of Henry VII (and therefore Henry VIII's sister). Until Mary was deposed from the Scottish throne in 1567 she had not appeared as a threat to Elizabeth, but once she had crossed the Northern border into England seeking refuge, she was transformed into a throneless queen, on the look out perhaps for another crown. At this point, in the view of the English court, there was no alternative but to lock her up. Hence Mary was imprisoned in a series of castles while Elizabeth grew increasingly uneasy about her cousin's political intrigues. Eventually, of course, Elizabeth's advisers, those 'whose foresight falsehood finds' uncovered the Ridolfi plot and Mary was finally and categorically identified as the 'daughter of debate', the woman who constantly threatened political 'discord'.

There can be little doubt about Elizabeth's unease with the subse-quent decision to execute Mary. Apart from the consanguinity of the two queens, the political advisability of condoning the death of an anointed monarch and one moreover whose faith could claim substantial sympathy at home and abroad was always uncertain. And the poem participates in this sense of unease, for as if evading the stark fact of Mary's inevitable execution, Elizabeth slips back into the gardening metaphor, depicting the two women as maids, sowing and reaping the alternate crops of peace and war. It is only when the poem swings back once again to external circumstance – to a possible invasion by the forces of a 'foreign banished wight' and to the covert actions of the 'seditious sects' – that the sharp focus of political reality returns. The harsh necessities are sustained in the conclusion with the threat of further executions, even though they are simultaneously combined with the horticultural trope. Thus, while Elizabeth's 'sword' of justice might have grown 'rusty' with lack of use in times of peace, she is ready to decree further beheadings as she prepares to 'poll' the rebels' 'tops'. The image of the decapitations is partially softened with the gardening metaphor, the vision of the bloody neck being veiled with the alternative picture of a gardener pruning the unwieldy branches of the tree. Yet there is a more politically astute reasoning behind the combination, for the whole discourse of horticulture serves to naturalise an act of political expediency, allowing Elizabeth to present an uncompromising punishment as a caring, necessary and inevitable act. As in Shakespeare's *Richard II*, the garden becomes a metaphor for the state and rebel lords are compared to plants that have grown too high:

> Go . . . and like an executioner
> Cut off the heads of too fast growing sprays,
> That look too lofty in our commonwealth.
> (III.iv.33–5)[1]

Shakespeare's play is dated to around 1595 and as such is unlikely to refer to the Catholic unrest of the 1560s that engendered Elizabeth's poem, although the text was in its turn to be used in one of the challenges to Elizabeth's power.[2] Nevertheless Elizabeth, like Shakespeare, was able to draw upon a host of classical antecedents, including Livy's account of Tarquin's order to destroy the leading men of the Gabii, and Herodotus' account of Thrasyblus' warning to his enemy Periander. In general terms therefore, the gardening metaphor was an Early Modern commonplace. But Elizabeth transforms the metaphor in one significant respect, for while in all other examples the gardener/avenging ruler is male, as are those executed, in her poem both monarch and rebel are female. The Queen had certainly overturned expectations of gendered rule when she succeeded to the throne, but Elizabeth also reinforced the realities of her political power with a feminised reworking of those metaphors most closely identified with the monarchy.

Elizabeth's poem, when read in the context of the political realities of her time and the poetic discourses that were commonly employed in describing them, thus pivots, in more ways than one, about the phrase 'daughter of debate'. From a reading that drew upon the broad historical expanse of the English Reformation and its far-reaching impact, the poem may now be recognised as a text immersed in its own cultural and political immediacy. Moreover, such periodisation and the recognition of ideological positionings are essential to the understanding of such shifting interpretations. Thus, while in terms of historical awareness it is important to survey the overarching discourses that link our own age with the past, it is also essential to retain an openness to the detailed particulars of a unique time and place. And although for Elizabeth the 'daughter of debate' might clearly represent Mary Queen of Scots as she approached the block, the term immediately pushes past this well-worn image to the unease with which Early Modern Europe viewed all female monarchs, especially those who claimed a spiritual as well as a secular authority.

There are several moments in Elizabeth I's poem that allow us to perceive such shifting interpretations. Apart from 'the daughter of debate', the different views of 'grafting' and the awkward merging of the two queens as garden maids have been mentioned, but there is one further point at which meaning stirs incessantly. At the very end of the poem Elizabeth threatens to execute those who 'seek such change' (that is to overthrow her) or those who 'gape for future joy'. I would like to look more closely at the word 'gape', for its meaning slides in relation to its grammatical and contextual position. Coming immediately after the image of beheading 'gape' cannot help but evoke the graphic picture of the neck like a wide and bloody mouth yawning for its decapitated head. Moreover, while that truncated form could hardly be said to have any expectation of 'joy' on earth, its 'future joy' in heaven remains a possibility. Yet 'to gape for' is not quite the same as 'to gape'. The use of the word 'for' thus offers an alternative interpretation, one that suggests yearning for something, as indeed the Catholic nobles must have yearned for the overthrow of their Protestant queen. But 'for' is also an unstable signifier, since linked with the following phrase, 'future joy', it can change to mean 'because of'. This in turn precipitates a reappraisal of 'gape' into the act of staring in bewilderment, with wonder or with anticipation. Indeed, in the definition of 'to gape' as 'an open-mouthed stare' the OED cites Elizabeth I's use of the term in her 1593 translation of

Boethius: 'Paulin the consul from the *gapers* Jawes I drew' (my emphasis).[3] The rebels are thus belittled into mere 'gapers' staring on foolishly as Elizabeth efficiently polices her realm in the same manner as she deploys rhetoric in order to defuse the image of bloody throats with the comic picture of open mouths. But the round mouthed 'O' of the gaper itself demands a circular interpretation.

The first line of Elizabeth's poem presents her own fears: 'The doubt of future foes exiles my present joy', which are then expurgated from realm and text through the merciless function of state and rhetoric. Yet the last words, 'or gape for future joy' demand a return to the beginning, a cyclical process which is reinforced through the image of the 'O' as well as through the repetition of vocabulary. On one level, of course, there is a certain neat satisfaction in the movement from Elizabeth's assurance of her own 'present joy' through the precise act of negating the 'future joy' of her foes. In other words, she secures her throne by eliminating all opposition, a policy condoned by Early Modern court advisers and political dramatists alike. However, while such narrative neatnesses might have been desirable for the temporal realities of the European state, such a policing of boundaries was unsustainable within the poetic conventions of the day. The use of such cyclical devices was a commonplace in Early Modern court poetry and Elizabeth would have been immersed in a discourse that called upon the structural 'O' to denote a multiplicity of significations, from a simple narrative change, through an awareness of incessant mutability, to a glimpse of the gaping nothingness of negation. As such, if the gapers in Elizabeth's poem are the beheaded nobles, then the gaping mouth of the text also portends the constant shifting of power within the Elizabethan world. And thus the poem finally proffers a nightmare vision of a gaping hole in which bloodied neck mutates into the yawning chasm of death, nothingness and the destabilisation of meaning. Like the Queen herself, Elizabeth's poem becomes a 'daughter of debate'.

The analysis of Elizabeth I's short political poem has served to foreground the importance of understanding historical contexts and the shifting possibilities of such discourses. Political trends, the immediate material circumstances of the text's production, the dominant cultural mores of the period and a self-aware recognition of ideological positioning are all key elements in the interpretation of texts. In the remainder of this chapter I want to explore several of the contexts that have been introduced during the initial analysis: the influence of the court and the question of regionalisation, the religious schism between Catholic and Protestant, as well as the issues surrounding authority. Each of these particular Early Modern contexts will be explored through the writings of Philip Sidney, in particular his sonnet sequence, *Astrophil and Stella* (1581–82). However, the contexts discussed here re-emerge into later chapters, combining ideological analyses with an overall focus upon genre. Thus, the uncompromising divide between Protestant and Catholic is clearly perceived in the poetry of John Donne. The discussion of political and spiritual authority is reworked through a reading of the plays of Christopher Marlowe, William Shakespeare and Thomas Middleton in the chapter upon drama. And, finally with a return to the notion of circularity, the way in which women negotiated a changing identity is described with reference to the prose works of Mary Wroth and Margaret Cavendish. Inheritance and radical change thus formed an uneasy contextual alliance in Early Modern England and at this point I wish to turn to the specific textual debates engendered by these moments of ideological transitions.

Philip Sidney

'Phoenix thou wert'
(Mary Sidney)

On 22 September 1586 during a cavalry attack against an overwhelming number of Spanish troops, Philip Sidney (1554–86) was wounded by a musket ball. Blood poisoning developed and within four weeks he was dead, one of the many victims in the protracted war between the Protestant forces of the Netherlands and her allies, and the Catholic armies of Spain. Philip Sidney was not, however, simply counted as another statistic on the long toll of English soldiers to die in that campaign. Rather, he was immediately heralded as a national hero who was mourned by his family and friends, as well as honoured at home and abroad by statesmen, philosophers and writers alike. As his sister, Mary Sidney (1561–1621), wrote in an elegy 'To the Angell spirit of the most excellent Sir Philip Sidney' (Mary Sidney 1998, I, 110–12), he was the:

> wonder of men, sole borne perfection's kinde,
> Phoenix thou wert, so rare thy fairest minde

Heav'nly adorn'd, Earth justlye might adore,
    where truthfull praise in highest glorie shin'de:
    For there alone was praise to truth confin'de;
    (Mary Sidney 1998, I, 111)[4]

The adulation evidenced in Mary Sidney's poem might be explained away by a sister's grief and a degree of bitterness against the monarch, that other 'Phoenix' Elizabeth I, during whose campaign he had died. But such eulogies were to become a commonplace when describing Sidney's death. His friend and biographer Fulke Greville described Sidney's death metaphorically, as 'the fire of [a] *Phenix*' for which there could be no 'equall' (Greville 1907, 136). Sidney's fellow courtier poet, Edmund Spenser, gathered together an elegiac tribute in pastoral verse for Sidney, which included among others his own poem, 'Astrophil' and another elegy by Mary Sidney, 'The Dolefull Lay of Clorinda'. As Spenser indicates, at the death of Sidney all 'shepherds' that is poets, grieved:

And every one did make exceeding mone,
With inward anguish and great griefe opprest:
And every one did weep and waile, and mone,
And meanes deviz'd to shew his sorrow best.
That from that houre since first on grassie greene
Shepherds kept sheep, was not like mourning seen.
(Spenser 1943, I, 184–8)

Even present-day biographies succumb to the same romantic rhetoric at the point of Sidney's death; for example, James Osborn's account notes that,

Soon his death was expected daily, to the grief of his friends and the garrison alike. As a devoutly religious man he faced the end peacefully, filled with anticipation of future bliss. When news of his death reached England his family and admirers were numb. (Osborn 1972, 516)

Indeed, such was the esteem in which Philip Sidney was held that his funeral became almost a state occasion, an event unprecedented for a minor nobleman. A magnificent 10-metre scroll commemorating the funeral procession depicts the coffin followed by 700 mourners, among them some of the foremost nobles of the age (Lant 1587).[5]

Several months later general mourning for Sidney was still respected; the courtiers continued to wear dark clothes and the flow of tributes from Europe persisted.

The reasons for such an immediate widespread outpouring of grief and subsequent mythologising have been repeatedly analysed. Dennis Kay, for example, sums up the 'lengthy and complex' mutation of Sidney's reputation:

> His image at the time of his death and burial was of a national hero, a Christian soldier and patron. The publication of his literary works in the 1590s led to a substantial modification of that image, and the conjunction of the religious, political, and literary values he was held to represent turned him into a figure who could be invoked as an authority, a privileged ideal, in political discourse for the best part of a century. (Kay 1990, 67–8)

Such responses have not, of course, been unique to Philip Sidney. Nelson was memorialised in a similar fashion and, even in the late-twentieth century, the death of Princess Diana provoked a parallel united sense of loss, a belief that somehow she was 'the people's princess', identified not with monarchical authority but with the populace. At Diana's death astute political speeches secured popular appeal and wrong-footed the monarchy until the Princess too was accorded a royal funeral, recorded not on an elaborately engraved scroll but on video tapes around the country. In a further parallel Princess Diana's brother, Earl Spencer, in a fashion reminiscent of Mary Sidney, made an impassioned funeral oration that eulogised his sister and bitterly castigated the monarchy he saw as responsible for her death. The limits to the comparison must be drawn at this point, for the two idealised figures were as different in life as were the ideas that they came in death to represent. The key point is that in each instance a single identity could develop a homogeneous integrity that served as an idealised mirror used to reveal the flaws of those debased figures of authority left behind. In Philip Sidney's case certainly these perfections appeared to have been considerable. In many ways he was after his death portrayed as the perfect Renaissance man. Sidney was held to have believed in the humanist tenet of the innate dignity of humankind, while at the same time being a resolute Protestant who brought his own faith and beliefs into every aspect of his life. He excelled in physical and chivalric skills, yet was also mentally agile and learned in the classics and languages, as well as being able to express himself in word and on the page with erudition and elegance. Finally, he was dutiful to his country and an admired politician abroad. In this perfected elegiac vision Philip Sidney could almost be matched to the description of the ideal courtier in Castiglione's manual for courtly behaviour, *The Book of the Courtier*, that was translated into English in 1561 by Thomas Hoby, as 'of noble birth, graceful, charming, and expert in so many exercises' (Castiglione 1959, 289). The transformation of Sidney into a flawless photofit image of the ideal courtier, however, reveals more about the need of the late-sixteenth-century society to construct an archetype that could be used as a sharp criticism for those in power, than it does about his reputation while alive. For if Sidney was in death the ideal courtier, a phoenix who arose through many poetic eulogies, then Elizabeth I must be seen as the debased ruler whose own emblematic feathers appear tarnished with the taint of imperfect mortality.

But this clear-cut dialectic was merely one of the discourses encompassing the relationship between the courtier and the monarch, between the court and the stately home, and between the city and the rest of the country. Indeed, a witty counterpoise to Castiglione's idealised vision was provided by John Lyly (1554–1606) in *Euphues: the Anatomy of Wit* (1578) in which the figure of the courtier is sharply satirised. For example, the courtly professions of love are ridiculed through a classic blend of Euphuistic superlatives and opposites:

> No, no, he that cannot dissemble in love is not worthy to live. I am of this mind, that both might and malice, deceit and treachery, all perjury, any impiety may lawfully be committed in love, which is lawless . . . Dost thou not know that the weak stomach, if it be cloyed with one diet, doth soon surfeit? That the clown's garlic cannot ease the courtier's disease so well as the pure treacle?
> (Lyly 1987, 140–1)

The ideals of courtly love are swept aside with a litany of dissemblance and deceit, an opposition that is itself commended as proffering a varied diet. And with a final satiric pun Lyly points out, through Euphues' unknowing verbiage, that rather than accepting the criticism that would cure their disease, the courtier prefers the flattering sweetness of treacle to the astringent taste of medicinal garlic.

Euphues was published at the time Philip Sidney was himself

exploring the role of the courtier poet/statesman. While never ignor-
ing European writers like Castiglione, in his writing Sidney
contributed a particularly English perspective that was happy to
embrace home-grown cynicism alongside continental intellectualism.
This does not suggest that Sidney condoned what he called the
'absurd . . . surfeit to the ears' (Sidney 1973, 139) of Euphuistic
discourse, but rather that he continually sets ideals alongside a
perceived reality, often using pastoral as a way of commenting upon
contemporary society. In the entertainment he prepared for Elizabeth
I, *The Lady of May* (1578), Sidney used the seemingly light masque
form to urge the Queen's support for the Protestant cause. In the
prose romance *Arcadia* (1580–93)[6] he created a complex pastoral
world that is successively infiltrated by trickery, gender inversions,
unbridled sexuality, death, and social upheaval. In *An Apologie for
Poetrie* (published posthumously in 1595)[7] Sidney attested to the
dignity of poetic writing, defended poetry against the charge of being
worthless fiction or lies, and surveyed the contemporary poetic situation. Most importantly he recognised that poetry could be used to
criticise contemporary ideologies and fiercely defended the writer's
autonomy to 'delight and teach' (Sidney 1973, 103). However, it is in
his sonnet sequence, *Astrophil and Stella* (1581–2), that Philip Sidney
focused specifically upon the role of the courtier and the recalcitrant
discourses that constructed his or her identity.

Astrophil and Stella consists of 108 sonnets and 11 songs that were
first published in a pirated edition in 1591, but which had been
composed a decade earlier and had circulated extensively in manuscript form. Indeed, although other sonnet sequences had been
produced before *Astrophil and Stella*, it was Sidney's work that had
both an immediate and a long-lasting impact upon English poetry. It
is a poetic address by the courtier poet Astrophil (star-lover) to his
lady Stella (star) in which he tells the story of their love. The sequence
can be subdivided into sections that conform to the narrative structure, although this is a sketchy estimation of content and should not
be seen to preclude more complex thematic interpretations. Roughly
therefore, sonnets 1 to 12 may be said to provide an introduction, 13
to 30 deal with Astrophil's isolation, and in 31 to 40 he loses control of
the relationship to Stella. In sonnets 41 to 68 overall Stella's voice
replaces Astrophil's, although in 63 he fights back and in sonnets 69 to
85 attempts to seduce her. Finally, while there is a possible consummation of their love in sonnet 81, Astrophil in 86 to 108 acknowledges

his failure and returns to court. The sequence as a whole was influenced by the continental tradition of Petrarch (Sidney was subsequently called 'the English Petrarch'), but the dramatic and personal voice of the poems is more akin to the immediacy of Donne than to the formal rhetoric of the Italian poet. On the other hand, Sidney chose to retain the Petrarchan sonnet form with its division into two quatrains and a sextet rather than the English version that preferred a concluding couplet. In order to understand the way in which the form and the positioning of individual sonnets contribute to the overall meaning of the text I would like to quote sonnet 30 in full.

> Whether the Turkish new-moone minded be
>   To fill his hornes this yeare on Christian coast;
>   How *Poles'* right king meanes, without leave of hoast,
> To warme with ill-made fire cold *Moscovy*:
> If French can yet three parts in one agree;
> What now the Dutch in their full diets boast;
>   How *Holland* hearts, now so good townes be lost,
> Trust in the shade of pleasing *Orange* tree;
>   How *Ulster* likes of that same golden bit,
> Wherewith my father once made it halfe tame;
> If in the Scottishe Courte be weltring yet;
> These questions busie wits to me do frame;
>   I, cumbred with good maners, answer do,
>   But know not how, for still I thinke of you.
> (Evans 1977, 14)

Within the sonnet sequence number 30 comes at the end of Astrophil's sense of isolation, and the last line of the sonnet is the first direct address he makes to Stella. Thematically the poem presents us with evidence of the autobiographical nature of the text; for example when Sidney refers to his father's post as Lord Deputy of Ireland in lines 6–10. Moreover, the whole piece, with its allusions to political conflicts at home (Ulster and Scotland) and abroad (the Turkish empire, Poland, Moscow, France, Germany and Holland) is deeply involved with the current public discourses of the Elizabethan court. As such, sonnet 30 has been the focus of a considerable range of critical attention and merits a detailed close reading here.

The most ready interpretation of sonnet 30, as indeed of the whole sequence, is autobiographical. There can be no question that in

Astrophil's rejected wooing of Stella, Philip Sidney describes his own unsuccessful pursuit of Penelope Rich. There are numerous allusions to personal details, such as the reference to his father's post, as well as puns upon the lady's married name 'Rich', as in 'Fame/ Doth even grow rich, naming my *Stella's* name' (sonnet 35; Evans 1973,16). Early critics judged an autobiographical interpretation as an important aspect to the understanding of the text; for example in her 1973 edition of Philip Sidney's *Selected Poems* Katherine Duncan-Jones notes that while,

> The realism of the sequence does not lie in the fact that Sidney uses biographical material . . . he certainly does this. (Sidney 1973, xiv)

But the relevance of such close identifications has increasingly been questioned. For example, Sidney clearly mocks Astrophil and the ideal courtly love conventions he aspires to, even as the character is cast as a poetic second self. In sonnet 30 the 'busie wits', whom Astrophil wishes to propitiate because he is encumbered with the good manners of a gentleman, suggest a court culture not too far from the verbose world of Euphues. And Sidney's compression of political allusions self-consciously engages with the superfluity of reference in Lyly's prose work. The most clear proof of Sidney's self-aware concerns about biographical poetry may be found in *An Apologie for Poetrie* where he argues that,

> Poets give names to men they write of, which argueth a conceit of an actual truth, and so, not being true, proves a falsehood. . . . But that is easily answered. Their naming of men is but to make their picture the more lively, and not to build any history: painting men, they cannot leave men nameless.
> (Sidney 1973, 124)

In his sonnet sequence, therefore, Sidney might 'name' his courtier poet Astrophil and he might imbue Astrophil with some of his own personal qualities and individual history, but that is not the same thing as writing a poetic autobiography. On the other hand, if *Astrophil and Stella* does not represent 'an actual truth' why accumulate specific references to himself and Penelope Rich? Perhaps, as Sidney disingenuously suggests, the question 'is easily answered', since poets merely wish to make their characters 'more lively'.

With this directive in mind we are able to trace the responses engineered by the text. The allusions to real people and the puns on their names provide tempting clues so that readers, either contemporary fellow-courtiers or present-day critics with knowledge of Sidney's history, are encouraged to discover the true identities concealed within the fiction. But at the same time, the process of mocking Astrophil rebounds upon the readers who have already made the link between character and author and who now appear foolish for ever assuming that art reflected reality. If we imagine the poetic text as a circle, not unlike the gaping 'O' of Elizabeth I's lyric, a fluctuating shift of emphasis from inner and outer becomes apparent. Thus, there are two layers of meaning: an external narrative in which the characters of Astrophil and Stella are located and an inner, intimate circle where the seemingly true identities of Philip Sidney and Penelope Rich may be discovered. But even as the reader believes they have penetrated that closeted space the poet's mocking tone thrusts them back into the outer regions of artifice. The movement of Sidney's poem thus fluctuates continually between inner and outer, arousing the reader's desire yet producing only a continued sense of frustration. Moreover, such interplay exists not only in the shifting biographical interpretations but also throughout the thematic concerns of *Astrophil and Stella.*

Similar dualities are present in the sonnet sequence's stylistic features. For example, antagonism to a Euphuistic rhetoric is voiced in sonnet 3 where Sidney attacks the 'strange similies [that] enrich each line' of such verse and praises the single truth of Stella's 'Love and Beautie' (Evans 1977, 3). Yet Astrophil employs precisely the 'strange similies' that he castigates, allowing Sidney to move the text from the desired perception of inner truth back to the contemporary debased currency of hollow rhetorical display. Similarly, while Stella might be associated with Penelope Rich she is also an archetype, an idealised lady of the sonnets, just as Astrophil aspires to be the perfect image of a Renaissance man. Gendered roles for public consumption are, it is implied, very different from the real person within the accepted part. And this is precisely what Sidney draws our attention to in the last phrase of sonnet 30: 'for still I thinke of you'. The 'busie wits', whether the Elizabethan courtiers who first read the poems in manuscript circulation, or other later constructed readers, are left outside the inner sanctum of the text's meaning, for Astrophil addresses only Stella, thereby implying that the single true 'reader' of

Sidney's sonnets must be Penelope Rich. Or is she?

When used in a direct poetical address the word 'you' is particularly ambiguous. Placed within its narrative context it refers to whatever character is being spoken to and in the case of sonnet 30 this clearly means Stella. In texts that dally with personal allegory, however far those interpretations might be taken, the 'you' must also suggest a 'real' person, someone materially present within their chronological frame; and here we read 'you' as referring to Penelope Rich. But within the intimate form of a sonnet the 'you' is also transferred into the immediacy of the poem's present reader. Sidney's direct address is thus multiplied through his poetic second self, Astrophil to Stella, through the autobiographical allegory to his lady Penelope Rich, and finally through the vatic voice of the text to the reader of the poem. That 'you' conjures a seductive atmosphere that proffers a personal, intimate and privileged bonding between reader and author, in which we, like Stella and Rich, may believe ourselves to be the sole possessor of a single orgasmic moment of meaning. The only problem with such a reading of sonnet 30 is that in contentual terms it is hardly a love poem.

It is still possible to understand the detailed allusions in the first 12 lines of sonnet 30, although today it requires some historical background and an edition with full contextual annotation. Sonnet 30 is packed with contemporary political information, no doubt readily accessible to Sidney's contemporaries, but certainly not transparent to a present-day reader. The poem refers to the expected attack of the Turks in 1582; to the Polish invasion of Russia in 1580–1; to the three French political factions, Catholics, Huguenots and moderate Politiques; to the diet (assembly) of the Holy Roman Empire at Augsburg in July–September 1582; to the Prince of Orange's defence of the Protestant Netherlands; as well as to the conflicts in Ireland and Scotland. All events are particularised, reading more like a historical account than a courtly love poem. But the events are not randomly chosen, since the early 1580s were significant in the change of political policy in England, from a period of conciliation emblematised most clearly in Elizabeth I's proposed marriage to the Catholic Duke of Anjou that Sidney vociferously opposed, to the militant Protestant campaign in the Netherlands in which he was to die. In sonnet 30 Sidney paints a picture of Europe at war, with the divisions in allegiances being drawn upon religious lines, particularly the split between Catholic and Protestant states. And like his 1578 entertain-

ment 'The Lady of May', sonnet 30 is directed primarily at Elizabeth I
in order to 'teach' the importance of a continued loyalty to the
Protestant cause, especially those 'good townes' in the Netherlands.
Read in the immediate context of sonnet 30 the 'you' in the last line
thus becomes transformed into a direct address to Elizabeth I, and its
rejection of the 'busie wits' is couched in exactly the flattering terms
designed to 'delight' the Queen. Like Stella, Penelope Rich and the
reader, Elizabeth I is caught in the seductive movement of the text,
being drawn from the public machinations of the court world into the
private adulation of a courtier for his queen. But she, again like the
other readers of the Sidneian text, will be repulsed. For within the
narrative whole of the sequence the lovers remove themselves from
the court, its associated poetic rhetoric and the centrality of the
Queen, to the secluded and intimate pastoral verses at the heart of the
text. As with the other discourses, Sidney skilfully negotiates the
rhythmic internal/external positioning of the public and private
persona of Elizabeth. Although, as we have seen, the Queen was similarly adept at creating such veiled literary devices.

Given the wide scope of historical allusion in sonnet 30, a politicised reading of this text might seem inevitable, but most critics
continued to read the whole of Sidney's *Astrophil and Stella*, in
common with other Early Modern lyrics from Wyatt to the Cavalier
poets, as a sequence of love poems. It was not until the incursion of
New Historicist criticism in the early 1980s that political and materialist readings became fully accepted, even foregrounded, and this
provoked a marked alteration in the perception of Sidney's oeuvre.
Initially the critics Ann Rosalind Jones and Peter Stallybrass began to
move away from reading Sidney's sonnets as private love poems,
formulating instead an understanding of them in relation to 'the
public world of the court' (Jones and Stallybrass 1984, 54).[8]
Subsequently, in his historicist overview, *English Poetry of the
Sixteenth Century*, Gary Waller pointed out that Sidney had reworked
the Petrarchan convention in order to display:

> a self-conscious anxiety about the dislocation of courtly celebration
> and Protestant inwardness, between the persuasiveness of rhetoric
> and the self-doubt of sinful man, between the insecurity of man's
> word and the absolute claims of God's Word. (Waller 1986, 138)

Rather than a lover inscribing a confessional narrative, Waller, and

Jones and Stallybrass, depicted Sidney as a courtier poet engaged in a series of cultural, political and religious conflicts through his poetic discourse. By 1992 Alan Sinfield confidently affirmed that 'Sidney's preoccupation with issues of political control and ideological strategy appears throughout both his career as a courtier and his literary work', and that he belonged to a Protestant faction that was committed to cultural interventionism (Sinfield 1992, 85, 184). And, finally in relation to sonnet 30 itself, Patricia Fumerton asserted that:

> It is a testament to the essentially political nature of Sidney's rhetoric that he employs a high number of such 'tropes of state' in his representation of his private love. (Fumerton 1991, 99)

The autobiographical love poet was transformed into a radical politician who used cultural products to effect social and religious change. The critical shift that occurred about Sidney's writing was of course replicated across a range of Early Modern authors and their works. For New Historicism, as has already been discussed in the Introduction to this book, had by the late 1990s served to excavate and display the hitherto ignored political discourses of Early Modern texts. However, this renewed focus upon the historicised context of Sidney's poetry mostly concentrated upon his role in relation to Elizabethan court politics and the wider European arena. This was, no doubt, exactly where Sidney would have liked to place himself in his guise as Protestant statesman, influential diplomat and militarily adept courtier. Certainly it was the place accorded to him in his lavish state funeral and in the subsequent widespread eulogistic preservation of his memory. But it is not where Astrophil finds himself at the heart of the sonnet sequence, nor is it the place that Philip Sidney found himself occupying during his lifetime.

It is perfectly possible to become so enamoured of the legend surrounding Philip Sidney's death that the historical actuality of his life becomes a vague and distant image. But a rapid estimation of how and where Philip Sidney spent his time reveals a man divorced from the heady power of the inner court circles and alienated from the Queen through a series of political removes. From 1572 to 1575 Sidney had travelled on the continent broadening his political and cultural experience, but when he returned the Queen failed to employ him in the policy-making capacities he had hoped for. After a brief period as royal cup-bearer, he returned to the continent in 1577 as an ambassador at the court of Emperor Rudolph in Prague. Over the next seven years, although Sidney was involved in public affairs, his fortunes suffered a series of setbacks. In 1580 his association with Leicester's household led him to share that Earl's estrangement from the Queen. He then wrote a somewhat ill-advised letter to Elizabeth advising her not to marry the French Prince Alençon because he was Catholic. Then he quarrelled with Edward de Vere, Earl of Oxford, at a tennis match in front of the French ambassadors. Unsurprisingly, Elizabeth banished Sidney from court and it is likely that he spent his exile at Wilton, the country house of his sister, Mary Sidney. Although the political tide subsequently swung back in favour of the Protestant faction at court, Sidney seems to have felt passed over by the Queen. Even when, in 1585, he was sent to the Netherlands as Lord Governor of Flushing, this appointment was relatively minor. It was of course a posting from which he never returned. Philip Sidney's material circumstances when alive were, therefore, considerably different from the image he was to portray at his death. But while at variance with his own memorial, Sidney was not dissimilar from the other noble-men of his day. The Earl of Leicester had been alienated from the Queen in 1580 and the Earl of Oxford with whom Sidney quarrelled seems to have been almost perpetually out of favour with Elizabeth. More than any of the nobility it was the Catholic lords who came under constant suspicion, for those 'future foes' of Elizabeth's own poem had risked far more than banishment from court. Thus, while it became a commonplace of late-twentieth-century criticism to focus upon the court and city as sites for political concerns and cultural productions, the reality for many Early Modern nobles meant a perpetual shift between their regional estates and the court, or more baldly, between country and city.

It should come as no surprise therefore that Sidney's archetypal courtier, Astrophil, should find himself in the pastoral haven of a country house where his love for Stella might be allowed free rein. In sonnets 80 to 86 Astrophil celebrates the kiss Stella has bestowed on him with a retreat into an intimate world far away from the conventions of the court. The courtly lady of the sonnets is transformed into the 'Nymph of the gard'n' (sonnet 82; Evans 1977, 37), while Astrophil is overcome with joy to 'see the house' where they may:

> Let eares heare speech, which wit to wonder ties;
> Let breath sucke up those sweetes, let armes embrace

> The globe of weale, lips *Love's* indentures make:
> Thou but of all the kingly Tribute take.
> (Evans 1977, 39)

The pastoral setting, that 'globe of weale', offers a freedom both to speak and to display love in a manner that would not have been possible at court. Of course the delight of this retreat is that it may encompass and provoke a host of interpretations. On one level, Sidney's love for Penelope Rich, like Astrophil's for Stella, could not have been condoned by the Queen or by the social mechanisms pertaining to noble alliances. For a possible consummation, in fictive and real worlds alike, seclusion was a necessity. And genre here colludes with character, so that as the figures retire into a private world that mocks the conventions of the court, so too the pastoral song throws the elaborate but hollow mechanisms of courtly sonnet into stark focus. The pattern of internal/external, of that withdrawal to the intimate world at the heart of the text, is thus replicated through setting (court/country), genre (courtly love/pastoral) and form (sonnet/song). And as with the autobiographical and political discourses here again the reader seems to be promised access to a privileged sense of a stable signification.[9] Thus, even the poetic forms utilised by Sidney appear to stress the plain value of the country over the untrustworthy subtleties of the court.

The complex formulations of the sonnet, at once intimate and stylised, might unwind the course of passion in which 'eares heare speech', but they turn back upon themselves in a labyrinth of inter-pretation. For example, that most conventional of Petrarchan conceits – imagining the beloved's eyes are like the sun so that when she leaves the lover is cast into black night – is reworked through the multiple ambiguities of sonnet 89:

> Now that of absence the most irksome night
>   With darkest shade doth overcome my day;
>   Since *Stella's* eyes, wont to give me my day,
> Leaving my Hemisphere, leave me in night,
> Each day seemes long, and longs for long-staid night;
>   The night, as tedious, wooes th'approch of day,
>   Tired with the dusty toiles of busie day,
> Languisht with horrors of the silent night,
> Suffering the evils both of the day and night,

> While no night is more darke then is my day,
> Nor no day hath lesse quiet then my night;
>   With such bad mixture of my night and day,
> That living thus in blackest winter night,
>   I feele the flames of hottest sommer day.
> (Evans 1977, 50)

The first two quatrains follow the traditional pattern of describing the effect of the beloved's departure, so that day and night have both become 'tedious' and full of 'horrors'. Yet in the final sestet night and day become so intermingled, in terms of meaning, repetitive vocabulary and formulaic rhyme scheme, that Sidney's recognition that the text has produced a 'bad mixture' comes almost as a relief. Indeed, the first twelve lines of the sonnet through their dogged pursuit of the same metaphor seem almost to force the text into the alternative of the last two lines, where temperature and season are appended to the ubiquitous 'night' and 'day'. But there is a double irony at play here. The allusion to '*Stella*' in line 3 reminds us that the 'me' of the poem is not an unambiguous poetic voice, but the fictional product Astrophil, who is perfectly capable of writing stylised, almost Euphuistic verse. That Astrophil's choice of form and content should simultaneously mock the courtly conventions to which Sidney and his fellow courtiers ascribed underlines yet again the way in which the sequence's poetic selves parade the hollowness of the externalised public world in which they must act.

But if the court and all its appurtenances are a sham, does the pastoral retreat offer anything more solid by way of meaning? Again, the answer remains ambiguous, but the acute irony that plays through the sonnet form is replaced by the bleak bitterness and melancholy of the pastoral song. Between the moment in sonnet 82 when Astrophil identifies Stella as a nymph and the formal acceptance of her absence in sonnet 89 there are seven songs. In the whole of *Astrophil and Stella* there are only eleven songs, so the preponderance of the lyric form at the heart of the poetic sequence is significant. Moreover, songs 8 and 9 are pastoral, sung apparently by or about shepherds and their loves, into which the individual voices of Astrophil and Stella sometimes incur. And here the narrative does achieve a certain lucidity, for song 8's third person account tells exactly how Stella refuses Astrophil's advances, neatly parodying the breakdown of the courtly lover's poetic speech with the shepherd-poet's graphic depiction:

> There his hands in their speech, faine
> Would have made tongue's language plaine;
> But her hands his hands repelling,
> Gave repulse all grace excelling.
> (Evans 1977, 46)

The bodily mechanisms accepted by the pastoral voice, with all the anti-court, regional and personal connotations Sidney attaches to this vocal signifier, cannot help but attract and focus attention through our own desire to know whether or not the lovers do actually consummate their passion. Yet the very question of 'did they or didn't they?' again opens up a variety of possible interpretations, so that the fictional narrative is interwoven with biographical realism as well as social commentary. Do Astrophil and Stella make love? Did Penelope Rich commit adultery with Philip Sidney? Was it possible for the men and women of Early Modern England to evade the confines of arranged marriages and the moral strictures of the church and so fulfil their erotic desires? More than that, the text inevitably extends the proposition of consummation to the whole panoply of signification in which desire, postponement and the achievement of a satisfying moment of single meaning are constantly in play, or as Sidney puts it, 'more lively'. However, if the sonnets leave the matter open for speculation with that famous reference to 'absent presence' (sonnet 106; Evans 1977, 59), the pastoral song depicts a more defined reality in which:

> Therewithall away she went,
> Leaving him so passion rent
> With what she had done and spoken,
> That therewith my song is broken.
> (Evans 1977, 47)

There is no consummated passion, no continuation of erotic play, no perpetuation of difference, no poetic voice, just absence.

In the overall narrative sequence Astrophil returns disillusioned to the court and the resigned bitterness aired in the last sonnets of the sequence recalls the political alienation of the Elizabethan courtier and of Philip Sidney himself:

And as a Queene, who from her presence sends
Whom she imployes, dismisse from thee my wit.
(Evans 1977, 60)

Perhaps this is where *Astrophil and Stella* ultimately leads, for each
time the process of seduction begins with promises of biographical
revelations, the power of the reader to ascertain the truth of the text,
the argument for an honest and original poetic language, and the
superior validity of a private, country existence over and above the
hollow sham of public court display, Sidney carefully evades fulfilling
our desires. For a series of love poems the metaphor of sexual arousal
is not unapt, and the outcome of the continued postponement of
consummation is inevitably bleak frustration. Or so it was until Philip
Sidney's death recreated the image of the shepherd/courtier poet, the
melancholy lover, and the ignored diplomat, so that the ideal, whole,
rounded signifier rose from the fallen and debased pyre of the signified, just as Mary Sidney and Fulke Greville eulogised their
brother/friend as a 'Phoenix'.

It was precisely because Sidney's life appeared unfulfilled and frustrated in exactly the political, public and intimate arenas that exem-
plified the dominant discourses of the day, that his death was seen to
answer a need for an ideal that could never exist in reality. This is not
to say that Philip Sidney was not an honourable man and a fine poet,
but simply that the legend presents an impossible perfection that
might well have been desired, but which in the material world
remained perpetually unattainable. And what must have been especially appealing to those Elizabethan courtiers who marched solemnly
alongside Sidney's coffin was that the responsibility for this loop of
ambition, desire, rejection, and death could be pinned on the reign-
ing monarch's own inadequacies. For like Stella, Elizabeth I had
spurned Sidney's attempts to win political preferment, exiling him
from an idealised court into the harsh realities of the Netherlands
campaign. If Sidney's verse and prose questioned the values of the
monarch and her court, then his death might be seen to vindicate
those nobles who, like him, had been repulsed by their queen. The
ideal 'self' that was constructed by others after his death was, therefore, at a far remove from the identity Philip Sidney had fashioned
while he was alive.

But if Sidney's death enabled a widespread critique of Elizabeth why did she allow the lavish funeral to proceed? Why not hush up the affair, particularly since the manner of demise must also have posed awkward questions about her foreign policy? A possible answer lies in the dating of the funeral. As has already been noted, Philip Sidney died in October 1586 and his body was transported back to England at the beginning of November. But the grand and lavish funeral did not take place until mid-February of the following year, a hiatus of four months. The reason for the delay might be explained by the intervening Christmas period, or by the need for Francis Walsingham, Sidney's father-in-law, to realise enough cash or credit to pay for the funeral, but above all the Queen must have at least tacitly agreed to this delay. Why?

To a certain extent the reinforcing of the shepherd courtier/poet values that Sidney's phoenix-image was accruing through those four months would have served to reinforce the value systems of Elizabeth's court, even if at first they implied a tacit criticism of her own policies. But the Queen had more on her mind in February 1587 than the organisation of a minor nobleman's funeral. On the 8th of February in the remote castle of Fotheringay, Mary Stuart, that 'daughter of debate', was executed on Elizabeth's orders. Few biographers and critics comment upon the close juxtaposition between the execution and the funeral, however, as Alan Hager rightly points out:

> The ceremonial parade through the capital, lavish and well attended, would have helped turn the minds of the populace from the beheading of Mary. (Hager 1987, 53)

This deflection of interest would undoubtedly have been an important aspect of the propagandistic value of Sidney's funeral; but there is more. If we turn to what Elizabeth herself wrote about Mary Stuart in her poem 'The Doubt of Future Foes', it is clear that her fears were not concentrated upon the possibility of a mob uprising, but rather upon those 'aspiring minds' that had become 'dazzled . . . with pride [and] . . . ambition' (Wynne-Davies 1998, 12). Moreover the reprisal envisaged for such unrest occurs not in the multiple hangings that would have been deemed suitable for commoners, but in the ritualistic execution by sword that only the nobility could claim. Sidney's funeral might well have provided a show for the Londoners who thronged the streets to watch the procession of coffin and the 700 mourners, but Elizabeth's propaganda was directed more at the living participants in the show than at those watching.

This piece of theatre had therefore a series of uses that extended far beyond remembering Philip Sidney. For the courtiers the Sidney legend was already starting to form, and the combination of physical prowess, able diplomat and accomplished poet began to provide an image of perfection that served to assure the existing value systems of the court. For Elizabeth and her inner court of politicians, Sidney's death could be transmuted into a propagandistic display that impressed commoners, visiting diplomats and the English nobility alike. The assurance here was of the continued stability of the English Protestant throne and of Elizabeth's own reign. And if we recall those 'gapers' described at the start of this chapter, it can well be imagined how those lining the street, viewing from above, or waiting patiently in their pews at St Paul's Cathedral did indeed gape at the sheer magnitude and cost of the display. Moreover, this gaping amazement had been engineered specifically to detract attention from that other 'gaper', the beheaded body of Mary Queen of Scots. As a cultural construct therefore Sidney's funeral acted in the same manner as Elizabeth's poem 'The Doubt of Future Foes'. In each case the possible destabilisation of authority, both political and contentual, is elided by apparent closure, the circle is in this sense completed in order to give the sense of an idealised whole, of a perfect continuity. Yet there was another 'gaper' at the very heart of the procession. For all the ideals, the perfection, the claims to a phoenix-like resurrection in verse, Philip Sidney was dead. At the very centre of the procession, the court's ideology, the Queen's political policy and the overall signification of the trope, lay the gaping mouth of death, nothingness and the consequent undermining of precisely the stable and unified meaning all had hoped to ensure. For, by using one gaper to call attention away from another, the Early Modern queen and her court had succeeded, not in assuring their own cultural, social and political positions, but in throwing that whole ideology into question.

Notes

1. William Shakespeare, *Richard II* in the Arden Shakespeare series, ed. Peter Ure (London: Routledge, 1966).
2. Scenes from *Richard II* were staged in London during the Essex rebellion to rouse the populace against the Queen.

3. Elizabeth's translation of Boethius is reprinted in the *Early English Text Society*, 5.9.

4. There are a number of criticisms that deal with the effulgence of poetic tribute at Philip Sidney's death; a useful and comprehensive work is Jan Van Dorsten, Dominic Baker-Smith and Arthur Kinney (eds), *Sir Philip Sidney: 1586 and the Creation of a Legend* (Leiden: J. J. Brill and Leiden UP, 1986).

5. For a full account of Lant's funeral roll see Sander Bos, Marianne Laye-Meyer and Jeannine Six, 'Sidney's Funeral Portrayed' in Van Dorsten, Baker-Smith and Kinney (eds), *Sir Philip Sidney*.

6. The composition and publication history of the *Arcadia* are complex. Philip Sidney completed the first version (*The Old Arcadia*) in 1580; it comprised five books of verse and prose. He began to revise the text in 1584 but had only worked on three books before his death; these were corrected and published by his sister Mary Sidney in 1590 (*The New Arcadia*). Subsequently the last two unrevised books were added to the three new ones in order to make up a narrative whole and were published in 1593.

7. Another Sidneian text with a complex history: Sidney wrote it in the early 1580s at the same time as *Astrophil and Stella* and it was widely circulated in manuscript form. It was published under two titles in 1595 as *The Defence of Poesy*, brought out by William Ponsonby, and as *An Apologie for Poetrie*, from the press of Henry Olney.

8. Two other useful and influential analyses are: Arthur F. Marotti, '"Love is not Love": Elizabethan Sonnet Sequences and the Social Order', *ELH*, 49 (1982), 396–406, and Clark Hulse, 'Stella's Wit: Penelope Rich as Reader of Sidney's Sonnets', in Margaret W. Ferguson, Maureen Quilligan and Nancy J. Vickers (eds), *Rewriting the Renaissance: The Discourses of Sexual Difference in Early Modern Europe* (Chicago: Chicago University Press, 1986).

9. Sidney repeats this use of the pastoral setting in his prose romance so that with an almost satiric force the text is able to reveal the personal, moral and political inadequacies of Elizabethan aristocratic society.

2 Poetry

I The sonnet form and tradition

> 'The winds (as having gotten their mouths now free, and at liberty)
> spoke more loud'
> (William Strachey, *A True Repertory of the Wrack*)

The momentous and rapid changes that occurred in the Early Modern world emerge through the mutating identities of sixteenth- and seventeenth-century poetry. Such textual evidence is hardly surprising however, given the enormity of the period's social and cultural transformations. After all, at the commencement of the Early Modern period, within the space of 50 years (let's say, 1480–1530), handwritten manuscripts had been replaced with printed books, the earth had been displaced from the centre of the universe and, thanks to Galileo, was known to orbit the sun. Moreover, the hegemony of the Catholic Church had been split asunder by the Protestant Reformation. And, the hierarchies of class and gender were being challenged by an increasingly powerful bourgeoisie, by a newly educated body of women, and by the advent of a supremely self-contained form of individualism that reinterpreted the personal as political. Finally, even the image of the globe had changed, for the flat and recognisable map had been replaced with a spinning orb resplendent with new and exotic worlds. In the twenty-first century we often lament the accelerated pace of change, but placed alongside the upheavals facing Early Modern men and women, it is necessary to concede that the forces of transition move through peaks and troughs in a wave-like fashion, rather than along an accelerating forwards-moving track. In terms of historical movement, therefore, the late-sixteenth and early-seventeenth centuries appear at the very peak of a storm.

Indeed, the use of a storm at sea as a metaphor for social and/or personal change was commonly recognised in Early Modern writing. For example, the actual storm described in the quotation at the beginning of this chapter was used, most famously, by Shakespeare in his play, *The Tempest*. The historical account itself, *A True Reportory of the Wrack and Redemption of Sir Thomas Gates, Knight* (1610), describes the storm and subsequent wreck on Bermuda of a ship bound for Virginia. Although the crew and passengers were presumed lost, a year later they were able to travel on to America, and the narrative was transformed from a tragedy into a tale of miraculous salvation, the account of which was written by the ship's captain, William Strachey. The storm itself is described in detail, from the initial 'restless tumult', through the 'waters [which] like whole Rivers did flood in the air', to the winds that 'spoke more loud, and . . . malignant', which lasted for 'three days and four nights' (Strachey 1997, 105). Yet, the winds that thrust the mariners into the new world of the Americas are ultimately proved to be redemptive, ruthlessly propelling the old world into a metamorphosis that will be seen to be, if not its salvation, then certainly the source of profitable expansion. Given the combination of symbolism and exciting narrative, it is hardly surprising that Shakespeare adopted the tale. Yet the trope of storm and wreck had far earlier antecedents than Strachey's failed 1610 crossing.

Strachey himself, in describing the storm, was aware of these literary associations; for example, quoting one of Horace's *Odes*,

> *Ego quid sit ater Adriæ noui sinus, & quid albus Peccet Iapex.* [Full well I know what Hadria's black gulf can be and what the sins of clear Iapyx.] (Strachey 1997, 105)

The reference to 'Hadria' and 'sins' would have been interpreted by the Early Modern reader as allusions to hell (Hades) and damnation, from which in due course the crew would be rescued. But they would also have been able to access a panoply of literature and mythology in which storms at sea and shipwrecks functioned as mutating signifiers of threat and destruction. Indeed, one of the most frequently worked examples of this trope was based upon the Italian poet Petrarch's verses, in particular sonnet CLXXXIX, which begins '*Passa la nave mia colma d'oblio*' (Petrarch 1979, 240–1). This sonnet and its associated conceit proved so successful and influential that it was reworked in England alone by the poets Thomas Wyatt, Henry Howard, Earl of Surrey, Edmund Spenser, and Michael Drayton. It is also alluded to by, amongst others, John Donne, Walter Ralegh, Philip Sidney, Mary Sidney, Samuel Daniel, Mary Wroth, and William Drummond. Further, while the trope might have remained recognisable, its signification was as turbulently shifting as the seas of the storm it evoked. Indeed, the social and cultural upheavals of the period were all, to a certain extent, explored in this particular sonnet type, including, of course, the final sense of actual exploration and geographical mutation. The image of the storm/wreck is, therefore, a useful starting place from which to begin a navigation of the way in which poetry, in particular the sonnet, participated in the major transitions of the Early Modern age.

II The Petrarchan sonnet

In order to examine the way in which the sonnet participated in the major transitions of the Early Modern age, it is useful to start with the image of the storm and shipwreck. Simultaneously, however, it is essential to understand the way in which the sonnet's form developed and the manner in which it acquired an international identity. To a certain extent, the sonnet is always larger inside than it is without, for while it remains bound by its 14-line, formally rhymed structure, its significations multiply through a spectrum of linguistic and imagaic referents. Although the exact source of the sonnet form is unknown, the earliest examples emerged in Europe during the thirteenth century, travelling alongside the cultural sweep of the Renaissance north west and finally reaching England around the 1530s/40s. The most well-known exponent of the early sonnet form was the Italian humanist poet, Francesco Petrarch (1304–74). At first, it might appear that Petrarch by both race and period exists outside the definition of this volume, yet his overwhelming influence and the enduring popularity of the particular sonnet form that he developed make a brief analysis essential. Thus, even in its ancestry the sonnet refuses to be contained within either logistical or temporal frames.

The Petrarchan sonnet as a structure laid down certain conventions that were to become commonplaces of Renaissance poetry. To begin with, it was aligned with the more widespread Early Modern move away from religious poetry written in Latin, towards secular verse composed in the vernacular. At the same time, a focus upon individuality was combined with a cosmic and elevated conception of the beloved, allowing the (possibly) harmonious reconciliation of a set of two oppositions. Classically, Petrarch's lady, Laura, is envisaged as being able to combine these dualities: the material with the spiritual, the earthly with the elevated, and the physically beautiful with a metaphysical divinity. Consequently, Petrarch's love allows for the uniting of lust and reverence, passion and purification, the transitory and eternal, and the worldly and heavenly. Yet even as the poetic voice proffers a reconciliation of these irreconcilable concepts, a bittersweet realisation of breakdown becomes unavoidable, so that understanding exists only in recognising that pleasure cannot exist without pain, and that life cannot be compassed without a realisation of death. These themes were displayed in the Petrarchan sonnet form in which an unequal bipartite division was presented through the rhyme scheme: abba abba/cde cde (although the last sestet could vary between two or three rhymes). In this way two seeming opposites could be introduced in the first two quatrains, and then subsequently reconciled and/or drawn apart in the sestet. The whole poem could thus revolve about a single theme with an associated prolonged metaphor or conceit. For example, Petrarch used the image of the sea voyage with its possible storms and wrecks as an allegory for the journey through life and love. In order to understand the way in which Petrarch developed this conceit, the sonnet will be examined in more detail.

The poem is usually identified today as CLXXXIX in *Rime Sparse*, although in earlier editions and critical works the overall title may be noted as *Canzoniere*. Although the majority of Petrarch's poetic output was in Latin, the most influential works were written in Italian and gathered together in the *Rime Sparse* or in the *Trionfi* (Triumphs). The former includes 317 sonnets, as well as a range of other verse, which focus mainly upon Petrarch's ill-fated love for Laura. Sonnet CLXXXIX occurs over halfway through the whole and belongs roughly to a section in which antitheses of form and image were foregrounded in order to represent the frustration, both sexual and moral, of the lover as he tortures himself with thoughts of his unyielding lady. In Italian the sonnet runs:

> Passa la nave mia colma d'oblio
> per aspro mare, a mezza notte il verno,
> enfra Scilla e Caribdi; et al governo
> siede 'l signore, anzi 'l nimico mio;

> a ciascun remo un penser pronto e rio
> che la tempesta el fin par ch' abbi a scherno;
> la vela rompe un vento umido, eterno
> di sospir, di speranze, e di desio;
>   pioggia di lagrimar, nebbia di sdegni
> bagna e rallenta le giá stanche sarte,
> che son d'error con ignoranzia attorto.
>   Celansi i duo mei dolci usati segni;
> morta fra l'onde è la ragion e l'arte,
> tal ch'i 'ncomincio a desparer del porto.
> (Petrarch 1979, 240–1)

['My ship, which is loaded with oblivion, passes through a tempestuous sea, at midnight, in winter, between Scylla and Charybdis; and at the helm sits my lord, or rather my enemy; at each oar is a thought ready and perverse that appears to despise the tempest and the [journey's] end; a humid wind tears the sail, eternally of sighs, of hopes, and of desires; a rain of weeping, a mist of disdain, bathe and loosen the wearied sails that are made of error and twisted out of ignorance. My two sweet accustomed stars are hidden; dead among the waves are reason and skill: so that I begin to despair of [reaching] the port.'][1]

The Petrarchan rhyme scheme divides the sonnet up into the expected octave and sestet. The first quatrain presents a vivid image of the ship, which is steered by a concealed enemy, sailing perilously through a midnight storm between two dangerous rocks. At the same time we become aware that the ship is a metaphor for the poet's mental state, since it is loaded with 'oblio' and is governed by a lord, who might be external to the poetic voice, perhaps Cupid the God of Love or another aspect of the self. The combination of image and metaphor imbue the first quatrain with a powerful sense of movement and foreboding, for whatever journey we and the poet are embarked upon, it will certainly be dangerous. The second quatrain, closely linked to the first through the replication of the rhyme scheme (abba), focuses more specifically upon the forces that should move the ship forwards, only to find that they are impeding progress. The oars move against the 'tempesta' and the 'fin', suggesting almost a backward movement, while the wind ('vela') tears the sail with a retrograde force of 'sospir', 'speranze' and 'desio', rather than filling the canvas with a puissant blast. Again, the allegory suggests a human stasis, in which thoughts (oars) and words (wind) serve to hinder progress towards the goal, rather than enabling success. The sonnet then turns towards the sestet with a clearer link between the image and the underlying meaning, so that the rain itself now becomes 'lagrimar' and the sails are twisted in 'ignoranzia'. The dualities of the octave have thus been pushed into the close conjunction typical of a Petrarchan sonnet and the last lines serve to replicate and entrench this enigma. Stars were conventionally the eyes of the beloved and with their retreat the poetic voice loses 'ragion' and 'arte', so that he begins to despair of ever reaching his destination. Here the image of the ship lost at sea is coupled with the sense of the lover who will never win his lady. But beyond that, Petrarch's choice of reason and 'arte', with their overtones of literary creativity, suggest that the poetic voice also fears that the text itself will not be completed. Yet, in the final moment of the sonnet, closure is achieved and the poet/ lover/traveller does reach the 'fin', while claiming that he despairs of exactly that which he has achieved. Personal and cosmic are thus brought together in an irreconcilable combination through a conceit that links the individual with nature, exploration, love, and art itself. Given the multiple possibilities that emerged from the Italian original it was not surprising that Petrarch's sonnet CLXXXIX proved so popular.

III   Sir Thomas Wyatt

Petrarchan conceits proved popular throughout Early Modern Europe, re-emerging in the writing of the French sonneteers such as Pierre de Ronsard (1524–85), in the works of Scottish writers such as William Drummond (1585–1649), and in the English sonnets of Thomas Wyatt (1503–42) and Henry Howard, Earl of Surrey (1517–47). In this section, I wish to trace briefly the impact of the Petrarchan sonnet on English poetic discourse, beginning with the translation of sonnet CLXXXIX by Wyatt.

Sir Thomas Wyatt was a courtier and diplomat whose travels in Italy in 1526 and 1527 acquainted him with continental Renaissance litera-ture, especially the works of Petrarch. The combination of Wyatt's lyrics, which followed an earlier English tradition, and his translations and adaptations of Petrarch's *Canonziere*, together served to form the basis of Elizabethan poetic conventions. It is important to remember that the Early Modern understanding of translation was very different from our own. While we use the term to mean a transposition into another language that remains as true as possible to its original, for Wyatt the word would have inferred the text as a mere base for his own literary imagination. Moreover, Wyatt's versions of the sonnet form seek to work out an English equivalent in terms of line, stress, metre and rhyme scheme. Thus, Wyatt retains the 8/6 split into octave and sestet, but transforms the Italian metre into English iambic pentameter. In addition, he turned the interwoven Petrarchan sestet into a complex movement of quatrain and couplet that reflected back on the original octave, turning it into a douzain. The effect of these changes in form becomes apparent when interpreting the verses themselves.

Wyatt's translation of Petrarch's sonnet CLXXXIX is commonly known by its first line, 'My Galley Charged with Forgetfulness':

> My galley charged with forgetfulness
> Thorough sharp seas in winter nights doth pass
> 'Tween rock and rock, and eke mine enemy alas,
> That is my lord, steereth with cruelness,
> And every oar a thought in readiness,
> As though that death were light in such a case.
> An endless wind doth tear the sail apace,
> Of forced sighs and trusty fearfulness;
> A rain of tears, a cloud of dark disdain
> Hath done the wearied cords great hinderance,
> Wreathed in error, and eke with ignorance.
> The stars be hid that led me to this pain,
> Drowned is reason that should me comfort,
> And I remain despairing of the port.
> (Wyatt 1975, 25–6)

The sonnet is, on the surface, quite similar to Petrarch's. Certainly, the image of the ship making a dangerous journey while the poetic voice despairs of a safe conclusion seems identical. There are, however, a number of alterations in terms of both form and content. For example, the rhyme scheme (abbaabbacddcee) makes it clear that the poem has two possible axes. The first occurs after the two abba quatrains ('apace' was written 'a pase' in the original manuscript, allowing it to sustain the 'b' rhyme). The second comes after the third quatrain, which although it follows a separate rhyme scheme (cddc) has more in common with the preceding pattern (abba) than with the final couplet (ee). In terms of form, therefore, it becomes possible to switch the third quatrain so that it could belong either to the Italian (octave and . . .) sestet structure, or to the emerging douzain (. . . and couplet) English tradition. The sonnet enacts, therefore, a transition between literary types, but it also heralds a shift in overall significa-tion.

The first quatrain retains the central image of the ship, yet the clas-sical references to Scylla and Charybdis (the Greek Gorgons) have been replaced with the more general danger of 'rock and rock'. This substitution serves to undermine the subsequent interpretation of 'signore' as the classical God Cupid, since Wyatt's 'lord' seems to be as generalised as 'rock'. Placed in context with Wyatt's other sonnets, which are often subtly political, 'lord' could quite easily signify the monarch whom Wyatt must serve, that is, Henry VIII. It is possible to date 'My Galley Charged with Forgetfulness' since the sonnet appears in the Egerton Manuscript that was copied in 1537 or earlier, and it contains some corrections made in Wyatt's own hand (Wyatt 1969, xi–xii). We know therefore that the sonnet could well have been trans-lated at the time of Wyatt's imprisonment in the Tower of London in May 1536 in connection with the fall of Queen Anne Boleyn from the King's favour. Wyatt was cited as one of the Queen's lovers, but was soon released and sent to Spain as ambassador. Accurate details of Wyatt's romantic involvement with Anne Boleyn will never be fully uncovered, but it is probable that he did develop an attachment during 1525/6 and found the King to be his rival for her affections. Wyatt's successive removals from court could well be explained by his earlier relationship with the Queen and a number of his poems appear to make specific reference to the poet's powerlessness in the face of Henry's courtship of Anne. For example, the reference to Caesar's possession of the deer in 'Whoso List to Hunt: I Know Where is an Hind' makes little sense unless it depicts Henry's successful wooing of Anne Boleyn (Wyatt 1975, 7). This sonnet is a translation from Petrarch's CXC in which the word 'Cesare' also occurs (Petrarch 1979, 242). More importantly, the connection of 'signore', 'lord', 'Cesare', and 'Ceasar' is reinforced by the fact that 'Whoso List to Hunt' is a translation of the sonnet that immediately follows 'My Galley' in the Petrarchan original. As such, if 'Caesar' in the Egerton manuscript may be identified with Henry VIII, then so may 'lord'. This means that even in the first quatrain of Wyatt's sonnet the personal has been infiltrated by the political, and that the voyage of the courtier is revealed as having to chart the tempestuous waters of court politics, just as the Petrarchan lover must combat the storms of passion.

The sonnet's second and third quatrains, however, serve to yank apart the formulaic progression of the Italian original. Lines 5 and 6 in particular form an almost self-sufficient unrhymed iambic pentameter, as they hold the rhythm of the lines in a 'readiness' as precarious as the oars. Indeed, the original sense of the oars working against the storm and towards an attainment of the final harbour is radically altered, so that 'fin' takes on the more ominous meaning of 'death', and the 'thoughts' or 'oars' become ready to challenge death, even though the tempest rages. Instead of the lover working against himself, as in Petrarch's original, for Wyatt, the poetic self struggles heroically against the forces of nature and monarchy combined. In Wyatt's sonnet the courtier still carries the noble identity forged through the English lyric, but it is now combined with the emergent individualism of the Early Modern political world and the self-effacing agony of the Petrarchan lover. It is almost as if Wyatt asks us to acknowledge another faux 'turn' at the heart of the douzain, so that while at the close of line 6 the poetic self may still blazon his identity forth, at the beginning of line 7 the sonnet turns us towards the despair of 'tears' and disdain'. Thus, even though the rhyme scheme and the conventional Petrarchan form divide lines 7 to 10, in terms of content they move with imagaic unity from wind, to rain and clouds. The image of the storm dominates the second half of the douzain, allowing Wyatt to transform the sonnet into a dark and perhaps unconquerable battle against the elements – political, natural and emotional.

The alteration in form is echoed by Wyatt's increasingly free translation from the Petrarchan original, so that while in both poems the sails are torn, the Italian wind of 'sospir' (sighs), 'speranze' (hope) and 'desio' (desire) is replaced with the more ambiguous English, 'forced sighs' and 'trusty fearfulness'. And to add to the complexity, the Egerton manuscript gives us 'forced sightes'. Thus Wyatt omits 'umido', adds 'forced', offers an ambiguous reading with 'sighs/sightes', translates 'speranze' as 'trusty', and changes 'desio' to 'fearfulness'. The allegory of the original, which describes the succession of sighs, hope and desire applicable to love, is thus transformed into two sets of opposites that, ironically, are more 'Petrarchan' in convention than is the original by Petrarch. The natural exhalations or visions of the lover become 'forced' and possibly faked, while trust is combined with its antithesis, fearfulness. Moreover, the points of reference remain open throughout these lines, so that each response might be applied to both political and love discourses. For example, the lover may both trust his mistress and fear her rejection, just as the courtier must rely upon but also doubts his prince. For Wyatt this Petrarchan conceit might have had personal resonances, and such a biographical reading serves to affirm further the overall private/political dialectic of the sonnet as a whole.

The open translation continues through the final lines of the sonnet, particularly in the last English couplet. Yet the clearest of Petrarchan images remains, for the stars, which in Petrarch's original represent Laura's eyes, are still the lady's eyes in Wyatt's version. In each case the light provided has been removed as the lady withdraws her favour, leaving the lover in despair. This metaphor recurs repeatedly in many European sonnets, as for example, in Philip Sidney's 'those two stars in Stella's face' (Philip Sidney 1962, 178). The last two lines of Wyatt's translation, however, prove remarkably different from the Italian. To begin with Wyatt omits 'arte' and adds 'that should me comfort' (the Egerton manuscript reads 'consort'), and continues with a subtle, but significant alteration of 'begins' to 'remain'. It is possible to interpret Wyatt's translation if we read 'arte' as the skill necessary to guide the boat to harbour, which would align with the word 'consort', which in nautical terminology means to accompany a ship into port. As such, a personified Reason could well have accompanied and guided the despairing lover/courtier to safety, which would, of course, also have brought comfort. But the key difference with the Italian original remains, in that Wyatt envisages movement in the term 'consort', whereas Petrarch refers to a talent, albeit a personified one, that has been lost. Thus, the last line's conclusive stasis, in which the poetic voice 'remain[s]' in despair, follows inevitably upon the loss of Reason as a consort to guide the ship, with all its attendant metaphoric significations, to shore. Without a consort, the 'galley' must remain at sea, without a human 'consort' the lover remains alone, and without supporting company the isolated courtier stands apart. And this was precisely what happened to Wyatt, for after the loss of his lady (Anne Boleyn) and of his prince's (Henry VIII's) favour he was banished overseas, remaining stranded away from the English shore, in France, Italy and Spain. If Petrarch's sonnet presented the ship conceit as an impossible combination of continuation and closure, Wyatt alters the meaning to suggest a bleak and despairing isolation in which movement becomes impossible.[2] Moreover, Wyatt had introduced a distinctly political discourse to the English sonnet that was to prove an overwhelming influence for over a hundred and fifty years.

IV   Henry Howard, Earl of Surrey

The introduction of political discourse to the English sonnet may have begun with Thomas Wyatt, but he was followed closely by Henry Howard, Earl of Surrey. Like Wyatt, Surrey served at the court of Henry VIII, but unlike the earlier sonneteer, he was unable to avoid the dangers of the Early Tudor world. Along with his father, the Duke of Norfolk, Surrey was persistently in conflict with Henry VIII mainly because of the Norfolks' entrenched Catholic sympathies, although court intrigue and factionalism were also important factors. Ultimately, Surrey was executed for treason in 1547 upon a tenuous charge that was grounded more in the Seymour family's (a rival faction) wish to discredit and disempower the Norfolks, than in any misdemeanour on Surrey's part. Although all his goods were confiscated and distributed amongst his enemies, Surrey's poetry appears to have survived in manuscript form, and while this is no longer extant, most of his poems was published, with a few emendations, in a collection entitled *Tottel's Miscellany* (1557).[3] This compilation was hugely influential and went through nine successive editions between 1557 and 1587. It began by naming Petrarch as 'the Prince of Poets' and invoked an intense literary discourse of Petrarchanism that laid down its own exclusive rules of poetry. Surrey's sonnets served an important function within the whole Petrarchan endeavour, since they both provided loose translations of the original in a readily accessible language, and established a smooth and sophisticated English sonnet form. The rhyme scheme was expanded from the usual five endings to a more flexible seven rhymes, structured as: ababcdcdefefgg. Surrey, like Wyatt, preferred the concluding couplet, but the divisions between the quatrains are more clearly demarcated. Thematically, Surrey retained the focus upon a poetic self that belonged simultaneously within political and love discourses, yet

Wyatt's fraught, emotional tone was replaced with a sense of detachment that demonstrates the greater impact of Surrey's verse on the Elizabethan sonneteers. As such, Surrey is often contrasted or set against Wyatt in a reading of the development of the English sonnet, but this fails to take into account his considerable debt to the earlier poet.

For example, three of Surrey's sonnets and one song are elegies written in praise of Wyatt. Not only does Surrey extol Wyatt's poetic skills, as in 'The great Macedon that out of Persia chased', but he also condemns the corrupt court politics that brought about Wyatt's downfall in 'Diverse thy death do diversely bemoan' (Brooks-Davies 1992, 91–2). Yet the most poignant evocations of Wyatt occur in Surrey's ethical and religious poems that were written during his own successive imprisonments. The first poem, which begins 'Of thy life, Thomas, this compass well mark', takes up the image of the ship in 'storms dark' and advises courage in 'strait estate'. It functions as an address to his own son, Thomas, as well as to Wyatt (Brooks-Davies 1992, 114). The second work, while not directly referring to Wyatt, presents a close parallel to 'My Galley Charged with Forgetfulness' and was written while Surrey was in the Tower of London awaiting execution on the charge of high treason:

> The sudden storms that heave me to and fro
> Had well near pierced Faith, my guiding sail,
> For I, that on the noble voyage go
> To succour Truth, and Falsehood to assail,
> Constrained am to bear my sails full low
> And never could attain some pleasant gale;
> For unto such the prosperous winds do blow
> As run from port to port to seek avail.
> This bred Despair, whereof such doubts did grow
> That I gan faint, and all my courage fail:
> But now, my Blage, mine error well I see:
> Such goodly light King David giveth me.
> (Brooks-Davies 1992, 118)[4]

There are a number of obvious parallels with Wyatt's verse. The storms that tear the ship's sail, the winds that are depicted as contradictory, here a 'pleasant gale' to Wyatt's 'trusty fearfulness', and the final dominance of 'Despair', all recall the key images and themes of

'My Galley Charged With Forgetfulness'. Moreover, Surrey would have been acutely aware of the similarities between his own perilous position and Wyatt's incarceration by the same monarch, Henry VIII. And like Wyatt, Surrey insists through the metaphor of the storm that the personal voyage through life must be recognised as affected by external political factors. Indeed, Surrey is much more direct in his autobiographical representation of this conjunction, particularly in the final rhyming couplet. The address to 'Blage' is made to Sir George Blage who had been a key figure for the prosecution in Surrey's trial, and the allusion to the biblical '*King* David' (italics mine) draws attention to King Henry VIII who allowed the execution to proceed. But the tone of these lines remains ambiguous, for it is difficult to know whether Surrey's seeming confession to Blage, 'mine error well I see', is ironic, particularly when coupled with the shift from a material (King Henry) to a spiritual (King David) authority. Further, the circumstances of Surrey's trial would certainly suggest that he had every right to feel wronged.

In 1545–6 Surrey had commanded English troops in a campaign against the French, but although he showed great personal courage, he was defeated and forced to retreat to Boulogne. Shortly after he was recalled home and was superseded by the Earl of Hertford, with whom he soon found himself in conflict. Henry VIII was dying and, as uncle to the young Edward, heir to the throne, Hertford contrived to assume the influential position of Protector. Surrey seems to have objected to this, wishing instead that his father, the Duke of Norfolk, should have the 'rule and governance of the Prince', although here the court relied upon Blage's testimony. Interestingly, the extant account also notes that Blage responded that the Prince would be 'evil taught' if he was placed under Norfolk's care (Surrey 1964, liii). Of course, Blage was not implying that Norfolk was a poor teacher, or even that he would not provide sufficiently scholarly supervision. Rather, Norfolk's teaching was perceived as 'evil' because it would have been Catholic and that commitment to the old faith was to the reformist Blage and the Protestant Hertford an 'evil' that compounded political difference with spiritual division. Read again, Surrey's poem takes on a further signification that, to those aware of the circumstances, would have been obvious by the second line, as the 'guiding sail' of 'Faith' is 'pierced'. The political and personal had been brought together by Wyatt before the Protestant Reformation took hold in England, but by the mid-sixteenth century, court power was indivisibly entwined with personal faith. And it was not only Surrey's ship that suffered the storms of religious persecution over the next fifty years. Moreover while the association of secular and spiritual journeys with political identity had been fully established, the way in which these signifiers related to one another was to shift continually.

V   Edmund Spenser, George Herbert, John Milton

One of the most dramatic shifts in the relationship between the spiritual, secular and political location of individual identity occurs in the writing of Edmund Spenser (c.1552–99). Unlike the Tudor authors discussed earlier, Spenser's writing encompassed a variety of forms and stylistic techniques, most obviously in the romance epic poem, *The Faerie Queene* (1590 and 1596). Moreover, he may be identified closely with the Elizabethan age and the cultural discourses that pertain to this later period. The role of the courtier was still important, but it had evolved from a dependency upon the medieval feudal hierarchy to encompass a gentleman drawn from the lower nobility or even the middle classes. As Spenser points out in the prefatory letter to *The Faerie Queene* in which he addresses Walter Ralegh:

> *The generall end therefore of all the booke is to fashion a*
> *gentleman or noble person in vertuous and gentle discipline.*
> (Spenser 1977, 407)

This 'fashioning' depended more upon inherent and personal moral worth than upon inherited status, and the value-systems that align with such an ideological shift emerge in Spenser's poetry. Rather than examine the more famous and lengthy works, however, I wish to look at one poem in Spenser's sonnet collection, *Amoretti*, which was published with the *Epithalamion* in 1595.

Both works were addressed to his second wife, Elizabeth Boyle, whom he had married in 1594. Sonnet 63 will be immediately recognisable in terms of influence:

> After long stormes and tempests' sad assay,
>   which hardly I endured heretofore,
>   in dread of death and daungerous dismay,

> with which my silly barke was tossed sore;
> I doe at length descry the happy shore,
>   in which I hope ere long for to arryve:
>   fayre soyle it seemes from far and fraught with store
> of all that deare and daynty is alyve.
> Most happy he that can at last atchyve
>   the joyous safety of so sweet a rest,
>   whose least delight sufficeth to deprive
> remembrance of all paines which him opprest.
> All paines are nothing in respect of this,
>   all sorrowes short that gaine eternall blisse.
>   (Evans 1977, 141)

Not surprisingly Spenser's sonnet invokes the image of the poetic self as a ship, the 'silly barke', which encounters the storms of life while looking to the peace and security of the 'happy shore', a trope which had by the late-sixteenth century become a commonplace of Petrarchan convention. Yet, the tortured lover of the Petrarchan original, or the doomed and despairing courtiers of the English tradition are absent, for sonnet 63 concludes with the triumph of 'eternall blisse'. Taken as a whole the poem moves through four sections with the first three being interwoven and answered by the final couplet, as the ababbcbccdcdee rhyme scheme suggests. The first quatrain introduces the conventional Petrarchan theme, allowing the reader familiar with the tradition to foresee the usual despairing conclusion. The second quatrain does nothing to disturb this pattern as it looks at the 'fayre soyle' from a distance. But the third quatrain, which is linked to the second through its rhyme, begins to suggest the possibility of attaining that 'sweet rest' and thereby the possibility of forgetting the 'paines' that have gone before and kept the poetic self 'opprest'. Yet it is the final division of the sonnet into the last couplet, divided by both punctuation and rhyme, that establishes the immediate presence of salvation, that unspecified 'this' of line 13, which is translated in the exultant 'eternall blisse' at the very end of the poem. To a present-day reader, this happy ending might seem a pleasant change from the desolation and hopelessness of the earlier poems, but to an Early Modern reader such flouting of a poetic discourse that had stood unchallenged for almost a hundred years would have appeared both radical and disturbing. So why did Spenser break the rules?

The most obvious reason might simply be that the love poems and subsequent marriage text were written for his wife, with whom he was clearly very happy. The role of the despairing or unrequited lover would have been inappropriate in such circumstances, although he might still have wished to employ the Petrarchan discourse given the way that it idealises the loved one. However, there is a further, concealed meaning within the *Amoretti*. As the subsequent verses progress the consummation of love and the perfection of the beloved is sustained and increased, through the 'sweet odour', 'sacred bowre', perfect 'light' and 'gentle [and] mylde[r] deare' of sonnets 64, 65, 66 and 67. It is not until the first lines of sonnet 68, however, that the alternative discourse of Christian love becomes apparent as Spenser commences what is now known as his Easter sonnet with:

> Most glorious Lord of lyfe that on this day
> didst make thy triumph over death and sin.
> (Evans 1977, 143)

At this moment the sonnet sequence reverses upon itself, demanding that the previous 67 poems be reworked in the light of an overwhelming and positive Christian narrative. The beloved shifts from a material location in the figure of Elizabeth Boyle and takes on the vividly New Testament image of Christ, who may now be fully recognised as the 'sweet . . . sacred . . . light . . . gentle [and] . . . mylde' subject of the whole work. Spenser Christianised the Petrarchan love sonnet so that it shed the worldly constraints of court politics and was transformed into a spiritual hymn.[5] In this almost prayer-like invocation of Christ, Spenser draws upon the neoPlatonic doctrine of an ideal and unified love that was able to reconcile spiritual and secular within a Christianised harmony.

But the poetic representation of such otherworldly perfection was not unproblematic. The traditional sonnet signifiers, particularly the Petrarchan elements of secular and at times erotic love, as well as the oppositional conceits such as hope and despair, could not be completely eradicated from the discourse. While sonnet 63 might claim that 'eternall blisse' meant the purging of painful memories, the twelve lines that go before remind us that 'death and daungerous dismay' is our inheritance in both poetic and spiritual terms. Thus, just as the reader remains in the fallen state exiled from an Edenic happiness, so the Petrarchan sonnet discourse reminds us that despair is not so easily dismissed from our minds. The use of the storm metaphor in particular proved recalcitrant to an idealised Christian discourse and this problem was directly addressed by another religious writer, George Herbert (1593–1633).

Herbert is an early seventeenth-century writer, who has been categorised as one of the Metaphysical poets, but whose writing should also be recognised for its strong devotional tone, rather than for dislocations of meaning and colloquial language, although these are both aspects of his verse. Nearly all Herbert's poetry was published in the posthumous volume, *The Temple* (1633). The overall context of this work is the worship of God and the tone shifts continually, displaying the various stages of the soul's relationship to devotion; for example, from the confessional 'The Sinner', through the elevation of the pictorial 'Easter Wings' to the angry rebellion of 'The Collar'. The poem that concentrates upon the metaphor of the tempest is entitled quite simply, 'The Storm':

> If as the windes and waters here below
> > Do flie and flow,
> My sighs and tears as busie were above;
> > Sure they would move
> And much affect thee, as tempestuous times
> Amaze poore mortals, and object their crimes.
>
> Starres have their storms, ev'n in a high degree,
> > As well as we.
> A throbbing conscience spurred by remorse
> > Hath a strange force:
> It quits the earth, and mounting more and more,
> Dares to assault, and beseige thy doore.
>
> There it stands knocking, to thy musicks wrong,
> > And drowns the song.
> Glorie and honour are set by till it
> > An answer get.
> Poets have wrong'd poore storms: such days are best;
> They purge the aire without, within the breast.
> (Herbert 1974, 143)

There are a number of differences between Herbert's verse and the Petrarchan sonnets of Wyatt, Surrey and Spenser. To begin with, the poem is longer, consisting of 18 lines of rhyming couplets divided into three verses, with a line pattern that echoes the ebb and flow of the storm. In addition, the storm is seen from land, and rather than moving towards the safety of an earthly harbour, the self ascends through the image of the stars to heaven and God's 'doore'. Yet there are also a number of similarities with the earlier works. Herbert internalises the storm immediately, so that we are aware of the parallel between the external forces of 'water and windes' and the personal 'sighs and tears' of the poetic self. Even the vocabulary reminds us of the earlier verses, with the repetition of storm, tempest, sighs, and tears, as well as the suggestion of an all-powerful lord. And as the mocking allusion to 'Poets [who] have wrong'd poore storms' in the last but one line denotes, the Petrarchan sonneteers have been summoned within the text's referents precisely so that they may be dismissed. The secular discourse is thus over-written with a devotional narrative that presents the storm as a necessary elemental force within man and nature, and as part of God's eternal and omnipotent design. Rather than reconciling opposites as in Spenser's *Amoretti*, Herbert's poem recognises dichotomies within a larger heavenly frame.

Devotional and spiritual poetry thus transformed the courtly and secular image of the storm into a devotional discourse praising God, yet of all the Early Modern poets to undertake this task it was perhaps John Milton (1608–74), in his poem *Lycidas* (1637), who completed the transition. Milton is best known today for his religious epics, *Paradise Lost* (1667) and *Paradise Regained* (1671), but he began writing poetry as a young man and in his early verse balanced the differing demands of Early Modern poetic discourses. *Lycidas* was written as an elegy for a young Cambridge colleague, Edward King, who drowned during a sea crossing to Ireland. The poem engages with classical antecedents, pastoral traditions, Italian influences including Petrarch, and other English writers, such as Spenser, while at the same time composing a Christian poem that ultimately praises God. The poet initially summons the classical God, Neptune, to ask the 'waves, and . . . felon winds' what has happened to Lycidas, but only 15 lines later St Peter, the 'pilot of the Galilean lake' regrets the loss of the 'young swain' (Milton 1971, 246–7). One of the most powerful images, however, submerges the text within the storm-ridden sea itself,

> Ay me! Whilst thee the shores and sounding seas
> Wash far away, where'er thy bones are hurled,
> Whether beyond the stormy Hebrides,

> Where thou perhaps under the whelming tide
> Visit'st the bottom of the monstrous world.
> (Milton 1971, 251)

Death is a stark reality here with the 'bones' being 'hurled' to the very bottom of the sea world. The despair of the Petrarchan sonnets becomes redundant in the face of a material image of death tied so closely to the lyrical vision of gods and nymphs. But it is precisely at the moment of negation and loss, when the self becomes dismembered and dispersed into meaninglessness, that salvation is offered. The 'monstrous world' of the watery depths recalls the biblical narrative of Jonah and the whale, with its redemptive associations, so that it comes as no surprise when we are told to 'Weep no more' since Lycidas will arise like the 'day-star [from] ocean bed' (Milton 1971, 252–3). Indeed, Lycidas returns to the present material world as a 'Genius of the shore' who will, Christ-like, be 'good/ To all that wander in that perilous flood' (Milton 1971, 253). The storm that kills Edward King is thus transformed through Milton's poetic language into a Christian allegory, whereby those who fall to the depths will be redeemed, in an overarching configuration that encompasses Adam and Eve, all humankind, Lycidas, and Christ himself. If *Paradise Lost* presents the reader with the concept of the fortunate fall, then *Lycidas* offers us the fortunate storm. But even if Milton transforms the Petrarchan discourse, the immediacy of contemporary allegory remains in place, as the place of the all-powerful monarch is taken by 'the grim wolf [whom] with privy paw/Daily devours apace' (Milton 1971, 249). For the wolf, apart from being the traditional enemy of shepherds is emblematically associated with Rome and therefore with the Catholic Church. Faith in Early Modern Europe was not a clear choice of elevating the spiritual over the secular, as it so often seems in the *Amoretti, The Temple* and *Lycidas*, but was, as Milton reminds us, a site of schism between Catholic and Protestant Churches.

VI John Donne

The upheavals in the spiritual lives of Early Modern Europeans had brought the acute schism between Catholic and Protestant churches into their lives and homes. It had riven families, destroyed whole towns and created enemies where before there had been friends. This division has already been explained briefly through Surrey's last verses, but the religious adherence of the Tudor poet had always been clear. Therefore, in order to examine the way in which the transition between faiths is represented poetically, I intend to look at the poetry of John Donne (1572–1631). As descendants of Thomas More, the English Catholic martyr, John Donne and his brother were brought up in the old religion. Indeed, Donne's brother, Henry, and his uncle, Jasper Heywood, both died for their faith. John Donne, however, became a Protestant and although the date of his conversion is uncertain it was probably soon after his brother's death in 1593 and before he volunteered to fight the Catholic forces of Spain at Cadiz in 1596. It would have been impossible for a Catholic to procure any advancement either in the universities or at court, but it is unlikely that Donne's conversion was an expedient or cynical act. Indeed, in his prose treatise *Pseudo-Martyr* (1610) he challenges the Catholic faith and any predilection towards martyrdom, particularly in his own family. John Donne's writing, therefore, often incorporates Catholic discourses even as it attempts to challenge them, and this dialectic became particularly emphatic after Donne's own ordination as an Anglican deacon and priest in 1615. Indeed, following his election as the Dean of St Paul's Cathedral in London in 1621, his sermons became set pieces of Anglican rhetoric, while retaining the vigour of intellectual and spiritual debate.

In addition to the spiritual divide Donne's writing is also known for its startling shift from the early erotic love poems, the *Songs and Sonnets*, to the devotional verses and sermons of his later years. And it is this transition that I wish to turn to particularly in looking at the poem, 'At the round earth's imagined corners'. The sonnet was probably written in 1609, shortly before *Pseudo-Martyr* and not long after the *Songs and Sonnets*, and is one of the *Holy Sonnets* that are commonly gathered with other devotional verses under the title, 'Divine Poems':

> At the round earth's imagined corners, blow
> Your trumpets, angels, and arise, arise
> From death, you numberless infinities
> Of souls, and to your scattered bodies go,
> All whom the flood did, and fire shall o'erthrow,
> All whom war, dearth, age, agues, tyrannies,
> Despair, law, chance, hath slain, and you whose eyes,

> Shall behold God, and never taste death's woe.
> But let them sleep, Lord, and me mourn a space,
> For, if above all these, my sins abound,
> 'Tis late to ask abundance of thy grace,
> When we are there; here on this lowly ground,
> Teach me how to repent; for that's as good
> As if thou hadst sealed my pardon, with thy blood.
> (Donne 1971, 311–2)

The sonnet is Petrarchan, although it follows the English rhyme scheme by adding a concluding couplet: abbaabbacdcdee. The first quatrain refers to God's Last Judgement, drawing upon depictions in Revelation and Corinthians of the four angels at the Four Corners of the world calling the dead to arise. Yet although the initial rhyme scheme concludes at line 4, the use of the caesura (after '. . . souls') and the corresponding enjambment demand that the first quatrain is pushed into an uneasy unity with the second. The rhyme scheme of the first 8 lines remains the same, following the chronological parity of the two sections, both focusing on the time before the resurrection. As such, the second quatrain depicts the 'flood' in Genesis and the all-consuming 'fire' of the Last Judgement, and then lists in detail the many causes of death, from war to chance events. Yet the image carried over from line 4 is of the infinity of souls who search for their 'scattered bodies'. Those bodies that are through the shifting reading of line 4, both scattered in themselves, their bones being torn asunder in the 'flood . . . war . . . tyrannies . . . Despair [and] law', as well as dispersed about the globe in their various graves. Only those who are alive on the Day of Judgement will escape 'death's woe', thereby evading the separation of soul from body with the horrific disintegration of the latter. The problem of the body's negation was returned to continually by Donne; for example, in a sermon preached on Easter Day 1626 he explains how:

> this body being fallen into a dissolution of dust, this dust falls into
> a dispersion, and is scattered unsensibly, undiscernably upon the
> face of the earth; and the resurrection from this death, is by way of re-
> collection; God shall recall and re-collect all these atoms, and grains
> of dust, and re-compact that body, and re-unite that soul, and so that
> resurrection is accomplished . . . (Donne 1990, 369)

Yet, the resolution of the sermon is never attained in the sonnet, for the third quatrain shifts the chronological position, drawing us back from the brink, so that the all-embracing Judgement Day and personal demise are projected into the future. Consequently, the past, present and future 'souls' are left caught between that moment of 'scattered' separation before the 're-collection' of their atoms, and the 'sleep' within which Donne contains them. Trapped in this gap between death and resurrection the infinity of souls remains as a troubling presence when we begin the third quatrain.

Instead of developing this theme, however, the poetic voice withdraws in an introspective moment, a 'space' in which the Day of Judgement is a threatening presence – 'When we are there' – but is simultaneously at a safe distance because we remain 'here on this lowly ground'. This dialectic of time persists, therefore, through the first 12 lines of the poem, shifting from a perception of an ultimate and dislocating finality, and the odd reassurance of a present, sinful and material existence upon the earth. Within the Petrarchan sonnet convention Donne appears to be happier to remain within the storm of 'flood . . . fire . . .', with the whole array of troubles besetting human existence, than to reach the port, that imagined heaven where we may behold God. Indeed, the dead are allowed to 'sleep' and Donne secures his 'space' for a little longer on the 'lowly ground'.

Of course, that space is perceived as necessary for the poetic self, and for all humankind, in order to offer the opportunity to repent, as the last couplet makes clear. Yet there is an unnerving opposition in these lines. The more positive reading tells us that true repentance is as powerful as a pardon sealed with Christ's 'blood' and therefore we have nothing to fear on Judgement Day, for our dispersed identities will be re-collected by God in a triumph of heavenly salvation. Yet the lines shift on the words, 'As if', undercutting the affirmative signification with lingering doubt. In this alternative form, repentance is still praised, but the emphasis is upon the absence, or failure, of Christ to seal that pardon with his death upon the cross. The very promise of everlasting life and the deliverance of humankind through Christ's suffering, must be read as simultaneously promised and withheld. And thus, like all the souls in the previous douzain, the poetic self is trapped at the interstice between faith and doubt; faith in salvation and fear of damnation, faith in God's re-collection of our bodies and fear that human identity will remain scattered in a final negation of subjectivity. The Petrarchan discourse is thus transformed yet again,

even in its spiritual form. It shifts back and forth between the ideal
unity of Spenser's *Amoretti*, Herbert's heavenly encompassing of
opposites in *The Temple*, and Milton's recognition of the necessity of
sin and damnation in *Lycidas*, to the doubts and fears of Donne's *Holy
Sonnets*.

Such doubts were not unique to John Donne. They recur throughout devotional poetry, not just in Early Modern writing, but also in
present day texts. However, I would like to turn back to the sonnet
once again, because doubt and despair were themes that projected
themselves into sixteenth- and early-seventeenth-century poetry
through the divided glass of Protestantism and Catholicism. If we
return to line 7, we find a list of the causes of untimely death, which
begins with 'Despair' or suicide. Taking one's own life was, in ordinary circumstances, seen as a sin for which no offer of salvation
would be made, but this was mitigated if welcoming death could be
identified as dying for one's faith. Indeed, the Catholic Church had
accepted the evils of martyrdom as a way of inspiring the faithful, and
the most well-known Catholic martyr in England was Thomas More,
Donne's ancestor. In his prose treatise, *Pseudo-Martyr*, which was
written at the same time as the sonnet, Donne explicitly denies the
interpretation of martyrdom as an allowable form of suicide, while
simultaneously using the text as a proclamation of his own Protestant
faith. As he points out:

> I have been ever kept awake in a meditation of martyrdom, by being
> derived from such a stock and race as, I believe, no family . . . hath
> endured and suffered more in their persons and fortunes, for obeying
> the teachers of Roman doctrine, than it hath done. (Donne, 1990,
> 190)

Moreover, *Pseudo-Martyr* itself was written and published specifically
to support James I's demand that all English Catholics should take the
Oath of Allegiance, despite the fact that the Pope had declared the
oath contrary to the Catholic faith. The fear of Catholics had increased
after the near-success of the Gunpowder Plot in 1606, and Donne
argues specifically that those executed should not be glorified as
martyrs. Being ready to die for one's faith could not, therefore, guar-
antee salvation and might be classed as suicide, or a 'Despair' following closely upon 'tyrannies'. Donne's sonnet engages with the
personal and spiritual concerns of the Christian faith, but at the same

time allows the political impact of religious schism to suggest a dialectic between welcoming death and the acceptance of a continued existence of earth. The poem not only challenges the Christianised version of the Petrarchan storm/port metaphor, but also relocates it within one of the most fraught debates of Early Modern Europe. For a Protestant, therefore, the storm must be endured, since by guiding one's soul-like ship to the heavenly haven was to court despair, suicide and the relinquishing of the very salvation that was most desired. And for John Donne this rejection of the spiritual discourse of Catholicism necessitated a simultaneous discarding of 'stock and race', and the consequential fashioning of a new Protestant identity for himself.

VII Sir Walter Ralegh

Of all Early Modern poets the most consummate self-fashioner must be Sir Walter Ralegh (1552–1618). Just think of the stories that surround him, such as the image of Ralegh throwing his cloak down over a muddy puddle so that Queen Elizabeth would not dirty her shoes. Or the tale of how he wrote a message to the Queen in a window, saying, 'Fain could I climb, but I fear to fall', and how when she found it Elizabeth wrote back, 'If thy heart fail thee, climb not at all', thereby encouraging her courtier in his ambitions. Or the story of how he discovered tobacco and potatoes and introduced them to the court. Or finally, the rumour of how he was such a passionate lover that a lady's reprimand, 'Sir Walter, Sir Walter', soon became the enamoured jumble, 'Swisser, swatter'.[6] Here we have the various images: a perfect gentleman, the consummate courtier, the bold explorer and the undeniable lover. Yet, there is no proof of any of these stories, no evidence to show that 'Swisser Swatter' displayed a single one of the perfections with which he has since been credited. The projection of a division between the real man and his constructed reputation is, however, precisely the point. For Ralegh was simply the quintessential self-fashioned Renaissance man. The discourses wrapped about him and his poetry are therefore as important to our understanding of a particularly Early Modern form of subjectivity, as to our appreciation of Ralegh as an individual author.

In order to identify the way in which Ralegh may be used to explain a broader concept of self-constructed identity it is useful to trace his history. He was a member of an obscure, but well-connected, country family, and after attending Oxford seems to have ascended the social ladder rapidly, becoming one of the Queen's favourites from the mid-1580s. Ralegh began to be interested in colonial exploration at this time, attempting to settle a colony on the eastern seaboard of North America in 1585. It was also around this point that his portrait was painted by Nicholas Hilliard; it shows a handsome man, with immaculately curled hair and moustaches, and a large, ornate ruff that offsets his dark features with a dazzling white surround.[7] This ascendancy came to an abrupt halt, however, in 1592 when Ralegh became involved with one of the Queen's maids of honour, Elizabeth Throckmorton, got her pregnant and married her secretly. When Elizabeth I found out, Ralegh was arrested and imprisoned in the Tower of London and, although he was soon released, the Queen's disfavour lasted for five years. After several unsuccessful attempts to win back her affections, two successful expeditions against the Spanish (1596 and 1597) finally reconciled Elizabeth to her erstwhile favourite. The respite was not enduring, however, for at the accession of James I in 1603 Ralegh was again imprisoned in the Tower, this time on a charge of conspiring with Spain against the King. The accusations seem to have been orchestrated more to ensure Ralegh did not actively pursue war against Spain, but he spent the next 12 years in the Tower, where he began his prose account, *The History of the World* (1614). In 1616 Ralegh was released in order to undertake an expedition to South America, and when this proved unsuccessful he returned to England only to be executed in 1618 on the original charge of treason.

Although many of his friends seem to have deserted Ralegh during his imprisonment, as a poet and writer he was held in high esteem. Francis Meres includes him in a list of poets who are, 'the most passionate among us to bewaile and bemoane the perplexities of Love', and George Puttenham refers to Ralegh as one of those:

> Courtly makers, Noble men and Gentlemen of her Maiesties owne servantes, who have written excellently well as it would appeare if their doings could be found out and made publicke with the rest . . .
> (Latham 1951, lix)

Obviously some of the poems written by Ralegh, such as those addressed directly to the Queen, could not have been published. But it would be wrong to assume that simply because verses such as

'Fortune Hath Taken Away My Love' and 'My Body in the Walls Captivated' (both addressed to Elizabeth I) did not appear in print that they were private works. Ralegh's unpublished works, in other words most of his poetry, were certainly not intended for general readership, but they would have been circulated in manuscript form at court. Moreover, such scribal publication would have been recognised as another aspect of the courtier's determination to fashion himself as an ideal gentleman.

The idea of an independent construction of subjectivity was fully explored in Stephen Greenblatt's path-breaking work, *Renaissance Self-Fashioning* (1980). This critical work has now become a standard point of reference for Early Modern literature, yet I would like to look briefly at the criteria described by Greenblatt to see how closely they match up with Sir Walter Ralegh. A full list of ten points is provided at the beginning of the book and the following quotation is a summary of the whole,

> 1 . . . all of these writers are middle-class. 2 . . . [it] involves submission to an absolute power or authority. 3 . . . [it] is achieved in relation to something perceived as alien . . . 4 . . . [this] alien is . . . always constructed as a distorted image of the authority . . . [5, 6, and 7 all deal with the replication and multiplication of both authority and alien] 8 . . . both the authority and alien are . . . always already internalised. 9 . . . [it occurs in] language. 10 . . . [it] involves some experience of threat [and] . . . some loss of self. (Greenblatt 1980, 9; 'it' refers to 'self-fashioning')

Some of the points are commensurate with the details of Ralegh's life. For example, his family was certainly more middle class than aristocratic, he created his own identity in relation to a figure of authority, that is Queen Elizabeth I, and an internalised sense of self-destruction is evident from the precariousness of Ralegh's existence at court and his final execution. Indeed, Greenblatt might well have had Ralegh in mind as he composed these criteria since *Renaissance Self-Fashioning* was preceded by an earlier criticism, *Sir Walter Ralegh* (1973), in which he had already been preparing the new theoretical concept. In this early book, Greenblatt writes,

> Ralegh's self-fashioning is paradoxical: it bends art to the service of life – advancing his career, justifying his actions, enhancing his repu-

tation – and it transforms his life into art, leading ever further from
the career toward symbolic characterisation and transcendent
meaning. It exists in time and in spite of time; it addresses a specific
historical audience and yet turns inward, cryptically mirroring the
self; it reflects the world and creates its own world. (Greenblatt 1973,
59–60)

Ralegh's projection of himself did indeed help serve his career at
court in a moment of historical influence and, as such, this self existed
at a chronological cross-section of material experience through an
immediate synchronic discourse. Yet at the same time, Ralegh pushed
away from this horizontal axis, along a vertical line that opposed and
questioned the restraints of time, suggesting that the self through its
symbolic signification could breach those limits. This diachronic
discourse involved a self-mythologising and an expansion of an inner
timeless world that demanded a recognition of the subject 'in and in
spite of time'. However, in order to test both Ralegh's role as a paradigm of self-fashioning, as well as the claim to the transitional nature
of this construction within the parameters of time and place, it is
necessary to examine his poetry.

The range of poems attributed to Ralegh is considerable, but given
the lack of holograph works (only four exist in the Hatfield manuscripts), few pieces can authoritatively said to be his. In choosing the
following sonnet for analysis, I have followed Agnes Latham and
Douglas Brooks-Davies in their creditation. This poem, however
relates to the storm metaphor only at a tangent (although the
Petrarchan discourse is fully evident) and I shall return to Ralegh's
poetic representation of a tempestuous sea later. The poem itself,
'Like to a Hermit Poor' was first published anonymously in *The
Phoenix Nest* (1593), but was later printed with Ralegh's name in *Sir
Walter Rawlegh's Farewell to His Lady* (1644). It was most probably
written during Ralegh's imprisonment or subsequent removal from
court after he displeased the Queen with his precipitous, although
happy, marriage to Elizabeth Throckmorton. The sonnet is a translation of 'Sonnet 8' from Book 2 of Philippe Desportes' *Diane* (1573).
The French original follows Petrarchan convention carefully and was
a popular verse, having been translated into English by Thomas Lodge
in 1589. While Lodge's poem offers a close rendition of Desportes' text
however, Ralegh's version gives us a much freer interpretation,

Like to a hermit poor in place obscure
I mean to spend my days of endless doubt,
To wail such woes as time cannot recure,
Where none but Love shall ever find me out.

My food shall be of care and sorrow made;
My drink nought else but tears fallen from mine eyes;
And for my light in such obscured shade
The flames shall serve which from my heart arise.

A gown of grey my body shall attire,
My staff of broken hope whereon I'll stay,
Of late repentance linked with long desire
The couch is framed whereon my limbs I'll lay:

>   And at my gate Despair shall linger still,
>   To let in Death when Love and Fortune will.
>   (Brooks-Davies 1992, 142)

Thematically the poem engages with the traditional Petrarchan concerns of love and power, in which the poet's lady is able to represent both a personal love and the authority of the Queen. Its rhyme scheme follows the conventional pattern of ababcdcdefefgg, dividing the poem into the three quatrains and final couplet of the English sonnet form developed by Surrey. Like the Tudor sonneteers', Ralegh's translation is not intended to follow the original slavishly and this is particularly apparent when compared to the two earlier versions offered by Desportes and Lodge. The French original reads,

>   Et tousjours, pour prier, devant mes yeux j'auray
>   La peinture d'Amour et celle de ma dame,

which Lodge translates as,

>   and daylie when I pray,
>   My mistris picture plac't by love
>   Shall witness what I say.
>   (Latham 1951, 106–8)

Both extracts imagine praying before the double image of the God of Love and the lover's lady. Ralegh, on the other hand, ends his poem by admitting both death and despair into the poem at a predicted future time when his love will be rejected. The dialectic created by this inclusion opens the sonnet up to Greenblatt's notion of self-fashioning, while also creating a link to a more widespread Petrarchan convention.

If we take the criteria for self-fashioning and apply them to the sonnet, several common elements become apparent. The representation of the poetic self as 'middle class', or certainly inferior to the lady, is apparent in the allusions to 'hermit poor', 'place obscure', and 'obscured', while the final reference to 'Fortune' suggests the hierarchical world of court privilege. The hermit thus comes to represent a self who is abased through class, love, and within the court. All Petrarchan poems contain a figure of authority and here the usual ones are repeated: the lady, a personified Love, and the monarch, who is here female and thus commensurate with the lady rather than in competition for her as in Wyatt's references to 'Lord'. The alien or other within the poem is figured, as it often is in Ralegh's verse, as death and despair representing a threat to his hopes for preferment at court as well as in personal love. The last couplet projects a deeply pessimistic view of life, almost tragic in its intensity, with Death and Despair 'linger[ing]' and always ready at the poet's 'gate'. Yet this otherness is a distorted image of the figure of authority in that it was precisely Queen Elizabeth who controlled Ralegh's fortunes, and while she might not have ordered his execution, there were plenty of others who died at her behest. Ralegh would have been all too aware that while his monarch could well offer the benign preferment of her love, at the same time she was perfectly capable of signifying death. But rather than blame the power structures of his time Ralegh internalises his fate, emphasising his own 'poor' and 'broken' self that remains in 'endless doubt'. And once again corresponding with the concept of self-fashioning Ralegh depicts his suffering in language, since this poem was most probably given to the Queen in the hope that she would recognise her courtier's despair and once more return his love. Indeed, Ralegh's use of the Petrarchan love sonnet shows not only that he was familiar with the convention itself, but also more especially with the way in which Elizabeth had personalised the tradition. By the 1590s Elizabethan sonneteers had become adept at offering political panegyrics to their monarch disguised as love poems to their lady. Within the Petrarchan form, therefore, Elizabeth was both the beloved and the figure of authority, both lady and queen, an embodiment of the inextricable combination of the personal and the political.

And it was as such that Ralegh addressed her in 'Like to a Hermit Poor' and the other poems he wrote while suffering her disfavour.

During his incarceration in the Tower of London, Ralegh seems to have written a long poem to Elizabeth I entitled *The Ocean to Cynthia*, of which only a part remains extant. Spenser certainly knew of the poem and makes reference to it in *The Faerie Queene* (Book III, Proem verse 4). It is impossible to know whether Ralegh entitled the extant verses as a part of a greater whole to give the impression of a longer and more substantial poem in order to impress the Queen further, or whether a considerable amount of the poem is actually lost. Whatever the extent of the work, its main import is the complaint of a lover at being forsaken, even as the moon goddess Cynthia appears to leave the ocean when she ascends into the night sky. The poem continually evokes Petrarchan storm/sea imagery:

> So my forsaken heart, my withered mind
> (Widow of all the joys it once possessed,
> My hopes clean out of sight) with forced wind
> To kingdoms strange, to lands far-off addressed,
> Alone, forsaken, friendless on the shore,
> With many wounds, with Death's cold pangs embraced.
> (Brooks-Davies 1992, 152)

The poet's heart and mind are imaged as a ship caught in the storm of a 'forced wind', cast adrift in a 'strange' land, and left to die. Yet the poetic self is also represented as the sea, as Ocean himself, whose personal grief is thus metamorphosed into 'floods of sorrow and whole seas of woe' which will drown the mind in 'depths of misery' (Brooks-Davies 1992, 154). The poetic self thus alternates in metaphoric terms: at one moment he is the object of the storm's destructive force, while at another he becomes the tempest itself and the active subject of the text. However, it is in the final lines of the poetic fragment, when Ralegh invokes the story of Hero and Leander, that the import of such transformations of the self becomes apparent.

> Against whose banks the troubled Ocean beat,
> And were the marks to find thy hoped port,
> Into a soil far off themselves remove
> (On Sestos' shore, Leander's late resort,
> Hero hath left no lamp to guide her love)

> Thou lookest for light in vain, and storms arise:
> (Brooks-Davies 1992, 162)

In addition to the original mythological allusion, the reference recalls Christopher Marlowe's erotic romance, *Hero and Leander*, which was in itself a fragment and was finally completed by George Chapman in 1598. By foregrounding the way in which the legend and its thematic concerns had been reworked, Ralegh's poem inevitably calls our attention to its own literary substance, and this self-referential conclusion demands a rereading of the role of the poetic self. For the poet is simultaneously the subject of the poem, the active author of the text, the all-encompassing Ocean, as well as being the object of the poem as the fraught lover whose death by drowning is predicted via a literary allusion. The poem's self-effacement is thus countered by an awareness of the power and continuity of language and text.

The poetic images in Ralegh's poems seem, by a twist of fate, to have come true, in that he did end his life on the order of the monarch. Yet, when he finally stood ready to face execution, Ralegh turned away from the material glories of self-fashioning. In his scaffold speech he claimed:

> The great God of heaven is my soveraigne, before whose tribunall
> seat I am, shortly, to appeare. (Ralegh 1829, VIII, 776)

And then he proclaimed his innocence and asked the crowd to pray for him. In that moment of actual despair, when death was finally encountered, Ralegh acknowledged that all the glitter and pomp of the self-fashioned Renaissance man was a hollow shell. Or did he?

Ralegh's scaffold speech is rhetorically skilful and stylistically adept. Yet it was in fact another facade, this time for posterity. For although Ralegh was right in proclaiming himself to be innocent of spying, it seems that he was involved in a conspiracy with the French. Indeed, on his return from Guiana to face sure execution, Ralegh wrote a plea to France to help him escape as payment for past services. Unfortunately, the letter was never delivered as the messenger was captured by pirates, and died giving the paper to a Jesuit. Until the nineteenth century the letter lay unread in a collection of church papers. Even in that final speech, therefore, Ralegh fashions himself as an object of injustice who turns in truth to God.

Ultimately, Ralegh was a perpetually self-fashioning Renaissance gentleman. Not only did he create particular identities for the benefit of Elizabeth I, James I, the court and his own family, he even constructed his own image for the future, as a brave, noble and honest man, who had been wronged by the omnipotent power of his king. Sir Walter Ralegh remains, therefore, an enigma, a series of bold and vivid self-depictions that were as flexible as his name. Yet these very images – with the cloak, as a lover and on the scaffold – ensured that Ralegh's identity was secured for posterity.

VIII Michael Drayton

While the legend of Swisser Swatter has persisted until today, the image and identity of Michael Drayton (1563–1631), another Early Modern poet, has been lost to posterity. Yet Drayton was far more prolific than Ralegh, and his published works fill four solid volumes, the fifth being devoted to copious annotation. Indeed, Drayton endeavoured to cover the full range of poetic genres, from geographical epic, *PolyOlbion* (1612–13 and 1622), through heroic histories, *The Barons Warres* (1603), to the sonnet in *Ideas Mirrour* (1594). Drayton, however, continually reworked and added to his compositions, so that in discussing any poem, especially the sonnets, it is important to note the changes, as well as to date those changes. For example, the sonnets were rewritten and finally republished as *Idea* in 1619. One of the reasons for these alterations was that Drayton recognised the contemporary changes in poetic style. Thus he rejected the elaborate and exaggerated conceits of the Elizabethan period for the more colloquial tones and philosophical debates of the Jacobean age. Nevertheless, Drayton's attempts at being up-to-date often seem half-hearted, and the literary allusions used show him to be deeply indebted to the major poets of the previous age. References to Spenser and Sidney emerge in Drayton's works through direct indebtedness as he copied the choice of form or rhyme scheme of the earlier poets. Moreover, a sense of nostalgia runs through all Drayton's writings and is particularly evinced in *Idea*. It is hardly surprising, therefore, to come across a ship and storm sonnet. Indeed, it appears as the first poem in the 1619 edition of Drayton's sonnet collection.

> Like an adventurous Sea-farer am I
> Who hath some long and dang'rous Voyage beene,

> And call'd to tell of his Discoverie,
> How farre he sayl'd, what Countries he had seene,
> Proceeding from the Port whence he put forth,
> Shewes by his Compasse how his Course he steer'd,
> When East, when West, when South, and when by North,
> As how the Pole to ev'ry place was rear'd;
> What Capes he doubled, of what Continent
> The Gulphes and Straits that strangely he had past,
> Where most becalm'd, where with foule Weather spent,
> And on what Rocks in perill to be cast:
>> Thus in my Love, Time calls me to relate
>> My tedious Travels and oft-varying Fate.
> (Evans 1977, 87–8)

In common with other sonnet collections of the period, *Idea* was dedicated to a real woman, Anne Goodere, whom he had served as a page when young and who subsequently became his patron. The affection seemingly displayed in the sonnets does not mean, however, that Drayton was in love with Goodere, for *Idea* does not carry the covert personal allegory of Sidney's *Astrophil and Stella* or the dedicated love of Spenser's *Amoretti*. Rather, *Idea* is, as its title suggests, about the idea of love, and even more, the idea of how love is encapsulated within poetry and poetic convention. It is in this light that Drayton's reworking of the Petrarchan sonnet should be read.

There is no question about Drayton's general indebtedness to the Petrarchan conventions as presented in the Italian, French and English sonnet discourses. But while allusions abound, Drayton never translated an earlier sonnet verbatim. Thus 'la tempestra' of Petrarch's original becomes the more colloquial 'foule Weather', and the rocks 'Scilla e Caribdi' are described as more conventional 'Gulphes and Straits'. Drayton's language thus shifts away from the dramatic tones and classical allusions of convention, suggesting rather the spoken discourse of early-seventeenth-century English verse. This transition to common experience is repeated in the construction of the poetic self of the sonnet, as well as in the poem's narrative. For example, the image of a courtier travelling with his lord is replaced by the 'adventurous Sea-farer' who commands and 'steer[s]' his own vessel. The poetic language of the court is thus fittingly transformed into the common tongue of the bourgeois mariner. Moreover, the text recounts the mariner's own description of his journey as he is 'call'd to tell of his Discoverie'. And it is here, in the central sections of the sonnet, that Drayton employs his most material and realistic formulations. The poem takes us from 'the Port whence he put forth', describes the directions and geographical areas he has traversed, gives an even-handed account of the weather, and finally returns to the act of telling, to the 'relat[ion]' of his 'tedious Travels'. Even the imagery depicts the necessary and prosaic 'Compasse' as the Sea-farer systematically indicates the points followed. The sonnet has been transposed from the concerns and language of the court to a decidedly lower-class discourse of real sailors, and the stuff of actual sea-faring.

Undoubtedly, one of the reasons for Drayton's use of a more realistic set of referents was his own social position, since he came from a yeoman family and was a professional poet. He was never financially secure, writing plays and poems for whatever cash he could secure, and although he attempted to gain the favour of both Elizabeth I and James I, his ambitions to become a court poet were never realised. Indeed, his praise for Anne Goodere can be read in light of his dependence upon patronage and his debt to her father, Sir Henry Goodere, who provided the poet with some formal education as a boy. For Drayton therefore, love and the adored lady of the sonnet were inextricably linked with the acute need for material sustenance.

By 1619, however, when Drayton added 'Like an adventurous Sea-farer am I' to the beginning of his sonnet sequence, *Idea*, literary vogues had abandoned the formal Petrarchan discourse that had been popular when he first published the collection in 1594. Drayton's persistence in using the sonnet form had been attacked specifically by fellow poets, Sir John Davies (1569–1626) and Joseph Hall (1574–1656), although they also satirised Petrarchan conventions in general (Drayton 1941, 137–39). Davies mocks Drayton as the overly 'audacious' 'Poet Decius' (Davies 1975, 139–40), and he also attacks the sonnet tradition in general when inverting 'la tempesta' and the 'sospir . . . speranze . . . [and] desio' of Petrarch's *Rime*, in the second of his *Gullinge Sonnets* (1594–6):

> As when the brighte Cerulian firmament
> Hathe not his glory with black cloudes defas'te,
> Soe were my thoughts voyde of all discontent
> And with noe myste of passions overcast.
> (Davies 1975, 164)

While employing the laboured rhetoric of an overly faithful Petrarchan sonneteer, Davies challenges the overall tone by pointing out that it was, in effect, a sunny day and that he was quite happy. Similarly, Hall in *Virgidemiarum* (VI. I; 1599) condemns the poet, Labeo, who is now recognised as representing Drayton, for,

> . . . filch[ing] whole Pages at a clap for need
> From honest *Petrarch*, clad in English weed.
> (Hall 1949, 94)

Although the criticism might seem unfair, Drayton was sufficiently stung by these characterisations as Decius and Labio to rewrite his sonnet sequence, in particular introducing sonnets that eschewed the earlier Petrarchan traditions for the more realistic, lively, and colloquial tones of 'Like an adventurous Sea-farer am I'.

Yet Drayton's sonnet does not conclude with this new reasoned language and the radical graphic descriptions. The final couplet follows convention by turning the poem's signification, and this shift is doubly entrenched within the Petrarchan discourse, for content echoes form and the familiar themes of love, time and fate are invoked in a series of personifications. The voyage has, it is now revealed, been through the trials of love, just as in the verses of Petrarch, Wyatt, Spenser and others. Moreover, the mariner's story has been demanded, not by a real person, but by the clichéd personification of Time, and the poet's 'Fate' has been as 'oft-varying' as any conceit-driven poem. Even as the poetic frame shifted about him, Drayton's recognition of those forces remained partial; he could not fully relinquish the traditional style, imagery, language and allusions of the Petrarchan discourse, any more than he could reject the very form of the sonnet itself. There remains a lingering nostalgia in Drayton's sonnet sequence that cannot be eradicated by the radical transitions of class and language that he both personified and echoed.

IX   Rachel Speght

The radical transitions of class and language that occurred at the beginning of the seventeenth century within London were echoed in the increasingly articulate and rebellious publications by women poets. The debate about the virtues and vices of women had continued

to engage writers from classical times, producing a range of oppositional stereotypes, such as the Virgin Mary and Eve, that can still be
recognised today. Until the Early Modern period, however, men had
produced the commentaries on both sides with very few women
writers, such as Christine de Pisan, offering a female perspective.[8]
Even then, as Helen Wilcox points out:

> It was . . . not straightforward for a woman to circulate or publish her
> own writings in the early modern era; to do so was a bold, much criti-
> cised and frequently isolated action. (Wilcox 1996, 2)

Nevertheless, by the early seventeenth century this situation had
altered marginally but irreversibly. The increasing number of women
who had received an education ensured that when they were attacked
in print, they were able to respond in kind. Thus, when Joseph
Swetnam produced his prose attack, *The Arraignment of Women*
(1617), the response was immediate and sharply perceptive.[9] The first
and only certainly identifiable response was by Rachel Speght
(b.1597), whose sharp prose treatise, *A Mouzell for Melastomus* (1617),
defended women against Swetnam's attack. The prefatory sonnet
turns the expected courtly discourse into a vehement accusation:

> **I** f reason had but curbed thy witless will
> **O** r fear of God restrained thy raving quill,
> **S** uch venom foul thou wouldst have blushed to spew,
> **E** xcept that grace have bidden thee adieu:
> **P** rowess disdains to wrestle with the weak,
> **H** eathenish affected, care not what they speak.
>
> **S** educer of the vulgar sort of men,
> **W** as Satan crept into thy filthy pen,
> **E** nflaming thee with such infernal smoke,
> **T** hat (if thou hadst thy will) should women choke?
> **N** efarious fiends thy sense herein deluded,
> **A** nd from thee all humanity excluded.
> **M** onster of men, worthy of no other name,
>   For that thou didst essay our sex to shame.
>   (Wynne-Davies 1998, 154)

Speght adopts a basically English sonnet form with seven rhymed
couplets, and she adapts the equally formal acrostic to refer to 'Joseph

Swetnam'. Several traditional themes from the sonnet discourse are also utilised, so that Speght refers to wit, even though Swetnam is described as 'wit*less*' (italics mine), and sets the whole poem within a religious context. Yet her terms are closer to the satirical vocabulary of Joseph Hall, than to the courtly language of the Petrarchan works. Swetnam is described as a 'witless . . . raving . . . Monster of men', who has been 'deluded' by 'Satan . . . [and] Nefarious fiends', so that he 'spew[s]' out 'venom foul . . . [and] infernal smoke'. Speght effectively transforms the sonnet from a verse form used to praise women into a poetic discourse that condemns men for attacking women. Gender relationships remain at the heart of the sonnet discourse, yet women writers preferred to invert the traditional poetic objectifying of their sex into an acute and self-aware response to such codification. The final line of Speght's sonnet encapsulates this shift, for it reaches out beyond the acrostic naming of Swetnam – thereby simultaneously undercutting the sonnet's couplet structure – with a rational and clear accusation that constructs the reader as sympathetic to 'our sex'.

The authenticity of Speght's defence of her sex was, however, doubted and it was thought that her father had written the work, putting the piece in his daughter's name for increased polemic efficacy. Speght responded to this renewed attempt to mute and objectify her sex by producing *Mortality's Memorandum* (1621), a long and scholarly poem, which corrects this misapprehension in the prefatory letter:

> I am now, as by a strong motive induced (for my right's sake) to produce and divulge this offspring of my endeavour, to prove them further futurely who have formerly deprived me of my due. (Speght 1621, no pagination)

Speght sees the recognition of authorship as her 'right' and 'due', and *Mortality's Memorandum* is presented to the reader as proof of poetic ability, scholarly knowledge and a continued determination to rework literary discourses from a female perspective. In the poem, the dream vision is re-sexed in order to show how women grieve over the loss of a maternal figure – Speght's godmother, Marie Mountford. Moreover it defends women's use of their intellect and abilities since the 'talent God does give must be employed' (Wynne-Davies 1998, 158). And Speght endeavours to display her 'talent[s]' as she consciously draws upon biblical, classical and vernacular literary works, in her evocation of the complex human response to death's inevitability.

Given the range of Speght's referents, her earlier use of the sonnet form, and the thematic focus upon human life within a spiritual context, the use of the ship's voyage as a metaphor for the journey of the individual towards death is expected. At the beginning of the poem, the dreamer feels disconsolate as:

> The haven of my voyage is remote,
> I have not yet attained my journey's end;
> Yet know I not, nor can I give a guess,
> How short a time I in this place shall spend.
> For that high power, which sent me to this place,
> Doth only know the period of my race.
> (Wynne-Davies 1998, 155)

The convention of the voyage, the distant haven, and the controlling power of the Lord, here referring to God, evokes the Petrarchan discourse within its Christian frame. Speght echoes the religious sonnets of Spenser and Herbert, rather than the courtly verse of Wyatt and Ralegh, although the allusions are not specific. By 1620 the ship/voyage/storm trope had become such an extensive and continually reworked image that, while tracing Petrarchan antecedents, the metaphor had spread far beyond its origins. Speght returns to the image throughout *Mortalities Memorandum*, as the idea of death is confronted:

> The mariner, which does assay to pass
> The raging seas into some foreign land,
> Desires much to have his voyage ended
> And to arrive upon the solid land . . .
>
> Men are as sailors in this irksome life,
> Who at the haven always cast their eye;
> As pilgrims wandering in an uncouth land;
> Then who is he, that will not wish to die?
> And he whom God by death does soonest call,
> Is in my mind the happiest wight of all.
> (Wynne-Davies 1998, 167)

The references to 'mariner' and 'sailors' are proverbial and no detailed analysis of the metaphor is necessary. Yet, the identification of all humankind as male, even though 'Men', given the period context, may be read as referring to women as well, is unsettling in a poem as conscious of gender difference as *Moralities Memorandum*. The distinction is underlined further in the last line of the quotation as the poet refers to 'my mind', which has already been firmly identified as a source of specifically female 'talent'. An uneasy duality begins to develop, in which the male seafarer represents the troubled human existence on earth, while the female poetic self, the mind, and the thought of the dream vision, reaches spirit-like to death and heaven.

These gendered roles are affirmed as the poem progresses, with men depicted as trapped by their material nature and a fear of death:

> Man's life on earth is like a ship at sea,
> Tossed on the waves of troubles, to and fro,
> Assailed by pirates, crossed by blustering winds,
> Where rocks of ruin menace overthrow,
> Where storms molest, and hunger pinceth sore,
> Where death does lurk at every cabin door.
> (Wynne-Davies 1998, 170)

The conventional storm images are rehearsed, with the winds and rocks threatening the sailor. But, in the context of Speght's work, the voyage and its literary predecessors are gendered, not only through the depiction of 'Man's life', but also through the use of a previously male-dominated discourse. As the poem draws to a close, the sea voyage metaphor is used finally in a biblical context,

> The dove, which Noah sent from forth the ark,
> Could find no rest till she returned again;
> Nor can the faithful, till they go to Christ,
> True rest and quiet without grief obtain;
> Heaven is the haven of the faithful wight,
> Christ's love the object of their soul's delight.
> (Wynne-Davies 1998, 179)

The story of the flood and the final successful search of the dove for land are taken from Genesis (8:9) in which the bird is described as female, as in Speght's poem. The interpretation of the biblical passage is also conventional, with Speght identifying the dove as the soul of the 'faithful' finding their spiritual home with God. The poetic verse thus appears to conform with expected readings of its biblical original, yet placed alongside the other uses of the storm/voyage trope, the language begins to look more radical. For the dialectic of male/body/material suffering and female/spirit/heavenly reward, is perpetuated by the biblical reference Speght has chosen, as the female dove succeeds in finding a 'haven', in contrast to the male sailors who remain 'crossed by blustering winds' and molested by 'storms'. The use of the archaic 'wight' to denote human beings further distances the possibility of male inclusion, since the word is used consistently throughout the poem to denote difference from the supposedly inclusive 'men'. If *Mortalities Memorandum* sets out to prove the talents of women, it does so by presenting them as the spiritual side of human existence and therefore nearer the 'haven' of 'Heaven'. Inevitably, the opposite of the thematic parallel is denoted as male: men are identified with the violence and trouble of life on earth, not too far distant, perhaps, from the 'witless' Swetnam. Rachel Speght was, therefore, not only one of the first women to defend her sex in the pamphlet wars of the early seventeenth century, she was one of the earliest Renaissance women poets to rework the sonnet and its Petrarchan discourses to display a distinctly female perspective.

X Mary Wroth

One of the first women to compose a sonnet sequence from a particularly female perspective was Mary Wroth (c.1587–c.1651). Indeed, Wroth's prodigious and innovative literary work has ensured considerable critical coverage over the last 15 years. She was the first Englishwoman to write an original prose romance, *Urania 1 and 2*, and an original comedy, *Love's Victory*, in addition to the sonnet sequence, *Pamphilia to Amphilanthus*, all of which were completed within a period of around ten years (c.1611–1621). In addition, Wroth was a member of the Sidney/Herbert family, whose political and cultural renown brought her attention in her own day as well as in our own. In order to understand Wroth's relationships with the other members of her family, some of whom are referred to elsewhere in this book, a family tree will be useful (Figure 1). The family members included in the diagram are only those who have a direct relationship or poetic connection to Mary Wroth; for example, William Herbert's brother, Philip, is not alluded to. The purpose of the curtailed family

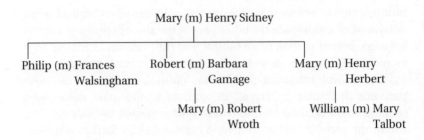

Figure 1   Sidney/Herbert family tree

tree given here is to show the way in which the Sidney and Herbert family developed the sonnet convention. In addition, it also uncovers how the Petrarchan discourse used by Wroth had its foundation, not in the writings of a broad group of authors, but within the limits of her own familial inheritance. However, it is important to recognise that such poetic echoes were not entirely nostalgic. As Gary Waller points out:

> To call the values and attitudes of the Sidney Circle reactionary, however correct, would however short-circuit an illuminating investigation of forces that were in fact becoming dominant in late sixteenth-century poetry and the wider culture. (Waller 1986, 164)

A balance between familial influence and successive transformations must, therefore, be retained.

The writings of both Mary Sidney Herbert (1561–1621) and her brother Philip Sidney (1554–86) have already been referred to, and their oeuvre certainly influenced their niece, Mary Wroth.[10] Until the end of the twentieth century, however, little attention had been paid to the writings of Robert Sidney (1563–1626) and William Herbert (1580–1630), or for that matter to Mary Wroth's own canon, yet over the last 20 years their work has been made increasingly accessible to literary critics. As such, it is now possible to ascertain the links between Wroth's poetry and the verses of her father, Robert, and her cousin, William. However, not only did Wroth allude to and quote her family, she chose to depict them as characters in her writings, thereby offering an autobiographical interpretation to the texts. It is, therefore, useful to explore some of the poetic and family history of Mary

Wroth, and her Sidney and Herbert relations, before undertaking an analysis of her sonnets.

Philip, Robert and Mary proved to be gifted siblings, although they seem never to have attained the political and personal success they wished for. Philip Sidney came after his death to be represented as the ideal Renaissance courtier, but was during his lifetime exiled from the court and overlooked by Queen Elizabeth I. Even his now-famous sonnet sequence, *Astrophil and Stella* (1581–2), portrays a poet courtier (Astrophil) who fails to win his lady (Stella), just as Sidney himself was unsuccessful in his attempt to wed Penelope Devereux, who instead married Robert Rich. This, of course, does not mean that the narrative events of the sonnet sequence can be superimposed upon Sidney's life, but sufficient similarities were incorporated in the poetry to allow for an intriguing play between the material and fictional worlds. Philip Sidney's poetry has already been discussed in Chapter 1, but it is important to note here his perpetuation of the sea-faring trope. For example, in *The Old Arcadia* the two male protagonists, Musidorus and Pyrocles, who are disguised respectively as the shepherd Dorus and the Amazon Cleophilia, sing comparative verses about love. Both invoke the sea-faring 'marchante man' who is accustomed to 'wyndes . . . [and] waves', yet Dorus concludes that even though he has suffered 'stormes':

> . . . now successe hathe gott above annoyes,
> That sorrowe's weight dothe balance up thies joyes.
> (Philip Sidney 1962, 70–1)

In contrast, Cleophilia argues that it is precisely when safety is at hand that the mariner worries most, concluding:

> Thus tossed in my shipp of huge desyre,
> Thus toyled in my work of raging love,
> Nowe that I spye the haven my thoughtes requyre,
> Now that some flower of fruict, my paynes do prove,
>   My dreeades augment the more in passion's mighte,
>   Synce love with care, and hope with feare do fight.
> (Philip Sidney 1962, 71–2)

In both poems the tempestuous voyage is marked as a metaphor for the passions of love in which acceptance by the beloved is envisaged as an approach to the shore. Yet such proximity to fulfilment produces differing effects, with Dorus claiming increased happiness and reassurance, while Cleophilia asserts that hope must always contain the fear of rejection. Within the prose romance the differing views develop the parts played by the two princes, yet Pyrocles' disguise as a woman imbues the songs with a gendered perspective. In this sense, the man's version foresees success, whereas the woman's response continues to doubt. Philip Sidney's adept manipulation of the conventional trope is apparent, yet these verses are also important because they were to become part of a broader familial discourse.

Mary Sidney appears to respond to the autobiographical context of her brother's poetry when she wrote 'To the Angel Spirit of the Most Excellent Sir Philip Sidney' (c.1599) as a memorial piece, and many of her verses echo the elegiac tone of this piece. As with Philip Sidney, Mary's writing has been looked at earlier in this book, and therefore only a brief indicator of her use of the sea voyage metaphor will be included here. In her translation of Psalm 46 *Deus Noster Refugium* the fears occurred because of tempests at sea or the storms of life are invoked:

> Yea soe lett seas withall,
> In watry hills arise,
>   As maie the earthlie hill appall,
> With dread and dashing cries.
> (Mary Sidney 1963, 110)

At the conclusion of the poem, however, God's love is presented as a comfort – 'Bee still saith he' – and a security – 'Our rock on Jacons God we found,/ Above the reach of harmes' (Mary Sidney 1963, 111). What is perhaps most interesting for Wroth's perspective is that the innovative reworking of the psalm form must be set alongside the conventional female role of pious translator, thereby presenting a dichotomy between public conformity and private radicalism. Moreover, this literary opposition seems to have been replicated in Mary Sidney's own life. She had married the older William Herbert as a young woman and was generally eulogised by her contemporaries as a woman of perfect piety and virtue. Yet, from contemporary letters we know that in 1614 after her husband's death, she went to the continental resort, Spa, and indulged in smoking tobacco, gambling with cards, shooting pistols and dancing. She was accompanied in these pursuits by a young companion, the physician Mathew Lester, with whom she was said to flirt incessantly, and court gossip certainly depicted them as lovers. In a close parallel to this dutiful/unconventional lifestyle, Mary Sidney appeared to adhere to the condoned female occupation of translating and editing, while actually reworking the material into a highly individualistic form. It was precisely this combination that Mary Wroth attempted to portray in the female characters she employed to represent her aunt, yet at the same time, the manipulation of a double self-image left its legacy upon Wroth's own thematic concerns.

While Mary and Philip have been the focus of critical interest, their brother Robert Sidney has remained in relative obscurity. Robert seems to have been the quiet and dutiful son, who after his romantic marriage with Barbara Gamage (against the Queen's wishes and completed only two hours before her messenger arrived forbidding the wedding), settled down to the mundanities of a nobleman's life. He served the Queen loyally at home, in the court, and in overseas campaigns. He nurtured his family at home, ensuring that all his children – boys and girls alike – benefited from a good education and promising betrothals. Indeed, his family home, Penshurst, was so famous as a paradigm of familial and courtly life that Ben Jonson wrote the pastoral eulogy 'To Penshurst' to commemorate it. The extant letters and account books depict a man who was concerned about all those in his care and who responded with loyalty and self-lessness to the calls made upon him by queen and country. Or so it seemed. In the 1960s P.J.Croft rediscovered Robert Sidney's holograph notebook in which were transcribed a collection of songs and sonnets that uncover the dichotomies of a man as torn between public and private, as were his famous brother and sister. Robert Sidney was similarly immersed in the poetic discourses of his day, a fascination which is demonstrated by his reworking of the Italian sonnet form with its octave and sestet pattern, but with an interwoven indebtedness to the English sonnet couplet via the rhyme scheme. In this harmonising of national styles, Robert echoed the choice of his brother, Philip, and foreshadowed that of his daughter Mary Wroth. His awareness of the origins of the Petrarchan sonnet ensured that Robert Sidney combined theme with form and, indeed, the storm and mariner trope is alluded to in three consecutive sonnets.

Rather than compact the metaphor of the lover's/humankind's

journey through love/life within a single poem, Robert Sidney extends
the metaphor through three sonnets (22, 23 and 24). The first quatrain
of Sonnet 22 invokes the mariner beset with storms:

> On unknown shore, with weather hard distressed,
> The fainting mariner so fears the night
> As I, who in the day's declining light
> Do read the story of my wrack of rest.
> (Robert Sidney 1984, 219)

The material fears of a sailor who must face a storm at night while
sailing close to the navigational dangers of an unknown shore are
compared to the poet lover's anguish as he faces a sleepless night in
the torments of love. Both are, of course, simultaneously linked to the
human fear of death, a meaning that is carried through the remainder
of the sonnet. The subsequent poem, however, returns to the seafar-
ing narrative in its first quatrain, depicting the mariner/lover now
shipwrecked and facing death:

> Absence, what floods of plaints 'gainst thee would rise –
> Which even the hellish wants dost make me taste –
> If perished bark on shore by tempest cast,
> Which late prayed for the land, now on its dies,
> (Robert Sidney 1984, 221)

The conventional Petrarchan opposites are presented at the end of
the poem suggesting that the 'present pain' of the lady's scorn is
better than the 'absent joy' of her removal. Thus the desired 'land'
becomes identified with the woman, whose rejection of the lover
causes his 'death'. Yet this 'present pain' and the 'tempest[s]' of love
are preferred to the calm nothingness of 'absence'. The final sonnet in
this group begins with the question:

> Canst thou from the haven of thy rest
> For bitter storms that beat thee from the shore?
> (Robert Sidney 1984, 223)

Sidney thus leaves the poetic self torn in the proverbial Petrarchan
formulation of preferring to love in torment rather than to seek the
peace of a sheltered haven in which love is relinquished. The image of

the mariner is sustained and the allusion to human nature clinging to life while welcoming death, is similarly developed throughout the three poems.[11] The sonnet discourse invoked participates, therefore, in the dominant Early Modern conventions, presenting Robert Sidney himself as a competent poet.

Yet Robert Sidney's 'unknown shore', his 'tempest' and his 'haven' all have their foundations within the political history of the times, and his own personal involvement in the power struggles of Early Modern Europe. During the second half of the 1590s, Robert was stationed in the Low Countries as the Governor of Flushing and, while he performed his duties with due attention, his absence from court allowed others to be promoted above him. This injustice concerned him, and Robert Sidney's letters throughout the period complain of the Queen's lack of recognition:

> I cold also say for my self that hauing bene there [Flushing]
> gouenor now almost ten yeares and nothing added vnto me either
> in reputacion or profitt, but rather diuers thinges taken from me,
> whereas all of myne own rancke haue bene preferred, and as such
> as were farr behind me made equall vnto mee, and some sett
> before mee. (1599; Robert Sidney 1984, 97)

The poems' references to being denied access to the beloved, who in sonnet 23 is referred to directly as 'my life's queen', demand that we reread the texts within this different frame. The storm-trapped mariner may thus be recognised as an autobiographical representation, partially depicting the very real predicament Sidney encountered and expressed in his letters, as for example, when in 1597 he wrote, 'I kan not saile against wind and tyde' (Robert Sidney 1984, 98). The relationship between the lover and his lady is thus, as in Wyatt and Philip Sidney, reworked within a political context to include the problematic power negotiations between the courtier and his ruler. Moreover, Robert Sidney expands this discourse beyond his personal dissatisfaction in sonnet 24 when he addresses an individual other than the lady. The addressee who must turn from the 'haven of thy rest' and forsake the 'golden store' would, as P.J.Croft points out, have enabled,

> any well-informed courtier in 1595–6 to recognise that the person
> being addressed is Sir Walter Ralegh, who had performed his cele-

brated voyage to Guiana in 1595 and who published his narrative of it
. . . in 1596. (Robert Sidney 1984, 99)

Ralegh's account describes the storms encountered on the journey
home, and these passages are clearly alluded to, although not quoted
directly, by Robert Sidney in sonnet 24. The 'mariner' must, therefore,
be reconsidered once more to include the sea-faring and colonial
exploits of Walter Ralegh, whose own poetic representations have
already been considered in this chapter. The parallels are clear:
Ralegh's poetic self is sent 'with forced wind / To kingdoms strange',
where he is 'Alone, forsaken, friendless on the shore, / With many
wounds, with Death's cold pangs embraced'. Similarly, Sidney shows
Ralegh as 'on unknown shore with weather hard distressed', cast up
on the 'shore' by a tempest 'on [which] it dies'. The multiple
discourses of Sidney's sonnet expand therefore to encompass autobiographical reading, political allegory, courtly love, spiritual dilemma
and poetic convention. Nor, as we have already seen through the
poets discussed in this chapter, was such a panoply of referents
unusual. What is particular about Robert Sidney's utilisation of these
forms is that his sources spiralled inwards to a personal and familial
space, at the same time as they extended out to the political and
poetic concerns of Early Modern Europe.

Of course, Walter Ralegh was a well-known adventurer within the
Elizabethan court, but he was also Barbara Gamage's cousin, and thus
a close relative of Robert Sidney. Thus, the sea-faring sonnets in
Sidney's notebook may be read as referring to two family members
(Robert himself and Ralegh), while at the same time emulating the
Italianate sonnet form favoured by another relative (Philip Sidney).
And, inevitably, they were to be taken up by another member of his
family, Mary Wroth.

Wroth's sonnet sequence, *Pamphilia to Amphilanthus*, invokes her
family's oeuvre, and this has sometimes led critics to defend her
against presumed attacks of plagiarism.[12] There can be no question,
however, that Wroth is individualistic in her reworking of male
discourses, inverting gendered identities in order to produce a
female-centred interpretation of love in the Early Modern period.
Sonnet 6, second series in *Pamphilia to Amphilanthus* (P68) is a good
example of the use of the voyage metaphor through a new gendered
perspective:

My pain, still smothered in my grieved breast,
    Seeks for some ease, yet cannot passage find
    To be discharged of this unwelcome guest;
    When most I strive, more fast his burdens bind.
Like to a ship on Goodwins cast by wind,
    The more she strives, more deep in sand is pressed,
    Till she be lost, so am I, in this kind,
    Sunk, and devoured, and swallowed by unrest,
Lost, shipwrecked, spoiled, debarred of smallest hope,
    Nothing of pleasure left; save thoughts have scope,
    Which wander may. Go then, my thoughts, and cry
Hope's perished, Love tempest-beaten, Joy lost:
    Killing Despair hath all these blessings crossed,
    Yet Faith still cries, Love will not falsify.
    (Wynne-Davies 1998, 213)

The sonnet begins conventionally in the first quatrain (abab) with the description of the lover's pain, whether at rejection, or because of the necessity for concealed affection, or both, is unclear. Moreover, the poetic self cannot escape 'burdens' and 'bind[s]', since the more 'she strives' the more she becomes trapped by her love. The second quatrain, again conventional (abab), concludes with the image of the vessel being 'sunk' just as the lover is 'swallowed by unrest'. The turn to the sestet begins with a self-contained couplet (cc) that sees the poetic self destroyed through a typically Petrarchan enumeration beginning with the seemingly final word, 'Lost'. Yet this ending, suggested by form and vocabulary, is twisted back through the caesura in line 11, from which the lover extends her voice, 'Go then, my thoughts, and cry'. The ensuing enjambment undercuts any sense of finality with a series of vocal outbursts that invoke the traditional opposites of hope/perish, love/beaten and joy/lost. As the dichotomy is reinforced, the sonnet turns to the last assertion of 'Despair' combined inextricably with 'Faith' and 'Love' (deed). Wroth's accomplished use of the Petrarchan convention includes the Italianate form (octave and sestet), the combination of opposites, the listing of emotions, as well as the trope of the sea voyage and tempest. Moreover, she invokes her own family's reworking of the discourse, including her father's representation of a ship 'perished' in the 'tempest', as well as his use of geographical reality. In Wroth's poem, for example, the shipwreck on the 'Goodwins' refers to an area off the

Kentish coast that was renowned for its treacherous waters. In addition, the spiritual elements of Mary Sidney's verse are inferred through Wroth's reference to 'Faith' and the spiritual aspect of 'Love'. Finally, the gendered responses, in particular Cleophilia's despair from Philip Sidney's *The Old Arcadia*, are rewritten in Wroth's final assertion of hope. The 'burdens' of love in Wroth's sonnet are ascribed to a male beloved, or possibly to Cupid, although both may be inferred. These are contrasted with the lover and ship, which are described as female. Gender identities are thus affirmed as traditional, with the despairing female lover concealing her desire. Yet while Cleophilia emphasises unhappiness, the poetic self in Wroth's verse inverts expectations and claims that love cannot 'falsify'.

The subject in Wroth's sonnet sequence may be identified with the eponymous Pamphilia, who also appears as the heroine of Wroth's prose romance, *Urania*. In both texts the character depicts the author herself, and this autobiographical identification is affirmed by a parallel linking of Amphilanthus with Wroth's cousin, William Herbert, with whom she had an affair. Indeed, the narrative lines of both sonnet sequence and romance appear to delineate the history of Wroth's relationship with Herbert. For example, in P68 the concealment of love might represent necessity, considering the illicit nature of the relationship between the cousins. In addition, Wroth's poetry often appears to interact with Herbert's verse, rather than reworking the material as she does with the oeuvres of Mary, Philip and Robert Sidney. Thus in sonnet 10 of the third series (P86), she enters the debate about 'Love and Reason' (Wynne-Davies 1998, 220), which was a poetic concern developed by Herbert, as if in answer to her lover.[13]

At first William Herbert's poem, 'It is enough, a Master you grant *Love*', might well be taken to participate in this poetic dialogue. However, placed in its context Herbert's poem is seen to respond not to the woman with her associations of family, love and inherited Petrarchan discourse, but to his male friend, Benjamin Rudyard. William Herbert's posthumously published volume contains verses written by the two men as a poetic dialogue, and the previous poem composed by Rudyard concludes:

> And now to you, Sir *Love*, your love I crave;
> Of you no Mast'ry I desire to have:
> But that we may like honest friends agree,

Let us to *reason* fellow-servants be.
(William Herbert 1660, 11)

The 'you [who] grant *Love*' of William Herbert's poem is unquestionably his 'honest friend' Benjamin Rudyard and not his cousin/lover, Mary Wroth. While women poets, therefore, were intent upon regendering the poetic discourses of the previous century, male writers had accepted the traditional roles, and as Philip Sidney devises a debate between the princes, Dorus and Pyrocles, so his nephew, William Herbert, constructed a dialogue with his friend, Rudyard. Familial use of poetic convention may thus be identified as both returning to earlier patterns, while at the same time, striving against those forms to develop radical reinterpretations. And it is precisely this notion of contradictory impulse that I wish to investigate with one final reference to Robert Sidney's notebook.

Before sonnet 11 Robert Sidney inscribed, 'A Crown of sonnets, but unfinished' (Robert Sidney 1984, 175). The 'crown' consists of four poems in which the last line of the first sonnet is repeated as the first line of the succeeding verse. The final 13 sonnets 'doth want' as Sidney notes (Robert Sidney 1984, 181), although had the crown been complete the final line would have returned the reader to the very first line of the sequence. In attempting this grouping Robert was emulating his brother Philip, who had composed the first crown or corona in English verse as a song of ten linked dizains in *The Old Arcadia*. Mary Wroth also used the corona in *Pamphilia to Amphilanthus* in a self-conscious acknowledgement of her Sidneian poetic inheritance. The crown was not by any means exclusive to the Sidney family, but its repeated use draws attention to the way in which Early Modern poetic discourse, in particular that of the sonnet, employed formal and often restricted structures in order to explore the possibility of undercutting and breaking through those limits. At the same time, writers were able to move into the heart of the work in order to excavate an inner vision that might itself be greater than the outside would suggest. The sonnet is a perfect example of such radical expansion and detailed introspection. It is almost as if the sonnet itself is both telescope and microscope combined, at one moment seeing the inner workings of the Sidneian family, and at the next charting a colonialist expansion that changed the understanding of the world. And it is the crown that encapsulates such a shifting perspective, for its points create an invisible circumference that bounds signification within, recognises the possibility of external meanings, and simultaneously exists between those two, the poetic lines between its points offering a unique linguistic border-crossing. The very lines of the poetic corona enact the transition between personal and public, old and new worlds, feudal aristocracy and growing middle class, and male and female authorship.

It will by now be apparent that the continuity and interconnectedness of the crown has been invoked in the structure of this chapter itself with its repeated vocabulary and its adoption of roman numerals for the subheadings. So that the first section, which introduced the sonnet form and the sense of radical exploration ended with:

> The image of the storm/wreck is, therefore, a useful starting place from which to begin a navigation of the way in which poetry, in particular the sonnet, participated in the major transitions of the Early Modern age.

While the beginning of Section II, which looked at the Petrarchan sonnet, began with:

> In order to examine the way in which the sonnet participated in the major transitions of the Early Modern age, it is useful to start with the image of the storm and shipwreck.

Initially such repetition might have appeared an oversight or simply linguistic laziness, but as the sections proceeded and the pattern persisted a sense of linked development would have been affirmed. The ideas and poets may be described in a linear form: the discussion of Petrarch's sonnet and the use of the ship trope (Section II) are taken up in Wyatt's reworking of these elements through a political and personal dialectic (Section III). While, subsequently, Surrey's indebtedness to Wyatt and his perpetuation of the sonnet discourse are discussed through the introduction of a spiritual element (Section IV). And so on. But an understanding of the corona's structural impact is better seen in diagram form as presented in Figure 2.

Identified as a circular structure, the limit of the poetic discourse is immediately apparent, as is the uniting metaphor and circularity of theme. Yet at the same time, the possibilities for a transition from within such enclosure may be recognised from the radial expansion of

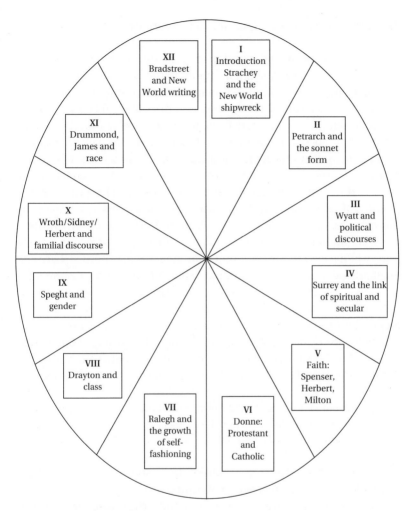

Figure 2 The corona

author and theme. Therefore, John Milton might incorporate Italianate sonnet discourses into his spiritual poetry, yet his understanding of religious themes and the works in which he presented them cannot be contained by the corona, even if suggested by it. The divisions are, however, more clearly marked in certain segments of the corona. In the final two sections of this chapter I intend to explore the contrast between the differences endemic upon national identity and the mutuality of poetic inheritance.

XI William Drummond, James VI of Scotland

During the inception and foundation of the mutual poetic Petrarchan discourse, divisions dependent upon national and racial identity appear to have had a limited impact. The proliferation of influence occurred across Europe, and the poetic discourses of Early Modern England cannot be divorced from the associated cultural developments in France and Scotland. The influence of Petrarch's love sonnets recurs in the poetry of a number of French writers, as for example in the sonnets by Pierre de Ronsard, often collected by present-day editors under the title, *Les Amours*. The image of the poetic self as a boat adrift on turbulent water is used regularly by Ronsard, as in 'Sonnet V' of *Le Bocage* (1554). However, the line between difference and mutuality is most distinct in its poetic expression when negotiating an understanding of the border between England and Scotland. For example, William Drummond's 'Sonnet IV' in *Poems The Second Part* (1616) is a translation of a sonnet by an Italian author, Sannazaro. Both works draw upon the Petrarchan original in their representation of life as a 'Fraile Boat . . . in a rockie Sea' that is 'expos'd to *Fortunes* stormie Breath'. But whereas Sannazaro repeats the Petrarchan dilemma of being caught between, 'Charbys e Scilla', Drummond follows the bleaker tradition of the English sonnet:

> Even, sith our voyage shamefull is, and short,
> Soone to strike Saile, and perish in the Port.
> (Drummond 1913, 53 and 208–9)

The metaphor of the ship is linked to a spiritual voyage, which concludes in the grim realisation of death.

The movement between continental and British discourses is also found in the poetry of James VI of Scotland (1566–1625), who acceded to the English throne as James I. James was certainly influenced by Petrarch and other continental poets such as Ronsard and Du Bellay. For example, James reworked Ronsard's original verse, through a self-aware use of Montgomery's translation, in a number of his poems. Thus, the 'cruell constellation that conspird/Before my birth my bale sa sharpe & saire' draws upon both Montgomery's 'Since the Hevins are hindererd of my hap', and Ronsard's 'Quel sort malin, quel astre me fit estre/Jeune et si fol, et de malheur si plein?' (James I 1911, 40, 99–100). Yet at the same time, James appears to favour the Spenserian sonnet form and certainly admired Philip Sidney, who is depicted as the epitome of 'manhoode, witt, and learning everie waye' (James I 1911, 1 and 29–30). But James's articulation of the tempest metaphor originated more from personal circumstance than from any adherence to poetic tradition.

In June 1589 a preliminary ceremony marrying James to Anne of Denmark took place with the Earl Marshal acting as the King's proxy. However, during the new Queen's journey to Scotland a storm caused her fleet to be scattered and in September she took refuge on the coast of Norway. On October 22nd impatience drove the King to set out on a secret voyage to rendezvous with Anne since, as he proclaimed, he was not an 'irresolute asse quah [who] can do nathing of himself' (James I 1911, 70). The two were united in Norway and the final ceremony took place in November. During this period James composed a number of sonnets that, not unsurprisingly, evoke the image of the tempest and describe how he was 'transported ou'r the stormie seas' (James I 1911, 2). For James I, therefore, the tempest metaphor was transformed first into reality, and then back again into the conventional Petrarchan trope. And in yet another transition between national and poetic discourses, the English writer, Henry Constable, responded in sonnet form to James's own versified presentation of his real predicament. Constable enacts a further self-conscious poetic shift when he claims he will in future abjure his 'sigh[s]' and 'teares shed in such abundant store', in face of James's justifiable complaints against the very real consequences of 'sea . . . [and] wind' (James I 1911, 71). The confluence of poetic influence thus simultaneously established and undercut national difference in Early Modern Europe. As William Drummond wrote:

> *Poesy* is not a Thing that is yet in the finding and search, or which may be otherwise found out, being already condescended upon by all Nations, and as it were established *jure Gentium*, amongst *Greeks, Romans, Italians, French, Spaniards.* Neither do I think that a good Piece of *Poesy,* which *Homer, Virgil, Ovid, Petrarch, Bartas, Ronsard, Boscan, Garcilasso,* (if they were alive, and had that Language) could not understand, and reach the Sense of the Writer. (James I 1911, xc)

Drummond is here attempting to resist change and bulwark the commonality and 'condescended' nature of poetry, citing in support of his argument a list of nations and poets who have contributed to the development of a united discourse. Yet, even as he wrote, Drummond's lists were outdated, for the American nations were already establishing their own literary discourses in the New World, and new poetic voices were soon being heard.

XII   Anne Bradstreet

The first American authors had their cultural origins in the Old World, yet the transition across the Atlantic demanded that new discourses be developed to answer the very different circumstances in which they existed. Indeed, it is at this point in the tracing of Petrarchanism, of the inheritance of Early Modern poetic conventions, of the ship/voyage trope, and even of this chapter's own corona, that the linguistic chain retaining the boundaries of similarity finally snaps. The experiential writing of the early colonists persistently breaks through any literary indebtedness to their European antecedents. In order to illustrate this difference I shall look briefly at the use of tempest images in the poetry of Anne Bradstreet (c.1612–72).

Bradstreet is rightly lauded as one of the first published poets of the New World, although ironically, in order to attain publication during her own lifetime, her work was taken back across the Atlantic to a London publisher. The first collection was published as *The Tenth Muse* (1650). The division between Bradstreet's English inheritance and her New World background is also blurred by the fact that she did not emigrate until 1630 and the library of 800 books that her family took with them ensured a continued connection to the cultural heritage of her youth. Indeed, Bradstreet tacitly acknowledges her debts to Ralegh, Spenser and Sidney; while in the prologue to *The Tenth Muse* she claims inferiority to the French poet Du Bartas:

> A Bartas can do what a Bartas will
> But simple I according to my skill.
> (Bradstreet 1967, 15)

The formal verse of another piece in the 1650 collection, 'The Four Elements', appears to bear out these European associations as Bradstreet refers to the 'wary merchant' who hopes to transport his 'wealthy freight unto his wished port', in the face of 'wasting floods and roaring torrents' (Bradstreet 1967, 28). The image and vocabulary recall much of the poetry already quoted in this chapter and it was appropriately included in the poems published in London. Bradstreet's canon is, however, divided between those poems included in *The Tenth Muse,* and the group made up by *Several Poems* which were published posthumously in New England in 1678 and other poetry that remained in manuscript form until the nineteenth century. In these later poems there is a distinct shift away from the concerns of the Old World in terms of tone, content and form. In place of the European literary allusions and references to British politics, there are a series of personal, colloquial and experiential verses which appear spontaneous and vivid by comparison.

Two of Bradstreet's later poems introduce the idea of a sea-faring journey and the threat of a storm in the personal context that characterises the group. The first is written as Bradstreet's husband, Simon, began the voyage home to England on January 16th 1661, and she prays:

> Lord, be Thou pilot to the ship
> And send them prosperous gales.
> In storms and sickness, Lord, preserve.
> (Bradstreet 1967, 266)

The marriage seems to have been intensely happy, with Anne addressing her husband with intense love in several poems, as in 'To My Dear and Loving Husband':

> If ever two were one, then surely we.
> If ever man were loved by wife, then thee;
> (Bradstreet 1967, 225)

Sorrow at parting and fears of a storm at sea were for Anne Bradstreet personal, material and heartfelt concerns. The relief and thanks to God expressed in the following poem, 'In Thankful Acknowledgement for the Letters I received From My Husband Out of England' is manifest,

> Thou hast relieved my fainting heart
> Nor paid me after my desert;
> Thou hast to shore him safely brought
> For whom I Thee so oft besought.
> Thou wast the pilot to the ship.
> (Bradstreet 1967, 269)

The Petrarchan dichotomies and paradoxes that had been revised and refined over the past century for English verse were certainly known to Bradstreet, as her earlier published work proves, but she chose to ignore convention in the immediacy of personal circumstance. The poetry produced by the writers of the New World could not abandon the traditions of European literature, yet by the mid-seventeenth century the older discourse had surely turned towards new forms, language, and themes. The transition in poetry was not confined to the Americas, of course, but the changes were perhaps more apparent when viewed through the distant remove of geographical difference.

Conclusion

Finally, if we return to the beginning of this chapter and recall the words of William Strachey, the implication of the storm trope will become apparent: 'The winds (as having gotten their mouths now free, and at liberty) spoke more loud.' Poetic discourses are perpetually in a state of change and transition. And poetic language, like the winds of Strachey's tempest, renews itself precisely by breaking 'free' from previous conventions and thereby proclaiming its 'liberty'. The sonnet form and its particular evolution through the Early Modern period, from Petrarch, Sidney and Spenser, through Donne and Wroth, to Milton and Bradstreet, encapsulates this evolution. So that at its English inception the sonnet was a radical proclamation of political and personal identity, the parading a self that could speak 'more loud'. Yet at the conclusion of the period encompassed by this book, the sonnet itself had become the restrictive tradition that was challenged by the writers of a new faith and a New World. Thus, the momentous and rapid changes that occurred in the Early Modern world emerge through the mutating identities of sixteenth- and seventeenth-century poetry.

Notes

1. The translation is my own and is intended to aid students following the text above in Italian, and not as a verbatim translation or for poetic felicity.
2. While Wyatt's sonnet, 'My Galley Charged With Forgetfulness' is

popular, it has often been considered a more simplistic and less carefully worked translation than some others. I hope that the analysis here has gone some way towards showing the poem's complexity, but also to contradicting Robin Kirkpatrick's assertion that the poem is 'less successful' since 'Petrarch produces, once more, an agonisingly open ending, as he emphatically "begins" to despair of the port – pointing to a process which will continue into silence after the end of the poem – where Wyatt resolves with a reiteration ("I remain") of the state which he has been exploring' (Kirkpatrick 1995, 131–3).

3. Some of Wyatt's verse was also published in *Tottel's Miscellany*, although the pieces were more heavily edited and current editors choose to use the printed versions only in conjunction with the more authoritative manuscript sources.

4. This poem is not a sonnet, but a 12-line lyric with the rhyme scheme ababcdcdcdee. It might well allude to the 14 lines of the sonnet, however, suggesting that the text, like Surrey's life, is curtailed.

5. The utilisation of a Christian discourse within love poetry had its antecedents in the courtly love lyric and so was hardly original to Spenser, but the Christian, neoPlatonic, secular harmony was initiated by him in the English sonnet tradition.

6. I am indebted to Terry Hawkes for this reference as well as for continued inspiration; see *That Shakespeherian Rag* (Hawkes 1986, 70–1).

7. Hilliard's miniature of Ralegh is in the National Gallery, London, and is dated to 1585.

8. For a rehearsal of this debate up to the sixteenth century see Alcuin Blamires (ed.), *Women Defamed and Women Defended: An Anthology of Medieval Texts* (Oxford: Clarendon Press, 1992).

9. The debate generated by Swetnam's publication is reproduced in Simon Shepherd, *The Women's Sharp Revenge: Five Women's Pamphlets from the Renaissance* (1985).

10. See above pp. 7–24.

11. There are similar uses of the ship image in sonnet 17 and song 24 (Robert Sidney 1984, 205 and 305).

12. See Wynne-Davies (1998), 363 for a summary of this defence.

13. The poetic debate between Love and Reason was initiated within the Sidney family by Philip Sidney in the second eclogues of *The Old Arcadia*. However, it is ascribed to both Sidney and Herbert, by Wroth, through their fictional self, Philisses, in her play, *Love's Victory* (Wynne-Davies 1996, 105).

3   D r a m a

Theatre History

> 'What you will have it named, even that it is'
> (Katherina in Shakespeare's *The Taming of the Shrew*)

While all literary texts alter their meanings over time, across regions, through linguistic shifts, or simply through the process of person-alised and individual readings, the possibility of variation is never more obvious than in the case of drama. Each production of a play offers new directorial insights, with further interpretations being added by the players themselves. Indeed, every separate performance will produce differences that depend upon the shifting rapport between those on stage, as well as upon each renewed audience. As such, a multiplicity of meanings becomes an inevitable product of the dramatic genre. It comes as no surprise, therefore, that in William Shakespeare's (1564–1631) *The Taming of the Shrew*, as the character Katherina is called upon to perform her husband's (Petruchio) script, calling the moon the sun and vice versa, in so doing she acknowledges that there can be no fixed signification: 'What you will have it named, even that it is'. But Kate's perception is not the only response presented in this scene for, as her words ironically indicate, a whole range of characters, Petruchio, Hortensio, Tranio and even the servants, represent an array of different interpretations.

The scene in question occurs towards the end of Act IV as the couple, accompanied by Hortensio, who hopes to wed a wealthy widow, return to Katherina's home. By this comparatively late point in the play the audience has become familiar with Petruchio's taming techniques. For example, his soliloquy at the beginning of Act IV has already indicated with irony that he intends 'to kill a wife with kind-ness', and his successive rejections of food, sleep and clothing on Kate's behalf have almost succeeded in 'curb[ing] her mad and head-strong humour' (Shakespeare 1984, 119). But by now both Katherina and Hortensio are keen to return to Padua; the former eager for the comforts of her father's house and the latter to procure the hand of the widow with all her supposed wealth. Petruchio, however, is determined to reinforce his authority, and he commences the scene by deliberately confusing night and day:

> Petruchio. . . . how bright and goodly shines the moon!
> (Shakespeare 1984, 137)

Katherina immediately corrects his error and they exchange quick-fire oppositions until Petruchio threatens to abort their journey:

> Petruchio. Now, by my mother's son – and that's myself –
> It shall be moon or star or what I list
> Or e'er I journey to your father's house.
> [*To Servants*] Go on and fetch our horses back again.
> Evermore crossed and crossed, nothing but crossed!
> (Shakespeare 1984, 137)

Given Petruchio's express intention to isolate, and so command, his wife, the unanimity of response, both on and off stage, to his outburst heralds a distinct shift in the play's allocation of authority. For Hortensio's weary, 'Say as he says, or we shall never go' (Shakespeare 1984, 137), echoes the audience's own desire for narrative movement, indicating that the unrelieved repetition of the taming trope is beginning to prove tedious. Katherina's subsequent resigned acquiescence offers the welcome possibility of progression, but Petruchio is not yet satisfied, insisting at this point that his wife admit a double-error. Finally, however, Katherine's reply satisfies him:

> Katherina. Then God be blessed, it is the blessèd sun.
> But sun it is not, when you say it is not,
> And the moon changes even as your mind.
> What you will have it named, even that it is,
> And so it shall be so for Katherine.
> (Shakespeare 1984, 138)

Thus, with Katherina's full admission of Petruchio's authority and Hortensio's congratulatory aside, 'The field is won' (Shakespeare 1984, 138), they resume their journey.

But if Petruchio and Hortensio believe that male supremacy and its complementary other, female submission, have been successfully reasserted, they are at variance with the audience's perception of what has actually happened. For like Katherina, we have been taught not so much how to ingest obedience, but rather the difference between overt verbal quiescence and inner contentual rebellion. Moreover, by returning to Petruchio's own speech it becomes possible to perceive that his own word-play incorporates a welter of puns, ambiguities, and innuendoes – indeed the whole panoply of verbal tools generally employed to destabilise meaning. He begins with a common pun on son/sun that, through a convoluted association of gender, class and natural law, affirms the power of the disenfranchised male ('my mother's son') over the richly endowed female ('your father's house'). It is, however, Petruchio's final lines, the carelessly sighed, 'Evermore crossed and crossed, nothing but crossed!' that uncovers the play's power relationships and whirls them into disarray.

The precise meaning of Petruchio's words remains doggedly unattainable. Does he, for example, mean that Katherina is always crossing, that is opposing, his will? Certainly given the context of the taming sequence this would be a perfectly respectable reading. But Petruchio provides the audience with neither subject nor object for this 'crossing'. Indeed, the very word 'crossed' suggests a string of possible interpretations. On the one hand, Petruchio might be cursing the fates for his adverse fortune, or he might be referring to Katherina's character and her propensity to be always 'crossed' or inclined to quarrel. In addition, given his own self-confessed taming strategies, we might equally assume that Petruchio refers to his own skilful deployment of a contrary disposition. Moreover, from Hortensio's jaundiced response and Katherina's immediate compliance, we might well assign the latter understanding to them, for at this point Petruchio appears ill tempered and perverse to his travelling companions. And the argument for narrative movement, together with the impatience of the audience to reunite a tamed Kate with her soon-to-be-surprised family, certainly associates the onlookers in the auditorium with their counterparts on stage, rather than with Petruchio.

These significations all assume, of course, that there are only three players on stage at this point with whom the audience may interact; Petruchio, Katherine and Hortensio, in other words, those who have been given lines. In fact, there are an indeterminate number, since the main characters are accompanied by their servants, and depending upon the wealth of the acting company, any number of these non-speaking parts could have been provided. Indeed, it could plausibly be argued, given that in his previous line Petruchio commands his servants to 'fetch our horses back again', that the master continues in the 'crossed' speech to address his men in a rhetorical fashion. Even though there is no specific addressee marked in the text, put into its context on the stage the speech would quickly be defined through a combination of Petruchio's movements, the direction and tenor of his voice and the positioning of the other characters. Therefore, depending on the decision of director and cast, Petruchio could address his peers (Kate and Hortensio), his servants, the audience, or all three groups.

Nevertheless, whichever interpretation of 'crossed' is foregrounded, what is clear from Katherina's first word of response – 'Forward' – is that all characters on stage have a clear understanding of the spatial implications of Petruchio's words. Thus put into action for both cast and audience, the verb to 'cross' inevitably takes on the material and locational signification of, 'to intersect or challenge the main direction'. This understanding is reinforced by the fact that Petruchio has used a similar phrasing at the close of the previous scene in which he and Kate have figured, when he accuses her of 'still crossing it' and orders his servants to 'let't alone' (Shakespeare 1984, 132). In this earlier scene Petruchio has called for the horses to be brought unto 'Long-lane end' and proposes that the company will walk before mounting. The symbolic meanings of both the long journey on foot and the restraining of horses would have been readily apparent to an Early Modern audience versed in a culture of moralities and emblems. Thus when Petruchio requests that the company walk along 'Long-lane' he asks for perseverance and moral strength, a point that is affirmed by the suggestion of bridling headstrong passions in the symbolic form of the horses. Similarly, in Act IV scene iii Katherina is described as 'crossing' Petruchio, and such a present-tense exhibition of self-will results in the journey being abandoned. After all, within the patriarchal reading of the symbolism, she is not yet ready to journey along the Long-lane of humility, nor is she able to curb her wilful female nature. In effect Katherina's verbal 'crossing' or contradicting Petruchio's will prevents the company from 'crossing' or traversing the stage as they progress to a symbolic moral ideal of female behaviour. Feminist criticism has been keen to point out the dualities of Patient Griselda and Katherina the Shrew, although the usual polarised opposites are now being usefully deconstructed. As Natasha Korda explains:

> I do not mean to suggest (following the play's so-called revisionist readers) that Kate's [final] speech should be read ironically, as evidence of her deceit, any more than (with its anti-revisionist readers) as evidence of her 'true' submission. Both readings, it seems to me, leave Kate squarely within the framework of the medieval shrew tradition. In the former she remains a duplicitous shrew, while in the latter she becomes 'a second Grissel'. (Korda 2001, 215)

My argument concurs with Korda's in that I would like to suggest here that there can be no single interpretation, or interested group, which is able to sustain dominance when placed in the context of movement or 'crossing' that is inevitably generated when the play is staged.

Between scene iii and scene v, Shakespeare revisits Padua and the romantic contortions of the sub-plot, but when we return to Petruchio's country house the characters we find there seem to be embarked upon exactly the same course, both material and moral, as they were when we last saw them. The audience might have crossed the five-hour ride between sophisticated Renaissance city and the quasi-Medieval world of the poor country estate, but the characters' attempts at movement appear to have been 'crossed' or thwarted by the mutual stubbornness of Petruchio and Katherina. Indeed, Petruchio's call for the horses to be brought back again suggests that the animals have stood ready to be mounted through whatever stage-time has elapsed. Although, of course, since horses were not generally used in Early Modern theatre, the animals carry a double symbolism, caught between the moral values of the text and the material movement of the staged play. Through a combination of widely ascribed perversity, therefore, the characters' movement across the expanse of stage with its imagined locational settings has been as 'crossed' as the narrative's movement through time and dramatic action. As Petruchio points out, everything is crossed. Although he actually says, 'nothing but crossed', pushing the vocabulary permutations still further, to imply that if every signification must be thwarted, then only 'nothing' can remain.

However, this still leaves the servants standing patiently, and perhaps with some bewilderment, at the side of the stage, caught between their master's orders to return the imaginary horses to their imaginary stable, and everyone's palpable desire for the cast to move across the stage and get on with the play. In most Early Modern dramas servants are expendable characters and would simply be called offstage again at the soonest opportunity in order to guise themselves as another minor group before returning. And the servants in Act IV scene iv of *The Taming of the Shrew* pretty much follow this pattern, reappearing recurrently in several of the wealthy Paduan homes. In Act IV scene v, however, these servants are, in one small but significant way, different from many of their kind, for the audience has been given a pretty good idea of what they might be thinking as they shuffle mutely offstage.

At the beginning of Act IV Grumio, Petruchio's personal servant, is sent ahead to the country house to prepare for his master and Katherina. Grumio arrives cursing 'tired jades', a punning double allusion to his horse and to the beleaguered new bride, and 'mad masters'. He is welcomed by Curtis, Nathaniel, Philip, Joseph, Nicholas, and Peter, who are all given speeches; as well as the non-speaking characters, Walter, Sugarsop, Gabriel, Adam, Rafe and Gregory. This group of servants greet Grumio with good-natured banter, and although Grumio remarks that Curtis has 'crossed' him, he still proceeds to recount the 'humourous' narrative of how Katherina's horse fell on top of her, broke its bridle and ran away (Shakespeare 1984, 113). The symbolic signification is clear, if not overly laboured by this point, as the shrew is held to be analogous to the wayward horse. Curtis' response and Grumio's conclusion are therefore surprising and perceptive:

> Curtis.   By this reckoning he is more shrew than she.
> Grumio. Ay, and that thou and the proudest of you all shall find
>   when he comes home.
>   (Shakespeare 1984, 113)

As Curtis surmises and Grumio predicts, when Petruchio arrives he shouts at them, abuses them and beats them. He calls them successively in the space of around 50 lines: 'knaves . . . logger-headed and unpolished grooms . . . whoreson malthorse drudge . . . rascal knaves . . . rascals . . . rogues . . . villains . . . rogue . . . whoreson villain . . . whoreson beetle-headed, flap-eared knave . . . rascal cook . . . villains

. . . heedless joltheads and unmannered slaves!' (Shakespeare 1984, 114–17). While he's railing at them Petruchio also strikes them and pelts them with the plates and food they have just placed before him. After such a prolonged bombardment the servants' amazed response ('didst ever see the like?'), their sympathy with Katherina ('she, poor soul'), and their ardent desire for escape ('Away, away, for he is coming hither'), appear completely understandable (Shakespeare 1984, 117–18).

Textual and theatre critics these days are often sympathetic to Katherina, but few comment upon Petruchio's treatment of his servants. Ideological shifts have served to uncover sexual inequalities, yet class difference at times still seems to be unquestioningly consigned to stage buffoonery and clown-like comedy. Nevertheless, Petruchio's treatment of his servants is too closely aligned to his baiting of Katherina for the sympathetic alliance between the 'unmannered slaves' and the wife with a 'mad and headstrong humour' to be ignored (Shakespeare 1984, 117 and 119). Nor is Petruchio alone in subjecting his servants to arbitrary violence designed purely to answer his own upper-class needs. Although Katherina defends Petruchio's servants she has shown herself capable of parallel attacks against those she sees as her inferiors. As the older and dominant sister Katherina binds Bianca's hands and strikes her; when Hortensio disguises himself as a music teacher she smashes a lute over his head; believing that Petruchio is her social inferior she hits him too; and she responds with violence when Grumio mocks her (Shakespeare 1984, 81, 85–6, 89, and 126). In addition, one of the rich Italian nobles beats his servant, while at the close of the play Katherina offers to place her hand beneath her husband's foot so that he may crush it, 'if he please'. And during the Induction the Lord's desire for amusement almost results in the buggering of his page Batholomew (Shakespeare 1984, 142, 153, and 57–8). The evidence proves conclusively that the abuse of servants and the lower classes by their so-called betters runs precisely parallel to the named concern of the play, to tame a shrew. This alliance of gender and class can hardly be considered surprising, although the neglect of its dramatic impact in *The Taming of the Shrew* has ensured that the play's dialectic of male/female opposition remains uncomplicated by the perverse and angry relationships between social groups.

But if we return to Act IV scene v, and to the impact of Petruchio's 'crossed' speech, it becomes possible to perceive an alliance building up against him, that runs from Hortensio's exasperated, 'Say as he says', through Katherina's sweetly ironic 'What you will have it named, even that it is', to the silent perseverance of the servants. Indeed, it is precisely the moment when Petruchio the husband and master are effectively, although covertly, crossed by his wife and servants, that he believes them to be most compliant. It is at this point, convinced of the natural acquiescence of those beneath him in the gender and class hierarchies, that Petruchio allows the action to proceed and they move forward across the stage. There are, of course, other mishaps before the company reaches the banquet with the uneasy concluding speech by Katherina. But at this point the dramatic perspective has shifted from its previous log-jam, presenting the audience with a cross-hatched series of significations and alliances, which are themselves breached as space and time are activated once more. Like Katherina and the servants, the audience learns from Petruchio's antics. But we do not learn how to accept a single patriarchal interpretation of universal harmony, rather discovering how to construct a web of superficial agreement that will both convince the figure of authority, while at the same time revealing a mutuality of oppression and justified complaint. Through this staged evocation of difference *The Taming of the Shrew* is, within a single scene, able to break away from that constricting textual battle of the sexes, towards a greater fluidity of interpretation and multiplicity of allegiance that only performance may allow.

It is not possible to date *The Taming of the Shrew* conclusively, although Ann Thompson argues persuasively in her introduction to the play that the script 'was written in or about 1590' (Shakespeare 1984, 9). This would mean that the play was most probably composed for the acting company, Pembroke's Men. By 1594, however, we know that it had become part of the repertory of the Chamberlain's Men and would most probably have been performed until 1597 at the first open-air playhouse in London, the Theatre. The amphitheatre-like design of the Theatre had been chosen by its builder James Burbage in order to evoke the classical grandeur of Rome. Therefore, while there are no absolute records relating to the construction of the Theatre, it is possible to surmise that the space 'crossed' by Petruchio, Katherina and their retinue would have conformed to the imposing, large extending square stage that we know existed in other Early Modern theatres. The audience would have sat mainly on wooden platforms erected around the roughly circular theatre walls, although the poorer customers would have stood directly around the stage in the 'pit', and the more wealthy patrons would have sat in the Lord's box immediately above and behind the main acting space. The cast's movement, or in the case of Act IV scene v of *The Taming of the Shrew* their distinct lack of action, would have been perceived differently by the various components of the audience. Unlike most present-day theatres with their careful consideration of viewing angles and all-round acoustics, the construction of Early Modern theatres took little account of whether all members of the audience could see and/or hear every part of the play. As recent productions in round theatres have discovered, a prolonged declamation by a single player standing still results in almost half the audience missing the full import of the speech. Thus, when Petruchio refuses to move, the urgency voiced by Hortensio and Katherina would have been particularly welcome to those members of the audience who were only able to see the actor's back. Crossing and recrossing the acting space was, therefore, essential for productions undertaken in Early Modern theatres, and to obstruct or 'cross' such continuity would most probably have produced a rather 'cross' audience.

A reading of *The Taming of the Shrew* demonstrates that, in order for us to understand the way in which Early Modern drama was able to produce such widely divergent and radical interpretations, it is essential to examine the way in which theatre space functioned. In particular, the way in which dramatic spaces altered and mutated during that heyday of Renaissance theatre, from the reign of Elizabeth to the Interregnum. The history of the English stage during these 75 years saw the development of a number of key transitions. Not only from Medieval drama to the complex power of Early Modern theatre, but also across a variety of spaces, from small to large and from public to private, as well as through a range of audiences, from eclectic to elite, and from common to noble. As Andrew Gurr explains, 'the different kinds of repertory that were maintained at the different playhouses confirm the evidence of . . . economic changes' (Gurr 1992, 14). In the subsequent sections of this chapter I intend to explore the ways in which individual plays used the theatrical spaces with which they were associated during the Early Modern period. The early public theatres, such as the Rose, are considered in relation to Christopher Marlowe and *Tamburlaine the Great*. Alternative dramatic spaces are explored through an analysis of the performance of Shakespeare's *Twelfth Night* at one of the Inns of Court. Finally, I will trace the shift from public to private theatre through an examination of Thomas Middleton's *The Changeling*.

Public theatre: Christopher Marlowe

> 'The scourge of God, must die'
> (Tamburlaine in Marlowe's *Tamburlaine the Great, Part Two*)

If any Early Modern dramatist epitomises the changes convulsing the English sixteenth-century stage, then it is Christopher Marlowe (1564–93). Even today his life is surrounded by myth. Was he a spy? Was he homosexual? Was he a Catholic, or a Protestant, or even an atheist? Who murdered him and why? Was he the real author of Shakespeare's plays? It is unlikely, although not impossible, that many of these questions will ever be answered. All we may adduce at present is that Marlowe's life remains shrouded in mystery. Still, there are a few ascertainable facts.[1]

Christopher Marlowe was born in Canterbury in 1564. He was the son of a shoemaker and therefore a member of the merchant classes. Marlowe studied at Cambridge, but did not go into the ministry as was expected, instead choosing to visit Rheims, which at that time was a centre for Catholic Jesuits. It was undoubtedly this link to Catholicism that caused him to be turned down when he applied for a Master of Arts degree in 1587. However, at this point the Privy Council intervened in his favour and he was granted an MA for 'good service' to the crown. It is highly likely that Marlowe's 'good service' referred to espionage work undertaken for Elizabeth and the Protestants against the Catholics. By 1593, however, his allegiances had become suspect and Thomas Kyd, another playwright with whom Marlowe lodged, accused him of treachery and atheism. However Kyd's testimony was obtained under torture, making it impossible to judge the truth of the allegation against the 'evidence' the crown now wished to obtain. But suddenly, only 18 days after Kyd's arrest on the 30th May 1593, Marlowe was killed in a brawl at a Deptford tavern apparently as he argued over who should pay the bill. With information uncovered by more recent research, we now know that all those noted as present during the murder were in some way involved in the world of intrigue and spying. Moreover, the men arrested for Marlowe's murder were quietly released. Had Marlowe become too problematic for the Privy

Council? Was he really a counter-agent? With a personal narrative of such drama and complexity it is hardly surprising that questions abound. Still, while queries over biographical particulars perforce remain unanswered, the issues that surrounded Marlowe's life and death may usefully be excavated. The conflicts of faith, the destabilisation of the social hierarchy and the radical privileging of individualism were concerns that emerged into the foreground of Early Modern ideology, just as they fragmented Marlowe's own life and energised, not only his own plays, but the dominant dramatic discourses of the day.

Christopher's Marlowe's works are often represented as bridging devices between a Medieval understanding of the world picture and the emergent Early Modern ideologies, although by the time his plays were written and performed such early transitions were relatively complete. Moreover, while certain dramatic devices, such as the hellmouth in the concluding scene of *Doctor Faustus*, recall the mechanisms of the Medieval theatre wagons, overall the plays demand the speed of movement and reliance upon character rather than props, which characterise Renaissance drama. Indeed, the production history of the two parts of *Tamburlaine the Great* is particularly informative about the way in which Marlowe's texts were open to a continued reproduction and updating of meaning.

It is likely that Marlowe wrote the first part of *Tamburlaine* while still at university, yet by the 1590s it had become one of the most successful plays in the repertoire of the Lord Admiral's Men as they played at the Rose theatre. Such popularity was difficult to sustain, for the Admiral's Men staged as many as thirteen different plays over a month, with regular new additions. So, for example, in 1594 they produced *Tamburlaine* alongside a number of other plays, including Shakespeare's *Titus Andronicus* and *1 Henry IV*, and by that point Marlowe's script was already seven years old. The success of *Tamburlaine* on the Early Modern stage is, however, even more surprising when compared to the neglect of the play by subsequent generations, both on stage and as a text for critical study. There are several possible reasons for the changing levels of popularity. The play's thematic focus upon the power of the individual to control his or her fate against established religious and social hierarchies clearly responded to the way in which the audiences of Early Modern London were investigating their own dominant ideologies, thereby suggesting a topical popularity. Yet I would like to suggest that the play's success was also due to the felicitous combination of theatre space and players' skills during those years in the Rose.

We are particularly fortunate in our understanding of the playing space at the Rose theatre since, during an excavation for an office block in 1989, its foundations were uncovered, allowing us to suggest a plausible reconstruction of dimension and form. It was a small theatre, particularly in comparison with the great Globe, and the stage would have covered an area 25 feet wide and 37 feet deep. The diameter of the whole was only 74 feet, so it is clear that the audience would have been in close proximity to the action at all times (Gurr 1992, 263–5). And the action in *Tamburlaine* was worth travelling across the Thames to the South Bank site of the Rose to see. For example, the first two scenes of the play immediately contrast the static and stately court of Mycetes, the rightful King of Persia, with the trophy-laden train of the shepherd Tamburlaine as he rips off his peasant's rags to disclose the armour and weaponry that proclaim him as a man ready for action. After this introduction, battle scenes rage across the stage, women bitch at one another over a throne, and Tamburlaine's enemies are pursued, trussed up, and tortured in front of the audience. The sequence in which Bajazeth is imprisoned in a cage like an animal and taunted by Tamburlaine is particularly dark, and when he finally commits suicide by braining himself against the cage the horror of the incarceration is fully realised. The sheer force of the warriors rushing around the small stage, the uncomfortable proximity of Bajazeth's cage to the audience, and the splatterings of 'blood' as the actor flung himself at the bars of the cage would have been immediately compelling. And through it all, the towering figure of Tamburlaine strides possessively about the stage in much the same fashion as he dominates the world within the text. Moreover, if we are lucky in our possession of details about the acting space in the Rose, then we are doubly blessed in that we also know which actor took the part of Tamburlaine. Edward Alleyn was one of the finest players to join the Admiral's Men and he is known to have performed the key roles of Marlowe's canon. Apart from being an actor, however, Alleyn was one of the new theatre entrepreneurs who had financial interests in several forms of public entertainment and he also went on to found Dulwich College in London. Indeed, the Dulwich Picture Gallery still owns a surprisingly tall full-length portrait of Edward Alleyn, which until recently was thought merely to flatter the sitter with a false sense of height. However, in her work for a biography of Alleyn, S. P. Cerasano demonstrates by measuring the actor's ring that he was probably about 5 feet 10 inches tall. Not a huge man by today's standards but, 'significantly taller than most men of his time' (Cerasano 1994, 67). Thus in his role as Tamburlaine, Alleyn would have appeared to be a giant, fully capable of inspiring fear in his enemies and profound loyalty in his followers.

Over the centuries the style of acting and the shape of theatres altered in a way that precipitated a reduction in the dramatic power of *Tamburlaine*. Static declamation would have favoured the King of Persia not the revolutionary shepherd, and the horror, immediacy and speed of the play would have been contained and distanced from the audience by a shift to a proscenium stage. Not surprisingly *Tamburlaine*'s popularity declined and it was not until the revisionist production of the play in 1992 that the text once more emerged fully into the forefront of Marlowe's canon. Significantly, this Royal Shakespeare Company production was shown in the Swan, a recon-struction of an Early Modern theatre with a small round acting space, which allowed the force of brutal action to be brought back into the centre of the audience's perceptions.[2] Moreover, Anthony Sher, the actor chosen to play Tamburlaine, even if not of comparable stature to Alleyn, emanated enormous physical force and magnetism. Thus, the combination of a small central acting space and a powerful leading player once more brought *Tamburlaine* back into the public frame. In addition, the play's themes of political power and the ability of an individual to overthrow their social origin in order to assume absolute rule proved particularly pertinent for the Thatcherite 1980s.

Alongside the recent reinstatement of *Tamburlaine* into the acting repertoire of Marlowe's plays, critical interpretation has begun to investigate what were previously supposed to be the relatively clear meanings of the text. It had generally been accepted that the play emphasised the immorality of the central protagonist and reinforced the dominant hierarchy with Tamburlaine's death in Part II. With the incursion of New Historicist criticism in the 1980s, however, and particularly with Stephen Greenblatt's radical rereading of the Marlovian canon, *Tamburlaine* was transformed into a play that negotiated directly with the social and political upheavals of sixteenth-century England. As Greenblatt notes,

> Of all Marlowe's heroes, only Tamburlaine comes close to defining himself in genuinely radical opposition to the order against which he

wars [and] he does so by virtue of a powerful if sporadic materialism. (Greenblatt 1980, 210)

This 1980s combination of astute critical analysis and powerful dramatic regeneration demands that Tamburlaine be interpreted as a 'an elemental, destructive force, driving irresistibly forward' (Greenblatt 1980, 216), yet at the same time, it would be reductive to ignore readings that might initially appear to be more conservative, since the play itself often appears to shift in allegiance.

The drama's narrative, however, is relatively simple. *Tamburlaine* is based on the life of Timur, the fourteenth-century ruler of Samarkand. Marlowe's protagonist rises to power through force of character, is followed by an army of strong-willed and utterly loyal men, and is loved by a beautiful and good woman. Part I of the play traces his rise to power, while Part II brings him further victories and death through illness. The dramatic crux of the play's thematic signification lies in the way the audience judges the ethical content of both Tamburlaine's life and the values he espouses. As the Prologue points out at the beginning of the play, 'applaud his fortunes as you please' (Marlowe 1999, 4).

Conventional Elizabethan values demand that he be condemned; for example, Tamburlaine does not have the traditional Christian principles of pity and humility that would have been valued by the church. This is particularly noticeable when Bajazeth is caged and when Tamburlaine orders the slaughter of four virgins who have been sent to beg for mercy. At such moments he seems devoid of human feelings, resembling almost a force of nature, and in Act II scene vi the Persian lords wonder if he is a devil:

> What god, or fiend, or spirit of the earth,
> Or monster turnèd to manly shape.
> (Marlowe 1999, 29)

A question seemingly answered by Tamburlaine in the next scene:

> Nature, that framed us of four elements
> Warring within our breasts for regiment,
> Doth teach us all to have aspiring minds:
> Our souls, whose faculties can comprehend
> The wondrous architecture of the world

> And measure every wand'ring planet's course,
> Still climbing after knowledge infinite
> And always moving as the restless spheres,
> Wills us to wear ourselves and never rest
> Until we reach the ripest fruit of all,
> That perfect bliss and sole felicity,
> The sweet fruition of an earthly crown.
> (Marlowe 1999, 30)

This is a speech written to inspire an audience. It directs the collective eye away from the surrounding 'wondrous architecture' of the theatre's microcosmic world, through the open roof to the 'restless spheres' and 'infinite' space beyond. Yet at the same time the vocabulary draws the audience's aural sensibility back to the 'Nature' that 'framed us' and the material reality of an 'earthly' reward. Indeed, the limits of human ambition are emphasised by the references to Christian ideology, with the human 'soul' questing after a form of 'knowledge' that is imaged as 'the ripest fruit of all'. The words recall the biblical narrative of humankind's fall from grace because they have eaten fruit from the tree of knowledge, and the subsequent expulsion from the garden of Eden. As the audience we are left with a paradox that sets the power of Tamburlaine's speech and his personage against the referential signification of Marlowe's imagery. Thus, what overall judgement can we make of the play's titular protagonist? Is he, as he notes himself, the tool and 'scourge and wrath of God' (Marlowe 1999, 38), or does he, on the contrary, question the most essential of Christian values? Before exploring possible answers to these questions concerning faith and morality, I wish to turn to the parallel idea of social hierarchy in order to discover whether the ambiguities are replicated across themes.

Distinctions in class are clearly indicated at the beginning of *Tamburlaine*, as Mycetes the King of Persia is contrasted with Tamburlaine the shepherd. The differences are sharply apparent, both to the audience and to the other characters on stage. Mycetes is a weak and cowardly king who relies on his men to fight for him and continually asks for approval, 'Is it not a kingly resolution?' A plea that provokes his brother Cosroe to voice the ironic aside:

> It cannot choose, because it comes from you.
> (Marlowe 1999, 5)

The audience is thus brought into complicity with Cosroe's judgement of the King, that Mycetes' words are 'kingly' only because he speaks as the monarch, and not through his own intrinsic merit. The contrast between inherited rank and individual worth is repeated when Tamburlaine refers to his own status:

> I am a lord, for so my deeds shall prove,
> And yet a shepherd by my parentage.
> (Marlowe 1999, 10)

Moreover, Tamburlaine, in direct contrast to Mycetes, is seen to inspire loyalty in his followers through the rhetorical power of his speech and his own personal bravery, not ruling as does the King, through an outmoded system of social rank. The advocacy of individual merit over inherited social status seems to be a clear message at the beginning of the play, and seems hardly surprising given Marlowe's own middle-class parentage and the overwhelming realignment of rank in Early Modern England to which his own shifting status contributed. Yet even here the narrative twists back upon its thematic allegiances. Cosroe successively betrays his brother to Tamburlaine so that he may become king, and is then himself killed by the warrior shepherd. Cosroe thus switches from fulsome praise for 'worthy Tamburlaine' to cursing the 'devilish shepherd . . . this monstrous slave' (Marlowe 1999, 21 and 28). Rather than an ideological elevation of personal worth over class and rank, the play demands that the audience recognises the way in which characters create and break allegiances in order to increase their own political power, rather than because of any support for or revolt against existing social hierarchies.

Signification in *Tamburlaine* is, however, not consistently skewed towards personal interest, and this is particularly true of Zenocrate, Tamburlaine's mistress and queen, who functions as a secondary, onstage audience to the shepherd's attainment of status and power. Female characters often take key roles in Marlowe's works, as for example in *Dido, Queen of Carthage* and in the homoerotic poem, *Hero and Leander*. In each case the women are trapped on the margins of expected conventionality, but are presented as sympathetic rather than disgraced. It is hardly surprising, therefore, that the Egyptian Princess Zenocrate also breaks with traditional female behaviour, although her radicalism takes her far beyond rejecting the

Renaissance commonplace of the chaste, silent and obedient woman. Zenocrate is captured and raped by Tamburlaine, yet she has grown to love him. Agydas, one of the Lords of her retinue, comments upon such unusual and unseemly behaviour:

> When your offensive rape by Tamburlaine –
> Which of your whole displeasures should be most –
> Hath seemed to be digested long ago.
> (Marlowe 1999, 34)

But Zenocrate points out that Tamburlaine's 'exceeding favours' would even 'content the Queen of heaven' and confesses her complete love for her assailant:

> Ah, life and soul still hover in his breast
> And leave my body senseless as the earth,
> Or else unite you to his life and soul,
> That I may live and die with Tamburlaine!
> (Marlowe 1999, 34)

Zenocrate articulates the conventional love discourses of Early Modern drama, wishing to merge herself with her beloved and to die with him should fate so decree. However, while such sentiments would be readily acceptable from a loyal wife or a chaste maiden, when they are voiced by a royal woman who has been raped by a peasant warrior, the resulting significations are both provoking and unsettling.

If we look at another play produced at the Rose theatre in the 1590s that focuses on a raped woman, Shakespeare's *Titus Andronicus*, it becomes clear that uttermost grief, shame and a desire for revenge/suicide were considered the 'natural' female response to sexual assault. Moreover, although the rape of Lavinia in *Titus* is an act of acute violence, unlike the wooing of Zenocrate by Tamburlaine, the basic Early Modern premise of shame remains a common response in both plays. For example, Zenocrate's father, the Egyptian Soldan, complies with the conventional attitude towards rape, seeing his daughter's situation as an insult to his own standing,

> The rogue of Volga holds Zenocrate,
> The Soldan's daughter, for his concubine,

and he demands to 'be revenged for her disparagement' (Marlowe 1999, 46 and 48). Similarly, Zabina treats Zenocrate with disdain:

> Base concubine, must thou be placed by me
> That am the Empress of the mighty Turk?
> (Marlowe 1999, 42)

Zabina claims precedence over Zenocrate, not only because she is an Empress, but also because she is legally married to the 'mighty Turk' Bajazeth. Zenocrate is deemed 'base', no more than a 'concubine', and as such is a social outcast unfit to be placed alongside decent women. Even if Zenocrate forgives Tamburlaine, the play's upholders of traditional values perceive the couple as no more than a rapist and a whore. Moreover, it would be as well to remind ourselves that a stage portrayal of a woman who falls in love with the man who raped her is hardly more acceptable today than it was at the end of the sixteenth century.

However, Zenocrate's support for Tamburlaine and her acceptance of his violence gradually begin to alter as the play's narrative evolves. There is a hint at the end of Act IV that her reactions to Tamburlaine are changing when as he attacks her home, she begs him to desist for the sake of her love:

> My lord, to see my father's town besieged,
> The country wasted where myself was born –
> How can it but afflict my very soul?
> If any love remain in you, my lord,
> Or if my love unto your majesty
> May merit favour at your highness' hands,
> Then raise your siege from fair Damascus' walls
> And with my father take a friendly truce.
> (Marlowe 1999, 56)

But when Tamburlaine rejects her plea, Zenocrate and the audience begin to question his motives and the nature of his love. Still, it is not until Act V that we finally appear to have been given a full perspective on Tamburlaine's moral downfall, regardless of all the victories he has achieved on earth. Again the key to the way the audience's allegiances are transferred is Zenocrate, although other female characters echo her role.

In Act V scene i, the governor of Damascus tries to win Tamburlaine's sympathy by sending four virgins to beg for peace. They repeatedly call on him to pity them, but he responds to them in terms that couple sex with death, 'Behold my sword. What see you at the point?' (Marlowe 1999, 62). And immediately he hears that his soldiers have 'on Damascus' walls . . . hoisted up their slaughtered carcasses', he begins a passionate soliloquy on Zenocrate. Tamburlaine's linking of violence with sexual desire, which might just have been acceptable to Zenocrate at the beginning of the play, has by Act V become dangerous and distasteful.

The unsettling aspect of the love between Tamburlaine and Zenocrate is thrown into sharper relief by comparison with the relationship between Bajazeth and his wife, Zabina. Their legitimate marriage and mutual suicide suggest, especially to Zenocrate, the inadequacy of the love between herself and Tamburlaine. The possible sham of affection between shepherd and princess is undermined further, when the King of Arabia dies proclaiming his true love for Zenocrate:

> And let Zenocrate's fair eyes behold
> That as for her thou bearest these wretched arms
> Even so for her thou diest in these arms,
> Leaving thy blood for witness of thy love.
> (Marlowe 1999, 70)

Thus, in the space of 100 lines, Zenocrate laments Tamburlaine's bloody victory over her 'father's subjects', the slaughter of the 'sun-bright troop / Of heavenly virgins and unspotted maids', and the death of 'this great Turk and hapless Emperess', as well as acknowledging her own 'deeds infamous' and that she has been the 'cursed object' responsible for the King of Arabia's death (Marlowe 1999, 67–70). Of course, in summarising Tamburlaine's pitiless treatment of his enemies and the vicious nature of his militaristic conquests, Zenocrate not only expresses her own grief, but also reminds the audience of the play's moral and social questions. Moreover, with only another 100 lines before part I of the play closes, any judgement on Tamburlaine seems destined to result in utter condemnation of the shepherd rebel.

It is at the precise moment when rejection by Zenocrate and the audience seems inevitable that Tamburlaine strides on to the stage and within those last 100 lines undermines each of the preceding suppositions. To begin with Zenocrate's father, the Soldan of Egypt, who has been saved in her name, accompanies Tamburlaine:

> Come, happy father of Zenocrate,
> A title higher than thy Soldan's name.
> Though my right hand have thus enthrallèd thee,
> Thy princely daughter here shall set thee free.
> (Marlowe 1999, 71)

Moreover, Tamburlaine reinstates the Soldan with the extra benefit of his own defence that will 'add more strength to your dominions' (Marlowe 1999, 71), prompting the Soldan in turn to welcome and praise his erstwhile enemy,

> Mighty hath God and Mahomet made thy hand
> Renowmèd Tamburlaine.
> (Marlowe 1999, 72)

Tamburlaine's role is thus transformed from an unholy alliance with the devil or an overly materialistic rejection of spiritual faith, into that of a man who is said to perform God's will.

Second, in a virtuoso somersault of narrative interpretation, Tamburlaine claims that he has not raped Zenocrate:

> Her state and person want no pomp, you see,
> And for all blot of foul inchasitity,
> I record heaven, her heavenly self is clear.
> (Marlowe 1999, 72)

At every other point in the play, from the princess's own admission, through the spurning of her by her female peers, to her father's call for revenge, no one has questioned that the relationship between Tamburlaine and Zenocrate has been sexual. Does Tamburlaine simply lie, or have the common expectations of society, both on- and off-stage, coerced us into believing the worst of a man who lays no claim to gentlemanly behaviour? The key to understanding how Tamburlaine's final speech is able to produce such questions lies in his ability to project an array of meanings that address some of the main ideological concerns of the day. For Tamburlaine couples his claim to have preserved Zenocrate's chastity with an offer of marriage, and within the legal framework of Early Modern England such a proposal immediately nullified any case of rape that a woman's family might choose to bring. In the 1590s the statute books still classified rape as a crime of theft against the father or husband of the abused woman, rather than as a violent assault against an individual. As such, the raped woman was regarded, not so much as a victim, but as damaged goods whose value on the marriage market had been seriously diminished. In these circumstances, if the assailant, or thief, offered to rectify the crime by marriage, the crime was considered void and the man was deemed merely to have employed his own property rights in the sexual use of his wife-to-be. Thus, when Tamburlaine offers to marry Zenocrate he immediately legitimises any previous sexual union between them, allowing him to claim with complete justification that she is still 'chaste'. The play both allows us to question the value systems that deploy women as commodities, while at the same time recognising the way in which Tamburlaine has manipulated contemporary value systems in order to serve his own interests. Moreover, as the Soldan welcomes him as a son in law, 'I yeeld with thanks . . . to thee for her love', and Zenocrate is crowned Queen of Persia, the full expediency of political power is laid bare (Marlowe 1999, 72–3).

Having won social status in time-honoured fashion, by marrying a woman of higher rank, Tamburlaine allows himself to honour others. The earlier treatment of Bajazeth and Zabina is, to a certain extent, recuperated through the organisation of a full state funeral:

> Shall we with honour, as beseems, entomb,
> With this great Turk and his fair Emperess.
> (Marlowe 1999, 73)

Thus, each mark against Tamburlaine that has been built up steadily throughout Act V and voiced by Zenocrate is undercut in this final speech of the play. The Soldan is saved, Bajazeth is honoured, Zenocrate's honour is redeemed, and chastity is valued. And as the play reaches its final moments, the characters prepare themselves to celebrate a wedding, twisting the tragedy that seemed all too probable at the beginning of Act V, into a conventional comedy. Nor is there a moral epilogue. The characters simply leave the stage, allowing the resonant power of Tamburlaine's final speech to remain with the audience as they depart from the theatre. At the end of the play the audience is left, not so much with an answer, but with the repetition of the Prologue's comment, 'applaud his fortunes as you please' (Marlowe 1999, 4).

There are two parts to Marlowe's *Tamburlaine*, of course, and in the second drama the Prologue reappears to tell us that all Tamburlaine's triumphs are overthrown, and that both shepherd warrior and princess will die. This sequel is often read as a more moral play, yet Tamburlaine dies expressing grief for Zenocrate, and his son rules after him. Indeed, his final speech is shorter, but as effective as the one in the earlier play:

> For Tamburlaine, the scourge of God, must die.
> (Marlowe 1999, 145)

Finally, any judgement about the moral and/or social messages of the play must come down to the performance of the actor playing Tamburlaine. If the power of the speeches is incorporated success-fully into a dynamic theatrical space then actors, like Sher and Alleyn, are able to address the issues of the day, allowing interpretation to shift and change with the political expediency of the part they perform. Debates over status, morality, gender, violence, politics and faith are thus caught up in the maelstrom of individual power and the force of language that emanates from a single protagonist. The imme-diacy and energy of such acting proved successful in the Rose theatre with its fee-paying clientele, but dramatic and ideological radicalism did not remain the prerogative of the public theatres in London.

Alternative performance spaces: William Shakespeare

'They're all mad here.'
(The Cheshire Cat to Alice in *Alice in Wonderland*)

In Early Modern Europe irreverence and mockery were condoned, even encouraged, in a way that might seem unfamiliar to us today. Whole courts, cities, communities and countries participated in a form of topsy-turvy celebration of that which might otherwise have been ignored, outlawed or punished. Social class was reversed, gender was inverted and madness took precedence over just and rational rule. Perhaps the nearest thing to such an occasion in present-day Britain would be 'Red Nose Day' when the comic spirit reigns on television and on the streets in aid of charitable causes. No such philanthropic cause was necessary for the Elizabethans, but their celebrations of misrule were attached to certain calendar dates, the most noted being Twelfth Night. Counting from Christmas, Twelfth Night falls on the 6th January and in the Christian calendar is celebrated as the Feast of Epiphany. The night was traditionally observed with disguises, music, dancing, and revels of various kinds, which allowed for chaos and disorder on the last night of the holidays. The Feast of Fools, as it was commonly called, thus brought the old year to a close with an unleashing of festive madness while at the same time predicating for the return to ordinary life in the morning. The title of Shakespeare's comedy *Twelfth Night* (1601) invokes this spirit of topsy-turveydom and would probably have been performed first on the January 6th. As such, the play, even in its title, makes us question the alternative values of radical inversion shifting and invert-ing in the darkness of the winter evening, and the alternative tacit acceptance of the dominant social and political hierarchy that would resume control in the cold light of day.

Twelfth Night opens with the play's heroine, Viola, shipwrecked on the coast of Illyria. She is bereft to have lost her brother, Sebastian, whom she believes to be dead, but is comforted by the sea captain who has saved her and who provides her with the information she needs to survive in this new land. It was this scene that caused Ann Barton to note:

> The sea-captain, appealed to by Viola for information about the country in which she has arrived, might just as well have said to her what the Cheshire Cat says to Alice: 'They're all mad here.' (RSC *Twelfth Night* Programme Notes 1991)

And in many ways the inhabitants of this strange country do appear to be 'mad' in the topsy-turvey manner of a Twelfth Night celebration. In order to protect herself Viola dresses as a young man and takes the name Cesario, and this cross-dressing in itself heralds a sequence of effects that centre upon gender inversion. Viola/Cesario joins the court of Orsino, Duke of Illyria, with whom she falls in love, but to whom she cannot declare her passion because of her disguise. In parallel, the Lady Olivia falls in love with Viola/Cesario believing her/him to be a young man. Lovers are thus confused, with women loving women and seeming-men loving men. The drunken antics of Sir Toby Belch, Olivia's cousin, and his friend Sir Andrew Aguecheek, add to the confusion as they joke, dance and duel their time away, recalling the activities of the Feast of Fools and, through their names, suggesting the physical consequences of alcoholic excess. Social inversion also emerges in the sub-plot that focuses upon Sir Toby's revenge against the censorious Malvolio, Olivia's steward. Malvolio is gulled into believing that Olivia loves him, thereby breaking down Early Modern marriage conventions that generally decreed unions within class. These illusions and this set of mistaken identities culminate in the final scene during which certain resolutions are achieved, although Viola/Cesario never removes her male costume even though she reveals that she is a young woman, and Malvolio leaves swearing that he will be revenged. As the Cheshire Cat says, 'They're all mad here'.

Even the full title of the play suggests the possibility of inversion, for Shakespeare appended the phrase *What You Will* to *Twelfth Night*, thereby suggesting that it was up to the audience to provide a suitable heading for the drama. By undermining the traditional function of the author to identify the text, Shakespeare simultaneously unleashes misrule into the inceptive moment of performance, and contains the multiplicity of naming within a tradition and a genre that is destined for closure. Thus even as the audience determines the meaning of the play, the variety and perpetual fluidity of their interpretations are destined to end with the drama's final speech, which is echoed in the closure of Twelfth Night itself and the dawning of the New Year. It comes as no surprise therefore that the first performance of the play was almost certainly on 6th January 1601 when Elizabeth I entertained Don Virginio Orsino, Duke of Bracciano, with the customary New Year's festivities. However, rather than undertake a performance at court, Shakespeare's company, the Chamberlain's Men, seem to have presented the play in Middle Temple Hall, one of the Inns of Court. There could have been any number of reasons why Elizabeth chose to entertain the foreign dignitary at an Inn of Court rather than in one of her palaces. For example, she could have wished to provide a variety of settings for the prolonged celebrations over Christmas and New Year, or her legendary parsimony might have suggested that spreading the cost of the revels would help to contain expenditure on these extravagant occasions. But there is a confluence of interpretation between the play's title, its content, the day of its performance, and the dramatic space chosen for its staging that together suggest that a discourse of misrule, or contained misrule, was in operation.

The Inns of Court were central to the development of Early Modern theatre in terms of the changing nature of dramatic spaces, and must have been conducive to budding dramatists as many playwrights began their careers at these various London sites. The opportunities for staging contributed to an overall atmosphere of theatrical growth, with each Inn offering a hall or courtyard that was easily converted to a stage. Indeed, Middle Temple Hall is still extant. It is therefore possible to reconstruct the way in which the space would have been used for a performance that might well have taken place before the Queen. The play was probably acted at the screen end of the hall, the doors allowing the actors to enter and leave a performance space, which would have been viewed primarily from the dais at the further end of the hall. Here noble visitors and distinguished members of the legal hierarchy would have sat to watch the revels at the close of the New Year's feast.

The combination of a theatrical arena associated with the changing face of drama, the timing of the performance for the only night of the year in which misrule was unleashed, and the play's central subjects of gender inversion and mistaken identities, all concur to suggest a first performance that proffered ideological challenges to the Queen and her court. By 1601 such dramatic critiques of the ageing Elizabeth I had become regular, although unwelcome, submissions. Moreover, while official censorship was able to contain the most extreme forms of political subversion, a static text displayed upon the page was very different from the live performance of a script. The staging of scenes from Shakespeare's history play *Richard II* at the beginning of Essex's rebellion in 1601 is a good example of how a seemingly innocuous text could be used to incite public agitation. Descriptions of this event are now commonplace in Shakespearean criticism and have served to uncover the way in which Early Modern dramatists were involved in the political events of the day. For example, Andrew Gurr writes that, 'the subject of the play [*Richard II*] was politically sensitive', although he is careful to note that these 'parallels were in the eye of the beholder' (Gurr 1984, 9 and 7). Thus, over the last 20 years assessments of the Shakespearean canon have shifted from a stress upon universal and human values to a focus upon the historical and political circumstances surrounding the production of the text. Chapter 1 of this book has already introduced the theory of New Historicism, but it is worthwhile discussing the impact this critical school has had upon Shakespearean criticism and Early Modern theatre studies in general. The idea that drama, particularly in its performance context, participated in the changing social discourses of the day has permeated many theoretical applications. In relation to *Twelfth Night* these theories are particularly attractive since they offer a way of understanding the radical elements of the play, while at the same time explaining how such seeming insurgence could be staged before the Queen. Although misrule might be unleashed, it is always contained when the dominant hierarchy resumes control at the end of the festive inversions. In this way *Twelfth Night* might offer, both as event and text, a challenge to authority, which was soon subsumed within the overarching social and political framework of the day.

Such contained misrule is evident in the cross-dressing sequences of the play, particularly in relation to Viola/Cesario and Olivia. The two female characters are similar in a number of ways. They have both lost brothers, the Duke Orsino loves both, and even their names appear as near-anagramatised versions of one another. When they first meet, as Viola/Cesario attempts to woo Olivia on Orsino's behalf, the 'lady of the house' immediately falls in love with the disguised 'gentleman' (Shakespeare 1975, 30 and 35). Olivia, however, does not welcome the recognition of this love when she rehearses the interview after Viola/Cesario has left,

> Olivia. 'What is your parentage?'
> 'Above my fortunes, yet my state is well;
> I am a gentleman.' I'll be sworn thou art:
> Thy tongue, thy face, thy limbs, actions and spirit
> Do give thee five-fold blazon. Not too fast: soft! soft!
> Unless the master were the man. How now?
> Even so quickly may one catch the plague?
> Methinks I feel this youth's perfections
> With an invisible and subtle stealth
> To creep in at mine eyes. Well, let it be.
> . . . . . .
> Fate, show thy force; ourselves we do not owe.
> What is decreed, must be: and be this so.
> (Shakespeare 1975, 36–7)

Olivia's recognition that she is starting to fall in love with Viola/
Cesario imparts unease rather than joy, as she compares passion to
'the plague' and depicts the object of her love as a thief whose 'subtle
stealth' has stolen her love. Moreover, while she realises that an
attachment to the 'man' rather than the 'master' will inevitably bring
problems, Olivia avoids dealing with the situation, trusting to fate 'to
show thy force'.

Viola/Cesario's response to Olivia's love is remarkably similar in its
abdication of self-will:

> Disguise, I see thou art a wickedness,
> Wherein the pregnant enemy does much.
> How easy is it for the proper false
> In women's waxen hearts to set their forms!
> Alas, our frailty is the cause, not we,
> For such as we are made of, such we be.
> How will this fadge? My master loves her dearly,
> And I, poor monster, fond as much on him,
> And she, mistaken, seems to dote on me:
> What will become of this? As I am man,
> My state is desperate for my master's love:
> As I am woman, (now alas the day!)
> What thriftless sighs shall poor Olivia breathe?
> O time, thou must untangle this, not I,
> It is too hard a knot for me t'untie.
> (Shakespeare 1975, 41–2)

In a series of defences Viola/Cesario blames her 'disguise', 'the pregnant enemy' (perhaps an allusion to love, or the heart), the 'proper-
false' deceivers who seduce women, women's 'waxen hearts', and
women's innate 'frailty'. All these, she/he decides have connived to
produce a 'fadge' of gender inversion and mistaken identity. Nor does
Viola/Cesario undertake to solve the problems, but calls on a personified Time to 'untangle this' for it is 'too hard a knot for me t'untie'. In
reality, of course, all Viola/Cesario has to do is 'untie' the strings of her
doublet and hose to reveal herself as female and therefore not the man
Olivia has fallen in love with, or the man Orsino trusts to pledge his
marriage suit. But, then again, in the reality of Middle Temple Hall if
Viola/Cesario had 'untangled' her 'disguise' she would have been
revealed, not as a pure and beautiful maiden, but as one of the boy
actors of the Chamberlain's Men. *Twelfth Night* might proffer the

possibility of sorting out problems, of restoring a sense of order to the Illyrian society, yet the actualities of performance suggest that such a realignment might never have been possible, for they are 'all mad here'.

The play's conclusion does offer a comic resolution to these entwined and 'twinned' complications as Viola/Cesario's brother, Sebastian, enters the play having been rescued from drowning. Olivia, at first unknowingly, transfers her affections from sister to brother, allowing Viola/Cesario to declare her true identity and win Orsino's love. The comedy's conventional ending, in which the harmony of love is bulwarked by the promise of marriage, appears to answer the titular question of identity with a firm assurance of genre. Moreover, in the play's narrative ending Shakespeare followed his source, using Barnabe Rich's happy resolution of the tale of 'Apolonius and Silla', to solve any gender problems with the resurrection of Silla's dead brother. At the end of the play, therefore, Viola/Cesario wins Orsino, while Olivia is happily married to Sebastian. Gender relationships are righted, the hierarchy is restored and misrule is contained. Fittingly, as the play closes and the company take their bows the festive season of Twelfth Night, when all might be 'what you will', draws to an end. Except that the play doesn't end there. It ends with a discontented Malvolio and a melancholic Feste.

In her erudite and challenging account, *The Stage and Social Struggle in Early Modern England* (1994), Jean Howard comments of *Twelfth Night*:

> The emphasis on the preservation of hierarchy is enacted in the text's treatment of class, as well. If unruly women and unmanly men are sources of anxiety needing correction, so are upstart crows. The class jumper Malvolio who dresses himself up in yellow stockings and cross-garters, affecting the dress of a courtly gallant, is savagely punished and humiliated, echoing the more comically managed humiliation of Olivia. (Howard 1994, 115)

And the tricking of Malvolio, with all its disconcerting class upheavals, has always been regarded as paralleling the interest of the main plot. The first production of *Twelfth Night* is notable for a tracing of performance history, not only because Middle Temple Hall is extant, but also because we have a first-hand account of the play, although from one month later. In his *Diary* entry for February 1601 the nobleman John Manningham, noted that:

> at our feast wee had a play called ... Twelue night or what you will ...
> much like the commedy of errors or Menechmi in plautus but most
> like and neere to that in Italian called Inganni ... a good practise in it
> to make the steward beleeue his Lady widdowe was in Loue wth him
> by counterfayting a lett^r as from his Lady in generall tearmes telling
> him what shee liked best in him and prescribing his gesture in smiling
> his apparraile &c. And then when he came to practise making him
> beleeue they tooke him to be mad. (Shakespeare 1975, xxvi)

Manningham's comments are useful in a number of ways, demon-
strating an awareness of the Shakespearean canon with the reference
to 'the commedy of errors' and an appreciation of classical comedy
('plautus') and European romance ('Inganni') traditions. However,
what is surprising about the account is that Manningham to a great
extent ignores the main plot and concentrates upon the sub-plot, in
which Malvolio is fooled and locked up as a lunatic. Sir Toby Belch,
his drinking companion Sir Andrew Aguecheek, the maidservant
Maria, and the clown Feste devise the plot. All have good reason to
dislike Malvolio since his puritan spirit and sombre self-satisfaction
have led the steward to castigate the drunken behaviour of the two
dissolute noblemen as well as the maid and clown who keep them
company. Maria describes Malvolio sharply as:

> a time-pleaser; an affectioned ass, that cons state without book, and
> utters it by great swarths: the best persuaded of himself, so crammed
> (as he thinks) with excellencies, that it is his grounds of faith that all
> that look on him love him. (Shakespeare 1975, 52–3)

And it is exactly that fault, the self-belief that 'all that look on him love
him', which Maria and the others use to fool Malvolio into believing
that his mistress, Olivia, dotes upon him. At first, the deceit begins
with the full festive panoply of misrule, as Malvolio's clothes are
presented in a topsy-turvey fashion with 'cross-gartered . . . yellow
stockings' (Shakespeare 1975, 95), which cause Olivia to interpret the
steward's changed demeanour as 'very midsummer madness'
(Shakespeare, 1975, 95). But as the lady returns to the romantic
concerns of the main plot, the sub-plot descends into a darkened hell
of lunacy in which Malvolio is bound, imprisoned in an unlit cell and
led to believe that Feste is a priest who has agreed to exorcise his
demons. The licensed madness of carnival thus shifts subtly into the

menacing unpredictability of lunacy, as Malvolio claims that 'I am as well in my wits, fool, as thou art', to which Feste responds, 'Then thou are mad indeed, if you be no better in your wits than a fool' (Shakespeare 1975, 126). The madness of the 'fool', the seasonal madness of carnival, and the lunacy of the possessed are thrown into close juxtaposition as Malvolio argues with a fruitless rationality to be given his freedom. For if the sane man is stranded in a world where all are mad, then it is he who comes to represent the otherness of lunacy.

It is hardly surprising that, when Malvolio has been given his liberty, he vows to 'be reveng'd on the whole pack of you!' (Shakespeare 1975, 152). Moreover, although Olivia acknowledges that, 'he hath been most notoriously abused', and Orsino calls for him to be followed and 'entreat[ed] . . . to a peace', (Shakespeare 1975, 152), the offenders seem to be rewarded rather than punished. We learn that Sir Toby has married Maria in recompense, and Fabian begs that their actions be seen more to 'pluck on laughter than revenge' (Shakespeare 1975,151). And the noble characters of the main plot leave the stage following their own romantic narrative line, rather than concerning themselves about the intricacies of the sub-plot with its minor gentry and middle-class servitors. The stage is finally left to Feste who sings the melancholic song of human life that traces existence from being 'a little tiny boy' to the final closure within 'my beds', with its constant sad refrain, 'For the rain it raineth every day' (Shakespeare 1975, 155–6). Thus, far from a comedic resolution, *Twelfth Night* ends with the apparition of tragedy, incorporating social division, an invocation of revenge, and a reminder of the inevitable momentum of time and death. Indeed, given the final scene, Shakespeare's play seems a somewhat incongruous choice for the light-hearted carnivalesque spirit of Elizabeth I's 1601 Twelfth Night festivities.

However, it is possible to interpret the discourse of licensed madness in terms other than those of the New Historicist theory of contained misrule. A treatment of the Early Modern understanding of carnival had been undertaken at least 20 years prior to the American New Historicism, by a group of Russian critic(s) who are now commonly recognised under the single name, Mikhail Bakhtin. In his book, *Rabelais and His World* (1965), Bakhtin discusses the Feast of Fools held on Epiphany:

> Laughter at the feast of fools was not, of course, an abstract and purely negative mockery . . . It was 'man's second nature' that was

laughing, the lower bodily stratum which could not express itself in official cult and ideology . . . From the wearing of clothes turned inside out and trousers slipped over the head to the election of mock kings and popes the same topographical logic is put to work: shifting from top to bottom, casting the high and the old, the finished and completed into the material bodily lower stratum for death and rebirth. These changes were placed into an essential relation with time and with social and historical change. (Bakhtin 1984, 75 and 81–2)

Bakhtin's description of the Twelfth Night festivities recognises that the Early Modern court festivities were part of a wider social celebration, which encompassed all levels of society in the material rituals of 'death and rebirth'. Moreover, he claims that the 'casting' down of the dominant hierarchies of nobility, age and formal social structures was an inevitable consequence of time, and of social and historical change. A Bakhtinian reading of Shakespeare's play, therefore, might uncover unleashed, rather than contained, misrule.

In attempting to interpret *Twelfth Night* in terms of Bakhtinian theory it is helpful to look back to an earlier Shakespearean comedy, *As You Like it.* Apart from the consanguinity of title, the shipwreck of Viola/Cesario on the coast of Illyria is paralleled with Rosalind's escape to the forest of Arden, and both heroines adopt a male disguise. Yet Rosalind never comes to regret cross-dressing as Ganymede and the whole pastoral ideal of the forest world is epitomised by a stasis of time, for 'there is no clock in the forest' (Shakespeare 1987, 75). The very opposite is true of Illyria. At the beginning of the play, Orsino recognises the mutability of art, love and nature:

> O spirit of love, how quick and fresh art thou,
> That notwithstanding thy capacity
> Receiveth as the sea, nought enters there,
> Of what validity and pitch soe'er,
> But falls into abatement and low price,
> Even in a minute . . .
> (Shakespeare 1975, 6)

That 'minute' is all-important in Illyria. The sense of time moving relentlessly on, is evoked by Viola when she plays with the country's name, desiring to be dead and in 'Elysium', rather than alive in Illyria

(Shakespeare 1975, 8). During the mistaken love scenes between Olivia and Viola, both rely on time to resolve the 'fadge'. Indeed, the clock actually strikes during the play, its chimes prompting Olivia to berate herself, 'The clock upbraids me with the waste of time' (Shakespeare 1975, 82). And finally, Feste's concluding song reminds us that human life moves inexorably from the cradle to the grave. There might not be a clock in Arden, but there is certainly one in Illyria and its very vocal presence questions the possibility of ever fully containing the material inversions of Twelfth Night.

As long as the madness of the feast of fools is perceived in a synchronic moment of stillness, as a single moment in time that both undermines, but simultaneously reinforces authority, then misrule may be contained. And so it is in Arden. But as soon as time is allowed to move, as soon as the temporal axis of the diachronic swings into action, then misrule becomes associated with the inevitable material changes of human life, as Bakhtin puts it, with 'the bodily lower stratum', that in turn necessitates 'social and historical change'. It is perhaps the knowledge that there is a clock ticking away the time in Illyria, the minutes that lead up to midnight and the end of Twelfth Night and all it represents, that makes the comment, 'they're all mad here' understandable. For in the topsy-turvey, upside-down world of the play that which has been cast down never fully returns to its pre-eminent state.

In this way time works in order to disrupt both social and historical axes in *Twelfth Night*. For example, at the beginning of the play the nobility and servitors know and accept their positions within Early Modern society. Such is the clear distinction that it is even possible to represent this class stratum diagrammatically as in Figure 3. The nobility are divided into two groups, those who combine status with wealth and power (Orsino and Olivia), those who are gentlemen and women but whose fortunes do not match their birth (Viola, Sebastian, and Sir Toby), and finally Sir Andrew who represents those who have rather more money than class. Within this noble framework it is perfectly acceptable for the poorer but well-born gentry to marry 'up' into the landed aristocracy. This is exactly what Viola and Sebastian do, proving that their adventures in Illyria, or onto the social sea of the Early Modern court, have proved successful. Moreover, the only member of the nobility whose desire seems destined to remain unfulfilled is Olivia in her impossible love for Viola/Cesario, yet even this is resolved through the narrative emergence of Sebastian, allowing

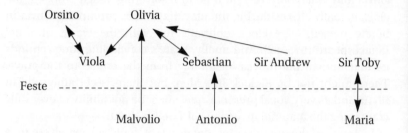

Figure 3

Olivia gratification. However, the breeding, rhetorical skills and upper-class accomplishments of Viola and Sebastian do not seem to be available to Sir Andrew, who therefore fails in his attempt to marry Olivia in spite of his fortune. Each character type was common in Early Modern drama and each, from noble lord through to the foolish country gentleman, was frequently paraded upon the English stage of the late-sixteenth and early-seventeenth centuries.

The servitors are similarly recognisable types within the dramatic conventions of the day. Malvolio is immediately classifiable as the stock puritan, whose self-opinionated seriousness makes him the obvious butt of the comic sub-plot. Except, of course, that he also tries to woo Olivia, thereby attempting to breach not only generic divides but also, more importantly, the division between two classes. Such an attempt is doomed to failure and he is severely punished for his presumption. Moreover, unlike Olivia, when his desire is thwarted at the end of the play he leaves the stage with increased frustration and deepest resentment. Malvolio's discontent is to a certain extent paralleled by the fortunes of Antonio, the captain of the ship, who rescued Sebastian, who loves the young man 'without retention or restraint' (Shakespeare 1975, 135) and who risks his life to accompany him to Illyria. The representation of homoerotic love between Antonio and Sebastian mirrors that which mistakenly occurs between Olivia and Viola, and like the affection between the women, that between the men is doomed to failure within the social conventions of the day. And after Antonio sees brother and sister side by side, asking 'How have you made division of yourself?' (Shakespeare 1975, 143), he remains alone and unanswered. Thus, if the nobility have their wishes fulfilled, the same cannot be said for Malvolio and Antonio, who at the close of the play remain alone with their desires frustrated.

There are, however, two characters who are not circumscribed by these class divisions, Maria and Feste. At the end of the play we learn that Sir Toby has married Maria, although neither appears to share the final promise of harmonious nuptials suggested by Orsino. After all, how could they? It would have been unimaginable that a serving woman should have attended the wedding of a Duke, even if she had married into his extended family. Expressed in this stark fashion the extent to which the class rules of Early Modern Europe have been transgressed becomes clear. Moreover, once the marriage of servitor and gentleman occurred there could be no containment of the misrule in the morning following the festivities, either those of a nuptial or of a Twelfth Night feast.

Yet Maria is not alone in her ability to cross social boundaries, for Feste too is a character drawn to a new pattern. Unlike Shakespeare's other fools, and here Touchstone in *As You Like It* is a useful comparison, Feste does not belong to a single household, nor is he dependent upon a single lord or lady. Throughout the play Feste moves between the courts of Olivia and Orsino, and as he does so he asks for economic recompense. Sir Toby and Sir Andrew give him 'sixpence' or a 'testril'; Sebastian gives him 'money'; he is given food and drink at Olivia's house; and is also paid 'for his pains' by Orsino (Shakespeare 1975, 44–5, 59, 74–7, 117). Moreover, when Viola/ Cesario asks Feste directly how he 'lives' and whether or not he is Olivia's fool, the clown proffers evasive answers, noting first that he lives 'by the church' and second that 'Olivia has no folly'. The play on words is, of course, the fool's traditional stock in trade, yet as the scene progresses it becomes clear that Feste has no wish to be identified with either 'master' or 'mistress', preferring to move freely between the two. When he leaves, Viola/Cesario describes for the audience how and where the self-employed fool lives:

> He must observe their mood on whom he jests,
> The quality of persons and the time,
> And like the haggard, check at every feather
> That comes before his eye.
> (Shakespeare 1975, 77–8)

And of course before Feste departs Viola/Cesario pays him 'expenses' (Shakespeare 1975, 76). Rather than being part of the feudal household, Feste represents a new class of servitors, those who work for whatever 'quality of persons' offer to pay them. Furthermore, the clown was not the only entertainer who had to 'observe the mood' of those who watched his performance, since the new acting companies had similarly achieved independence from noble households. As the actors of the Chamberlain's Men played through each successive scene in Middle Temple Hall, they too would have been alert to the mood of their audience. Perhaps as the sub-plot took shape they even exaggerated Malvolio's role in response to the obvious enjoyment of spectators such as John Manningham. There can be no possibility of recapturing the effect of these Early Modern performances, but Feste's final song brings out the collusion between his own role as a transgressor of class boundaries and the actors' evaluation of their own new position in society. The clown concludes the play with:

> But that's all one, our play is done,
> And we'll strive to please you every day.
> (Shakespeare 1975, 156)

Like Feste, the actors need to please the 'mood' of the audience so that they will return 'every day' and pay money in order to see the show; more particularly, they strive 'to please' and not 'to serve'. Within the palace of Westminster or in any of the great houses of the nobility, the old pattern of patronage would have been too evident for these economic changes of Early Modern England to be clearly demarcated. But in Middle Temple Hall with its tradition of professional training and dramatic invention, such feudal structures would have appeared arcane and out of place. In Bakhtinian terms therefore, an early-seventeenth-century production of *Twelfth Night* would have cast down the absolute power of the nobility and celebrated the insurgence of the servitor class. Rather than promising a return to the old hierarchy at the close of the festivities, the play ensures that the voice of the new self-employed class, with their insistent demands for fair monetary recompense, cannot be contained. In these circumstances the feast of fools becomes a liberating force for (as Bakhtin refers to it) the 'lower . . . stratum' of society, which is aptly embodied in the character of Feste, the fool.

When Bakhtin describes the impact of a Twelfth Night discourse, he

not only refers to social upheaval, but also to 'historical change'. The
two processes are, as has already been shown, inextricably linked, for
revolutions in class expectations depend upon the transformative
movement of time. Yet *Twelfth Night* is a drama that matches the
extension of its narrative line to the disruption of its class limits. Again
a diagrammatic representation of this process enables us to perceive
how boundaries are irreparably ruptured (see Figure 4). *Twelfth Night*

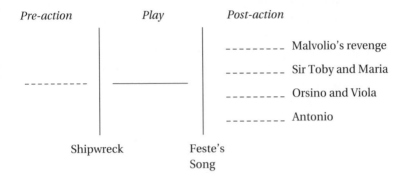

Figure 4

resists limitations in a number of ways, and the breaches of its narrative confines are examples of the way in which Shakespeare's version
of misrule refused to be contained. The suggestion of a pre-action
plot given by Viola/Cesario in the second scene of the play is conventional, depicting a world before the shipwreck when she and her
brother were happily united. Similarly, we become aware that previously Olivia's brother has died and that Orsino has wooed her with
little success. The shipwreck thus acts as the force that casts the world
of these romance protagonists askew and traditionally the play works
to resolve ensuing complications and to unite the two sets of
contented lovers at its close. And to a certain extent this harmonious
conclusion is accomplished, but there are a surprising number of
extra narrative pieces that refuse to be neatly closed off. For example,
in the final scene of the play Viola remains dressed in her boy's
clothes and Orsino continues to address her as Cesario when they leave
the stage. This presents a stark contrast with Rosalind in *As You Like
It,* for although she is given a complex and unconventional epilogue,
Rosalind appears at the end of the play appropriately reattired in her

female garb. Viola, who has consistently proclaimed distaste for her enforced role as Cesario, remains enclosed within a state of discontent until, as Orsino orders,

> . . . when in other habits you are seen,
> Orsino's mistress, and his fancy's queen.
> (Shakespeare 1975, 153)

For Viola and Orsino, therefore, Feste's song cannot herald a full consummation of their love, since she must wait to regain her female accoutrements before being accepted by the Duke. Thus, if the audience wishes to sustain the comedic conclusion they must imagine a post-action sequence in which Viola is reunited with the captain who produces her clothes, which she is then able to put on in order finally to become 'Orsino's mistress'.

Other post-action narratives have already been discussed in relation to the play's disruption of social hierarchy, and they serve similarly unsettling functions within the temporal discourse focused upon here. For example, the difficult circumstances ensuing upon the marriage between Sir Toby and Maria have already been noted. In addition, both Malvolio and Antonio present unresolved plot lines at the close of the play. Indeed, apart from being isolated and disgruntled, Antonio is about to be imprisoned and Malvolio departs swearing he will be revenged, making them appear more like characters about to enter a Jacobean tragedy, than ones departing an Elizabethan comedy. And while Antonio's brooding discontent might well be imagined as resolved, Malvolio's dark threats offer up the possibility of a revenge tragedy. In this sense, genre and time are simultaneously extended in *Twelfth Night*, as the work looks forwards to the problem plays that follow it in Shakespeare's canon.

Since time itself cannot be restrained, the carnivalesque spirit of Twelfth Night is propelled forward with the topsy-turvy swirl of temporality, demanding social, historical and generic change, as the high are cast low and art itself unleashes the forces of misrule. And as Queen Elizabeth returned to the security of her royal palace these forces of transformation were already at work in Middle Temple Hall and the surrounding Inns of Court. More dramatists began their careers, new plays were produced, and old ones were revived in political defiance of the crown. In the constant activity and perpetuation of misrule within the Early Modern theatre one might almost echo the words of the Cheshire cat, 'they're all mad here'. Yet even as the Bakhtinian understanding of a triumphant rise of the lower stratum appeared to gain force, the material contexts were once again shifting. As the Jacobean age began a new discourse of madness evolved and the forces of authority re-emerged in an attempt to control misrule, not with external constraints, but through a strategy of internalised manipulation.

Enclosed theatres: Thomas Middleton

> 'The black audience/Where howls and gnashings shall be music.'
> (Alsemero in *The Changeling*)

During the first 20 years of the seventeenth century theatres underwent a radical transformation. Instead of the open public stages such as the Rose and the Globe, or marginal and mutating acting spaces such as Middle Temple Hall, theatrical companies increasingly invested in small, closed buildings. The benefits of having a roof over the audience's head must have been desirable and, by the 1620s, when Thomas Middleton wrote *The Changeling*, small covered theatres had become accepted constructs. Inevitably, new performance strategies had to be developed to deal with the consequent change in audience expectations. For example, the space immediately before the stage altered from an uncovered pit where the poorest spectators stood, into the most exclusive seating area in the theatre. As such, from their earlier position of distance within the tiered seating of the open theatres, the audience now moved into close proximity to the theatrical action, and seat prices began to rise in relation to their closeness to the stage. The whole theatre structure appeared to have drawn in upon itself. The stage was smaller, the large pillars had been removed and balconies were used increasingly to present refined musical interludes. Instead of the active declamations suited to a production of *Tamburlaine* in the Theatre, the company who performed *The Changeling* could rely upon intimate asides and long moments of motionless expectation. The older-style theatres, such as the Rose, Theatre and Globe, remained profitable during the first part of the seventeenth century, but they were increasingly used to stage dramas that were popular with the citizens of London who were not able to leave the city during the summer months. The small closed theatres, such as Blackfriars, mostly produced plays that were viewed by the nobility, and might well be commissioned by the Master of the Revels for a court performance. The demands of this more exclusive audience and the closed acting space inevitably altered the textual contents and style of those plays that were written for the new theatres, and *The Changeling* both participates in and questions this transition of dramatic discourse.

Little is known about Thomas Middleton's life (1580–1627), although he was probably a law student and, given his age, he could well have been one of the young dramatists who worked with the theatrical space offered in Middle Temple Hall. We do know, however, that he wrote plays and masques, being primarily a collaborative writer, working with William Rowley, Thomas Dekker and others. *The Changeling* is co-authored by Rowley. Middleton's main works, *Women Beware Women* (c.1621), *The Changeling* (1622), *A Chaste Maid in Cheapside* (1613), and *A Game at Chess* (1624) are all dark satires, which focus upon class conflict, economic difficulties, ambiguous sexuality, and moral degeneration, while their tone is uniformly cynical and ironic. In addition, *The Changeling* revives a number of themes from the earlier works discussed in this chapter. The play as a whole therefore demonstrates political and social change, the impact of the alteration in theatre construction, and the radical transitions that were occurring in Early Modern dramatic discourses.

As in *Twelfth Night,* there are two class-related narrative strands in *The Changeling,* both tracing the entangled relationships of women. The main plot concerns the Lady Beatrice and is set at court, while the sub-plot centres upon the middle-class Isabella and her role as the wife of the physician-owner of a lunatic asylum. Within these settings the play explores themes that had already been established as dominant dramatic discourses of the Early Modern period. Class, economic standing, the role of women, spiritual faith, madness and autonomy all emerge as central concerns. Thus, while excavating these themes in relation to *The Changeling,* it is possible to refer back to the earlier plays discussed, tracing the changes that occurred in the dramatic traditions of the sixteenth and seventeenth centuries.

For example, the growing importance of a cash-based economy has already been discussed with regard to *Twelfth Night,* yet Feste's sixpences are insignificant in comparison to the recompense expected by DeFlores, the dark malcontent anti-hero of *The Changeling.* Indeed, economic imagery seeps insidiously through the play, infecting the other thematic discourses, just as the prospect of a 'reward' affects character and narrative choice. In such interests the play is influenced by the rapid early-seventeenth-century growth of a strong middle class in London, which had led to the increasing power of wealth against the traditional value placed on social standing. Dramatists had been quick to emphasise the repercussions of this shift in fortunes and 'gold' became a common focus of theatrical satire, Ben Jonson's city comedy *The Alchemist* being a good example.[3] Middleton, however, adopts a particularly dark tone in his satirical drama, depicting all relationships, even the most personal, as devalued through the emphasis placed upon wealth rather than moral worth. This is particularly apparent when Beatrice asks her servant DeFlores to murder the gentleman she is betrothed to, Alonzo, so that she might marry Alsemero, the man who has aroused in her a passionate love. At first Beatrice believes that DeFlores desires 'Gold' as payment, and she gives him an advance of money as well as promising that 'Thy reward shall be precious' (Middleton 1975, 172). But DeFlores desires Beatrice for himself and the 'reward' he asks for when he has committed the crime is her own body:

> DeFlores. For I place wealth after the heels of pleasure,
> And were I not resolv'd in my belief
> That thy virginity were perfect in thee,
> I should take my recompense with grudging,
> As if I had but half my hopes I agreed for.
> (Middleton 1975, 184)

DeFlores perceives sex with Beatrice as the only form of payment he will accept. Beatrice, however, is loath to go to bed with DeFlores, whom she despises and finds physically repugnant, and she begs him to release her:

> Stay, hear me once for all: I make thee master
> Of all the wealth I have in gold and jewels;
> Let me go poor unto my bed with honour,
> And I am rich in all things.
> (Middleton 1975, 185)

Beatrice's final offer is refused, however, as DeFlores reminds his lady that the murder has made her a 'woman dipp'd in blood' and 'the deed's creature' (Middleton 1975, 184–5). Act III closes with the couple retreating from the stage to pursue an inextricably entwined consummation of passion and payment of debt. At the very centre of the play, Beatrice recognises that her desire for Alonzo's death and the belief that she could 'buy' DeFlores with money has already damned her with a multitude of sins. The mixture of sex, money and murder was a common allegorical trope designed to highlight human corruption, and one that is as common to the salacious newspaper headlines of the twenty-first century as to the Early Modern stage. Yet, Middleton's satire was directed at a much more specific target, since *The Changeling's* dark satire of contemporary society, and particularly of Beatrice's plight, was based on real events.

Since the publication of David Lindley's insightful book, *The Trials of Frances Howard* (1993), it has become critically accepted that the character of Beatrice is based on Frances Howard, Countess of Essex. Howard obtained a divorce from the Earl of Essex in 1613 and subsequently married Robert Carr, Earl of Somerset. However, in 1615 Sir Thomas Overbury, who had consistently opposed the remarriage, was murdered and scandal ensued. In addition, Howard appears to have been involved in witchcraft, and a trial found both her and Carr guilty of murder, leading to their imprisonment in the Tower. The scandal was thoroughly disseminated by the court and London networks, ensuring that within the small theatres with their enclosed spaces and noble clientele, the story proved both apposite and popular. In tracing the origins of the play Lindley quotes DeFlores' claim that by becoming his accomplice in murder Beatrice:

> . . . must forget your parentage to me:
> Y'are the deed's creature; by that name
> You lost your first condition, and I challenge you,
> As peace and innocency has turn'd you out,
> And made you one with me.
> (Middleton 1975, 185)

Lindley then proceeds to analyse this speech pointing out that:

> DeFlores' words are an accurate summary of Frances Howard's fate in subsequent narratives. She has been represented ever since 1616 as 'the deed's creature', and the deed that defines her is the murder of Overbury. The later-known crime is imported back into the

reading of the divorce, which then becomes a sign of Frances Howard's essential moral turpitude. DeFlores' lines hint also at another powerful cultural motif which plays a significant part in determining the response to Frances Howard. The 'first condition' of which he speaks is also the original female 'deed' of Eve's betrayal in the Garden of Eden. (Lindley 1993, 78–9)

While Lindley's focus is upon the female paradigm that was applied to Frances Howard, his comments have important repercussions for an understanding of the way *The Changeling* evokes concerns with sex, death, and faith. Thus, while the events were seen as referring to a particular scandal, they were also, through the play, expanded to become emblematic of court corruption, female immorality and sexual licence.

Yet, even if the immediate source of *The Changeling* was the Overbury affair, its overall thematic concerns were backed up by a whole tradition of condemning women for their overt sexuality and sin. Jacobean tragedies are replete with female characters who, like Beatrice, are portrayed as sexually rapacious, self-willed and immoral. Moreover, these characters often 'change' from good to bad in narrative strands redolent of Middleton's dramatic plots. For example, Beatrice may be linked to Evadne and Aspati in Beaumont and Fletcher's *The Maid's Tragedy* (1612), the Duchess in Webster's *The Duchess of Malfi* (1613), and Annabella in Ford's *'Tis Pity She's a Whore* (1630–1), since all are women who have been trapped by tragic circumstances. Within *The Changeling* itself, Beatrice is contrasted with Isabella, who remains chaste and constant throughout the play. Although William Rowley most probably wrote the sub-plot, the coincidence of theme and the clear focus upon character difference suggests a close pattern of mutual production with Middleton. Isabella's role as the steadfast and loyal wife of the jealous doctor Alibius provides a commentary upon Beatrice's moral decline, just as the sub-plot's lunatic asylum offers a tacit and critical observation of court life in the main narrative. The moral judgement is underlined at the end of the play when Beatrice displays an acute self-awareness of her own change and moral decline as she addresses her father:

> Oh, come not near me, sir, I shall defile you;
> I am that of your blood was taken from you
> For your better health; look no more upon't,

> But cast it to the ground regardlessly,
> Let the common sewer take it from distinction.
> (Middleton 1975, 209)

The medical metaphor suggests that the good blood, which Beatrice has inherited from her father, has been tainted and corrupted, so that in death she is removed from him, just as a surgeon would bleed a patient to expel the bad blood of contagion. From being a noble-woman Beatrice has sunk to the 'common sewer', brought down by mortal sin. Moreover, the fact that Beatrice links death with sex, and that her actions must be contrasted with Isabella's married chastity, signifies that within the play women are represented in a conventional dialectic of whore and virgin. In addition, through the introduction of witchcraft (Beatrice is quite happy to use potions to gain her desires, as did Frances Howard), women are further linked to supposedly sinful activity. The acceptance of magic evinced by the Elizabethans had been overturned in James I's reign, which saw the incursion of witch trials, and as such, Beatrice's activity could well have been seen to carry a suggestion of satanic involvement.

The Changeling is not, of course, a play that centres upon witch-craft, although its title certainly brings the text within the overall discourse of magic. Rather the allusion colludes with broader contemporary social beliefs about women, as well as with the immediate example of Frances Howard, in order to represent women as a focus for mortal sin. In turn, this identification was reaffirmed by the growing puritan tradition that evoked Eve as the key example of female transgression. Just as *The Changeling* draws upon contemporary social discourse, it also participates in Christian ideology, for Middleton employs biblical figures in the characters of the play. Thus, as Adam and Eve 'fall' from their state of grace through the action of Satan they *change* from being innocent to being sinful. In parallel, Alsemero and Beatrice become aware of and are brought to sin through the action of DeFlores, and so are changed from the ideal lovers of the start of the play. Even as Beatrice accepts that she must go to bed with DeFlores she interprets her loss of virginity in biblical terms:

> Was my creation in the womb so curs'd,
> It must engender with a viper first?
> (Middleton 1975, 185)

Human creation is 'curs'd' even at its beginning in the 'womb' of Eden through the 'engender[ing]' of woman/Eve/Beatrice with the 'viper'/Satan/DeFlores. In this reading of the play, the chaste Isabella is associated with Mary, becoming the virgin to Beatrice's Eve-like whore. And at the close of the play Beatrice and DeFlores are damned to hell, in which they will perform their 'scene of lust' to 'the black audience/Where howls and gnashings shall be music to you' (Middleton 1975, 208). In summation, *The Changeling* may be interpreted as a dark attack upon the greed and depravity of human nature, which called upon actual events, contemporary views of women and biblical exemplars in order to produce one of the darkest and most cynical views of humankind produced on the Early Modern stage. A play so sinister that its 'scenes of lust' are deemed fit only for the 'black audience' of devils in hell. Yet this interpretation is unsettlingly rounded for a Middleton play, and several doubts linger amongst the more obvious moral conclusions. First, the biblical narrative does not end with Adam and Eve's eternal damnation in the Old Testament, for in the New Testament Christ dies on the cross in order to redeem humankind. Second, while critics are often tempted to focus upon the main plot, *The Changeling*'s sub-plot with its emphasis upon madness must be considered integral to the whole play, and its overtly comedic ending contrasts with the tragic deaths of the dominant narrative. Third, the scenes of lust referred to are not performed in hell, but in an enclosed space off-stage, while the main action continues in front of the audience. Thus, the play's self-referential formulations, its perpetual shifts between various social discourses, and its complex negotiation of the role of women in Christian ideology, demand further exploration.

The obvious 'fall' from grace enacted by Beatrice and DeFlores has often been allowed to overshadow the extended biblical narrative that may also be found in *The Changeling*. In the Bible, Adam and Eve are tempted to sin by Satan and are then expelled from the garden of Eden; they bequeath mortal sin to all humankind, condemning them to eternal damnation in hell. Thus, when Christ's death on the cross redeems humankind, the true value of God's grace is fully understood by those who had already understood the repercussions of sin. In this sense, the original fall may be seen as 'fortunate',[4] for humankind is able to appreciate fully the value of their redemption. If this Christian narrative is set alongside the plot of *The Changeling*, almost like a template, it becomes possible to see two alternative conclusions. In the main plot, as has already been noted, Beatrice and Alsemero are tainted by the manipulations of DeFlores. Beatrice in particular, like Eve who takes the apple from Satan, becomes aware of mortality and sex, and as such no redemption seems possible. Beatrice and DeFlores are thus condemned to hell, and the main plot ends with their deaths on stage in the conventional form of a tragedy. However, the play does not end exclusively with the main plot, for the story of Isabella and the lunatic asylum has wound its way towards a very different conclusion. In the asylum, Alibius and Isabella have a chaste marriage that conforms, particularly in the character of Isabella, to the social conventions of the time. However, when Lollio, Alibius' servant, begins to tempt Isabella to commit adultery, and threatens to expose the two noblemen, Antonio and Franciscus, who have disguised themselves as madmen in order to woo her, the parallel with the main plot and the biblical narrative becomes clear. Yet, unlike Beatrice and Eve, Isabella remains chaste, defying Lollio's attempts to blackmail her into sexual submission, and resolutely refuses the advances of Antonio and Franciscus. In a further link between the two plots, the disguised noblemen are accused of murdering Alonzo, and are only saved when Isabella reveals that they were locked up in the asylum, rather than fleeing punishment. Thus at the very end of the play, after the tragedy of the main plot closes, the characters of the sub-plot acknowledge their wrongdoing and proclaim themselves redeemed. Antonio recognises that he has been 'a great fool' and Franciscus says that he became 'stark mad', but both have been saved from death by their 'innocence'. Similarly, Alibius accepts that he has been 'a jealous coxcomb' and vows to become 'a better husband' (Middleton 1975, 210). The characters of the sub-plot learn the worth of socially accepted values, and the marriage of Alibius and Isabella is renewed and reinforced in the traditional manner of comedy. The comedic resolution of the sub-plot thus allows the New Testament narrative its full remit, which is that humankind may be redeemed. Moreover, for the characters of the sub-plot, the fall has been fortunate since they are now able to acknowledge their sins and vow to lead a better life. The sub-plot reworks the main plot's evocation of the biblical narrative, so that the New Testament promise of salvation is appended to the Old Testament damnation of humankind. But generically even if the play turns from a 'tragedy' towards a comedy, it never fully realises its comedic conclusion. Ultimately, *The Changeling* cannot sustain the forgiving tone of a tragi-comedy, but demands a double interpretation, in which the realisation of change creates shadows about characters, setting and language, even as redemption appears to be proffered.

The stark alteration in Beatrice's character has already been described, as she changes from a woman in love and honest to her father, into an unchaste, disobedient and articulate adulteress. In her final words she uses the metaphor of illness to describe how her blood, being corrupted, needs to be drawn from her father for his 'better health' (Middleton 1975, 209). Yet Alsemero also undergoes a transformation, for he begins the play scorning love, whereas by the final scene he accepts that he has been ruled by a passion that he describes as 'some hidden malady' (Middleton 1975, 153). Placed in the context of the sub-plot, such claims to illness imply that the discourse of madness has been allowed to seep beyond the confines of the asylum. As with *Twelfth Night* Middleton's play continually hints that 'they are all mad here'.

The main focus for the discourse of insanity in *The Changeling* is, however, the asylum run by Alibius. Middleton most probably based his description upon the first London madhouse, Bethlehem Hospital, which was founded at Camberwell in 1547 and commonly called 'Bedlam'. Today the conditions would seem appalling, with over-crowded rooms, and the chaining, whipping and starvation of inmates. In the Early Modern period, however, such sensibilities would have been quickly rejected, for it was considered a popular amusement to go and visit Bedlam to wonder and laugh at the lunatics. Middleton and Rowley were clearly aware of the realities of asylum life, for Alibius points out to Lollio:

> . . . those are all my patients, Lollio.
> I do profess the cure of either sort:
> My trade, my living 'tis, I thrive by it.
> But here's the care that mixes with my thrift.
> The daily visitants that come to see
> My brainsick patients, I would not have
> To see my wife. Gallants I do observe
> Of quick-enticing eyes . . .
> (Middleton 1975, 160)

The 'gallants' who come 'daily' to visit the asylum may gawk freely at the antics of Alibius' 'patients' since that is an accepted amusement, but they are not to be permitted to see Isabella, because a wife's chastity must be continually guarded. Additional references to the everyday activities of the madhouse build up a realistic portrayal of 'Bedlam' with its 'chimes', and the use of the 'wire' or whip (Middleton 1975, 163).

Although *The Changeling* is only separated from *Twelfth Night* by 20 years there had been a considerable alteration in the representation of madness. The incarceration of Malvolio in Olivia's house with the attendance of a fake priest (Feste) to exorcise his demons is very different from the institutionalised Bedlam that provides an income for its owner Alibius, who depicts himself as a doctor trying to cure patients. The midsummer madness of the Elizabethan age has been replaced by the lunatic malady of the Jacobean period, and in order to understand the way in which this transition developed it is useful to look at the theoretical exploration of madness in Michel Foucault's *Madness and Civilisation* (1961). In his path-breaking study Foucault explores how society disciplines and regulates itself, not by external force, but through the processes of self-regulation. In other words, we each carry a sense of control within us that determines our conformity with the social norms of our day. But in order to enable a recognition of appropriate behaviour, and to police our own boundaries, we need to perceive divisions between what is considered normal and what aberrant. Hence, distinctions between being mad and sane, ill and healthy, wrong and right are all necessary for an understanding of acceptable behaviour. The individual thus 'subjects' him/herself to these distinctions or laws. In this sense, we are subjects constructed by social, cultural and psychological forces. Moreover, given the regulatory aspect of the conventions it is possible to say that we are also 'subjected', in other words repressed, by these same forces. Foucault concludes by applying this understanding of subjectivity to madness:

> In a general way, then, madness is not linked to the world and its subterranean forms, but rather to man, to his weaknesses, dreams and illusions . . . madness no longer lies in wait for mankind at the four corners of the earth; it insinuates itself within man, or rather it is a subtle rapport that man maintains with himself. (Foucault 1961, 26)

Madness can no longer be explained as possession by external force, as in *Twelfth Night*, but must be recognised as an integral part of ourselves, something that may be restrained through a recognition of social boundaries, but which remains a constant threat within the frame of human weakness. This is the madness that Alibius hopes to cure, the folly adopted by Antonio and Franciscus, the malady that affects Alsemero, and the badness of blood represented by Beatrice and DeFlores. *The Changeling* is not so much possessed from outside by an infernal spirit, as infected from within by the human propensity for madness and all forms of social transgression.

Foucault, however, proceeds to identify different forms of the 'madness' that we carry within us as part of our constructed subjectivity. One such form is, inevitably, 'love':

> Then the last type of madness: that of *desperate passion*. Love disappointed in its excess, and especially love deceived by the fatality of death, has no other recourse but madness . . . Punishment of a passion too abjectly abandoned to its violence? No doubt; but this punishment is also a relief; it spreads, over the irreparable absence, the mercy of imaginary presences; it recovers, in the paradox of innocent joy or in the heroism of senseless pursuits, the vanished form. If it leads to death, it is a death in which the lovers will never be separated again. (Foucault 1961, 30–1)

In the sub-plot, madness and love are clearly linked: for example, Antonio and Franciscus pretend to be mad because they love Isabella. Yet this is not the desperate passion described by Foucault. Paradoxically, it is in the asylum where madness should abound that social boundaries are reinforced, where Isabella retains her chastity and the disguised nobles finally accept their subject positions within contemporary ideology. Rather, it is the main plot that produces the excessive passion, the unrestrained mad love that can only be satisfied in mutual death. DeFlores and Beatrice together breach all the boundaries of normality/morality/sanity in their passion. At first, this unrestrained desire originates with DeFlores, as he tells Beatrice:

> I shall rest from all lovers' plagues then;
> I live in pain now; that shooting eye
> Will burn my heart to cinders.
> (Middleton 1975, 185)

But increasingly Beatrice responds to DeFlores' passion, asking 'who would not love him?' (Middleton 1975, 200). And at the conclusion of the play the 'twins of mischief' die together, DeFlores calling Beatrice to 'make haste' for he would 'not go to leave thee far behind', while she accepts that "Tis time to die' (Middleton 1975, 209 and 210). In the final moments of the main plot therefore, the two lovers die and, in Foucault's words, will 'never be separated again', although the 'black fugitives' are condemned by the Christian value system of their society to damnation in hell, where the 'howls and gnashings' of the devils will torment them.

Yet, if we accept Foucault's theories of Early Modern subjectivity in relation to madness and love, then DeFlores and Beatrice cannot remain entirely positioned as symbols of eternal sin within a Christian allegory. Rather than being possessed by Satan, their tragedy is seen to have come from within, representing a malady of excess that exists within us all. Moreover, taken from the preordained narrative structure of the Bible and Christian ideology, the refusal by Beatrice and DeFlores to accept social conventions begins to transform them into passionate human beings whose challenge to society may be interpreted as a romantic gesture towards individualism. By the early nineteenth century this passion and individualism would be acceptable, but in the seventeenth century such a claim to free will would have appeared as a dangerous challenge to the hierarchies of church and state. Thus, while the Early Modern establishment might strike us as investing in the binary system through which society teaches us to police ourselves, to the first audiences of *The Changeling* such assumptions might well have appeared alien and radical. Is it really possible, therefore, to reinterpret the play's incorporation of biblical forms, in particular the categorisation of women, as an Early Modern exposé of the way in which religion repressed the individual? Or, as an audience of today interpolated into our own society, is it possible to appreciate the values of an earlier society by rejecting DeFlores and Beatrice?

There can be no fixed answers to questions of interpretation, particularly in the case of drama, for as Katherina points out, 'what you will have it named, even that it is'. Yet by returning to the first performances of *The Changeling*, to the Phoenix theatre and the small covered buildings of the Jacobean stage, it becomes possible to excavate the way in which the play's language and the use of a predicted performance space evokes a particular form of subjectivity. The small acting arena of the new theatres with their darkened auditoriums and audiences clustered around the stage suggested a far more intimate atmosphere than had been possible in the larger open-air auditoriums. In such a closeted area it was possible to evoke a discourse of scandal and gossip, as *The Changeling*'s allusions to the Overbury affair make clear. Yet Middleton moves beyond contemporary allusion and exaggerates such confidences, in that the whole play is replete with innuendo and asides. For example, Act II scene ii, when Beatrice and DeFlores agree to murder Alonzo, makes extensive use of such devices. Beatrice believes that, once Alsemero has left, she remains alone on stage, although the audience realises from DeFlores' first words in the form of an aside, 'I have watch'd this meeting', that he has been present throughout. Whether the production makes his presence clear at this point, or if the audience has been privy to his concealment from the beginning of the scene, a mutual understanding inevitably develops between DeFlores and the spectators in the auditorium. Yet even as DeFlores concludes his lines, Beatrice commences her own aside, confessing to the audience that she 'loath'd him' but still wishes 'to serve my turn upon him'. At this point DeFlores has emerged from his concealment and upon seeing him Beatrice calls out his name. Over the course of the next 30 lines DeFlores gradually approaches Beatrice across the stage, yet he addresses all but two of his ten speeches away from her and towards the audience. Within the small, darkened space the audience must weigh the knowledge of Beatrice's manipulation of DeFlores against the passion he confesses to us alone. It is in this context that the two characters on stage construct a mutual misunderstanding about the reward Beatrice will give to DeFlores for murdering Alonzo. There is, however, no parallel confusion for the audience, since the asides quite clearly inform us that Beatrice is thinking in terms of 'Gold', whereas DeFlores interprets her words as 'wanton'. Meaning shifts according to the desire of the individual, and what might be an accurate 'name' in Beatrice's upper-class understanding of household loyalty and service, is quite different for DeFlores with his sense of salaried employment in which murder comes at a high cost indeed. But like Petruchio, DeFlores will teach Beatrice his meaning, and although he threatens violence, again like Shakespeare's comic character, he uses language alone to obtain his desire. Moreover, if language displays its instability in the play's use of the aside, it also weighs the balance of meaning towards the male characters, suppressing the female voice regardless of class or morality.

In the final scenes of *The Changeling* Beatrice and Isabella both become muted participants in the narrative. Although the audience knows that the sub-plot's fakeries have been uncovered by Isabella, it is Alibius who conveys the information to Vermandero, and although she is allowed a final four lines, even then her husband undertakes the closure of the sub-plot with his own rejoinder. In parallel, Beatrice is locked up in Alsemero's closet where he affirms that she will 'Be my prisoner only . . . [and] I'll be your keeper yet' (Middleton 1975, 207). At first Alsemero is uncertain as to what course of action he should follow, but when DeFlores informs him 'that she's a whore', the cuck-olded husband immediately incarcerates both wrongdoers within the closet. It is at this point that Alsemero employs the self-referential allusion to playing quoted at the start of this section:

> . . . rehearse again
> Your scene of lust, that you may be perfect
> When you shall come to act it to the black audience
> Where howls and gnashings shall be music to you.
> (Middleton 1975, 208)

Although Alsemero addresses these lines to the now-concealed Beatrice and DeFlores, he also unwittingly demands that the audience identify themselves within a convoluted and multiple-space under-standing of the performance. Initially, Alsemero presents Beatrice and DeFlores metaphorically as players in the process of rehearsing a play off-stage, although the material import of his words implies that they are having sex in the cupboard in which they have been locked. Yet the audience is fully aware that Beatrice and DeFlores *are* players who *have* rehearsed 'scenes of lust' on stage during the present perfor-mance. Thus, the closet in which the two 'perform' is transmuted into the small covered Phoenix theatre, requiring that the spectators recognise themselves in the allusion to the 'black audience'. The enactment of adultery within the small space off-stage is thus trans-muted simultaneously into the performance of *The Changeling* with its depiction of sexual immorality, as well as into a harsh judgement upon the corrupt activities of the Jacobean court. Moreover these depictions evoke a biblical narrative and its wider Christian ideologi-cal framework in which the world becomes a stage for all mortals with their perpetual presentation of sin that will finally lead them to the audience of devils in hell.

It is in this context that Beatrice's voice is heard from within the closet. The 'horrid sounds' that she emits are inarticulate cries, 'Oh, oh, oh!' (Middleton 1975, 209). As DeFlores enters the stage carrying a wounded Beatrice we learn that her cries have signified mortal wounds, but for those brief moments before we see her bloodied form, the cries remain within Alsemero's evocation of the 'scenes of lust', suggesting instead a violent consummation of passion. Thus death and sex combine through an absence of words in a moment of textual instability, which is represented in the concealed figure of Beatrice. Just as the closet devolves into the broader externalised spaces of theatre, court and the world, so Beatrice's inarticulate cry extends beyond her own material experience into a comment upon the volatility of meaning and the impossibility of fixing signification. As Terry Hawkes concludes of the genre of these broad stage directions,

> However ingeniously 'explained', those 'ah's and 'O's and 'thus's continue to subvert order, to disrupt sequence, to impede the linear flow of meaning because that is what their final referents – orgasm, disintegration, despair and death – finally do. (Hawkes 1986, 89)

Thus even at the end of the play Beatrice and Isabella offer the audience alternative conclusions. Isabella's silence with its tacit acceptance of the dominant patriarchal ideology, and the overall possibility of comic renewal within the sub-plot, combine to offer the audience subject positions that celebrate social convention. Yet Beatrice's cries and her ultimate compact with subversion and instability suggest that it is possible to break down those interpolated value systems, even if self-destruction is an inevitable consequence. While the persuasive power of self-regulation might determine the acceptable limits of social behaviour, existence on the margins, in the reprehensible space of madness, sex and death, maintained a powerful grip upon the Early Modern imagination.

Conclusion

In the period leading up to the mid-seventeenth century London had become the site for an explosion in theatrical activity. The early theatres with their vast public auditoriums, the smaller acting spaces that had sprung up in the Inns of Court, and finally the closed stages with their intimate atmosphere, had all been built and utilised in response to the increasing demand for dramatic activity. And as the size and shape of the theatres themselves had changed, so did the concerns and emphases of the plays performed in them. The mythic power of Tamburlaine, the topsy-turvey world of Illyria and the dark fascination of *The Changeling* succeeded each other in a pattern of transition that was echoed by the shifting form of the stages on which they were played. Even the thematic concerns of the Early Modern plays demanded that change, whether of politics, class, gender or religion, be brought to the forefront of the audience's perceptions. As such, sixteenth- and seventeenth-century England participated in an unprecedented surge of writing and production that retained a fluidity of form, content, performance and theatrical space. And as these works succeeded one another on the various stages, so the audiences themselves altered, from a wide cross-section of the Elizabethan populace, to the more restricted groups of the Jacobean and Stuart ages. Dramatic signification was thus propelled into a period of acute and powerful transition, in which meaning was destabilised with each successive performance. For the Early Modern audience, as Katherina points out, 'what you will have it named, even that it is'.

This period of accelerated change was, however, soon to come to a close. As the country became caught up in the turmoil of the English Civil War, dramatic representations of transition remained valid, yet the material impracticalities of their performance made them all but redundant. Moreover, the Interregnum, which followed the war, proved a politically hostile environment for the theatre, with sustained theatrical activity occurring only within the safety of individual households. It was not until the restoration of the monarchy in 1660 with the reopening of the theatres that plays once more began to participate in the construction of social and individual identity.

Notes

1. For a recent discussion of Marlowe's life see, Charles Nicholl, *The Reckoning. The Murder of Christopher Marlowe* (1992).
2. The use of space at the Swan in the RSC 1992 production both reinforced Stephen Greenblatt's 1980 reading of *Tamburlaine* as 'the equivalent in the medium of theater to the secularization of space, the abolition of qualitative up and down', but at the same time proved that

the play certainly did not have to rely upon 'unvarying movement' in which 'very little progress seems to be made' (Greenblatt 1980, 193–2).

3. Ben Jonson, *The Alchemist*, ed. Peter Bennett (London: Methuen, 1987).

4. Stanley Fish, *Surprised by Sin. The Reader in Paradise Lost* (Berkeley: University of California Press, 1967).

4 Prose

A map of Renaissance prose

> 'Heaven was too long a reach for man to recover at one step.'

The above quotation is taken from John Speed's *A Prospect of the Most Famous Parts of the World* (1627), which was the first world atlas to be compiled by an Englishman.[1] To the present-day reader the spiritual tone of Speed's opening sentence appears anachronistic for a geographical text, yet as the passage progresses the link becomes clear:

> Heaven was too long a reach for man to recover at one step. And therefore God first placed him upon the earth, that he might for a time contemplate upon his inferior workes, magnifie them in his Creator: and receive here a hope of a fuller blisse, which by degrees he should at last enjoy in his place of rest. (Speed 1627, 1)

The purpose of this Early Modern atlas is, therefore, to allow the viewer to 'contemplate' the 'earth' as an inferior replica of heaven and by so doing begin to appreciate God's power and munificence, thereby preparing him/herself for the 'place of rest' at the end of life's journey. As such, maps are not only useful tools for navigation on earth, but also a guide on the spiritual path to 'heaven'. And understanding the world's diversity is necessary for a true appreciation of God's whole creation. Thus, for Speed and his readers the material and spiritual spheres merge inextricably on the page.

In *A Prospect* Speed undertakes a representation of diversity by amplifying the charts with historical descriptions of the continents, intriguing vignettes about the peoples and areas of the various countries, and a series of border engravings depicting the costumes and cities of the regions. For example, 'The Description of Africa' presents a debate between the Christian understanding that, 'Africa as it lay neerest the seate of the first people [Adam and Eve], so questionlesse it was the next inhabited', and the indigenous history:

> Give the people their owne asking, and they will have the glory of the first Inhabitants of the World. (Speed 1627, 5)

The peoples of 'Numidia' are described as of 'ingenuous disposition, and addicted much to Poetry', while the 'Land is full of sandy deserts, which lie open to the winds and storms'. The chart itself is similar to current maps of Africa, although the framework depicts a King of Madagascar with what looks like a basket on his head, as well as a series of ports whose plans recall European towns, rather than African cities. Finally, Speed adds further odd pieces of information such as, that one of the Canary Islands 'hath no water but from a cloud, that hangs over a tree, and at noone dissolves' (Speed 1627, 5–6). Thus, *A Prospect* combines cartography, history, spiritual treatise, characterisations, narrative accounts, travel writing and anything else John Speed happened to know about a particular location. In fact, *A Prospect* was a typical work of Early Modern prose.

Critics have recognised the hybrid nature of late-sixteenth- and early-seventeenth-century prose. R. W. Maslen points out that:

> Throughout the sixteenth century, prose fiction seems consistently to have been regarded, by its authors as well as its readers, as the most slippery of literary mediums. Its slipperiness lay partly in the difficulty of defining what it was. Prose fiction refused to conform to any of the generic categories by which contemporary textbooks charted the hegemony of what is written: tragedy, comedy, history, epic, satire, and the rest. It masquerades as anything but fiction. (Maslen 1997, 11–12)

Similarly, Roger Pooley comments:

> So, a history of seventeenth-century prose is a history of paradigms, of images, as well of styles, of rhetorics, of ideas, of faiths often in conflict. It is also a history of genres – autobiography, history, sermons, essays as well as fiction. (Pooley 1992, 7)

Maslen's description of the 'slipperiness' of sixteenth-century prose with its list of 'generic categories' is echoed by Pooley's inventory of 'paradigms . . . [and] genres'. In order to comprehend prose writing in Early Modern England, therefore, it seems we have to accommodate a confusing mass of often divergent and inconsistent genres, styles, and forms. For readers accustomed to reading novels, with their solid generic foundations (even when those are challenged), the earlier prose works appear overly complex and made almost impenetrable with these multiple parts. Yet it is precisely here that John Speed's atlas might be able to help.

If we imagine a work of Renaissance prose, not as a linear narrative, but as a route across a hugely detailed map then the process of reading becomes more manageable. The map must be contemplated at intervals so that the reader will be able to follow the correct route to the journey's end. In the same way, the narrative line of the prose work must be halted at regular intervals so that theme may be considered on the way to a final sense of knowledge and understanding. And in each case proceeding along the path and finding one's way infer an array of thematic paradigms, from spiritual quest to political satire. Indeed, the image of the map is particularly apt since the first Elizabethan prose fictions were often set in distant or imaginary lands, such as John Lyly's *Euphues* (1578 and 1580) and Philip Sidney's *Arcadia* (1590). In each case the 'foreign' location offered the opportunity to comment upon the authors' own Elizabethan society, and the adventures of the main characters in both works represent the concerns of the late-sixteenth-century courtier. Geographical distinction was further suggested by the fact that Lyly and Sidney were influenced by English translations of the Italian pastoral romances of Boccaccio, Ariosto and Tasso. The Spanish picaresque form also proved influential, resulting in, among other works, Thomas Nashe's *The Unfortunate Traveller* (1594), that itself depicts a journey across Europe. The idea of mapping out themes occurs through a range of other genres, including travel literature, essays, diaries, biographies and autobiographies, allowing authors to extend textual commentary beyond personal narrative to a wider range of contemporary discourses.

There seems, however, an inevitable dichotomy in a comparison between reading a map and reading a prose work. The process of map reading requires the reader to undertake two simultaneous, yet antithetical positions. First, they must have a static and elevated overview of the whole and a sense of the final goal in order to plan their journey. Yet at the same time, the map reader must also be aware of the material conditions of movement along the actual route, recognising features from their symbolic replication upon the chart so that they may attain their, as yet unseen, destination. As such, the map reader appears to be both stationary and moving, both aware of and yet distant from the conclusion. While this more complex process of map reading can never fully equate with reading an Early Modern prose work, there are again certain useful analogies. An initial overview of the text might well incorporate a kaleidoscopic range of referents (genres, themes, and styles), yet the method of understanding them demands movement and the recognition of changing meaning. Thus, *Euphues* might offer a multitude of individual set pieces and phrases, presenting a static and satiric vision of the Elizabethan court. Yet at the same time, the reader must move from episode to episode, thereby increasing his or her own appreciation of Lyly's sharp wit and of the individual moral lesson. That linear journey through the sequential literary features of the text is a familiar one for readers of the novel, yet to understand Early Modern prose, we must be ready to halt occasionally along the way and study the broader compass of the map.

The Early Modern period revolutionised the production of prose, undertaking expansionism through genres that equalled the rapid enlargement of the charts that depicted the known world. Yet such multiplicity was to prove difficult to sustain and as the seventeenth century wore on rifts began to appear. Margaret Cavendish's *The Blazing World* (1666) and John Bunyan's *The Pilgrim's Progress* (1678 and 1684) were two of the last prose works which attempted to bridge these various discourses. For example, philosophy, science, autobiography, fiction, gender polemics, history, language and geography are all disciplines which occur with Cavendish's work, but rather than forming into an understandable map, they collide in a series of impossible patterns. If John Speed could imagine the earth as 'one step' away from heaven, by 1680 the fragmentation of the way in which the world was understood meant that, although time had moved forward, heaven seemed even further away.

John Lyly

In his prose treatise on humanist education, *The Scholemaster* (1570), Roger Ascham famously wrote:

> Ten *Morte Arthures* do not the tenth part so much harme, as one of
> these bookes made in *Italie* and translated in England. (Ascham 1863,
> 82)

Ascham had visited Italy himself and had been shocked by the
'corrupt maners and licentiousnes of life' that he believed himself to
have encountered (Ascham 1863, 74). This blurring of text and location was common in Early Modern England and extended beyond
travel books, to other works of prose, drama, and poetry. Yet if
Ascham found European differences threatening, many more writers
welcomed the opportunity to translate and rework the Italian prose
romances, just as their compatriots increasingly travelled abroad.

Continental romances were often read in their original language,
but there was a growing market for translations into English. The
enterprising and well-travelled gentleman or scholar was thus able to
consolidate their reputation and increase their income through a
witty balance of translation and astute reworking of Italian, French,
and Spanish prose novellas. This vogue had begun with a collection of
translated romances by William Painter, *The Palace of Pleasure* (1566),
which contained 66 romances that were enlarged at subsequent
publications in 1567 and 1575. Two further compilations followed
quickly, Geoffrey Fenton's *Certaine Tragicall Discourses* (1567) and
George Pettie's *Petite Pallace of Pettie his Pleasure* (1576), consolidat-
ing the popularity of the genre. These anthologies included, among
others, translations from the Italian authors, Boccaccio and Bandello,
as well as the French translations of Bandello by Belleforest and
Boaistuau. In each case the narratives describe, often with considerable relish, a catalogue of sexual, violent and illegal adventures. Yet
the author distances him/herself from the original text through
his/her position as a moral narrator. So, even if women commit adultery, while men rape and murder, the narrator is able to point out that
such salacious stories are presented only so that the reader may avoid
possible temptation. In terms of map reading, therefore, the translated prose romance might well have a clear destination – moral edifi-
cation – but the path detours through a host of pleasure-rich sites en
route.

As the pulp fiction of its day, the prose romance's combination of
immoral tale and moral author proved hugely successful, and numerous translations of continental works followed. It would be wrong,
however, to imply that all the romances, either in their original or

translated versions, emulated this popular formula, and there are some clear examples of carefully wrought and thoughtful works. For example: Tasso's *Amyntas* (1587) translated from Italian by Abraham Fraunce; Ariosto's *Orlando Furioso* (1591) translated from Italian by John Harington; and Montemayor's *Diana* (1598) translated from French by Bartholomew Young.[2] Moreover, these works and others like them proved not only popular in the market place, but also influential upon the developing form of the English prose romance. Perhaps the most well known of these English works today is Philip Sidney's *Arcadia* (1580), although Mary Wroth's *Urania* (1621) is now being studied as a female alternative in a male-dominated genre. However, since the writings of both Sidney and Wroth are dealt with elsewhere in this book, I intend here to concentrate upon equally influential works of their time, although ones not read so often today.

John Lyly's (1554–1606) *Euphues* (1578) and its sequel *Euphues and his England* (1580) followed the line of generic development begun by the compilations and translations, in combining narrative descriptions of the eponymous hero's wanton behaviour with a regular influx of didactic speeches from more moral characters. It was, of course, an immediate success. The plot itself is simple: Euphues, a young gallant, makes love to his friend's (Philautus) lady, Lucilla. When betrayed by Lucilla, who subsequently dies, the original male friendship is affirmed through the reconciliation of Euphues and Philautus. The second part depicts Euphues seeking to share his newfound wisdom through a series of didactic letters, advising his friend on a series of courtships. Their earlier roles are, however, duly rewarded at the end of the narrative, with Euphues being left estranged and 'musing in the bottome of the Mountaine', in contrast to Philautus who is happily 'marryed in the Isle of England' (Lyly 1902, II, 228). Lyly utilised a number of sources for this overall structure as well as for the numerous episodic stories that embellish the text. In terms of character and plot Lyly drew upon classical authors, the Italian romances, as well as Painter, Fenton and Pettie. In addition, Lyly was indebted to the translators for the development of his stylistic techniques, in particular Thomas North's *The Diall of Princes* (1576) and Pettie's *Pallace of Pleasure*. The former was based upon a French translation of the Spanish original by Antonio de Guevara that consists of a conventional romance told with close attention to rhetorical techniques. It was, however, the signal stylistic devices of Pettie's work, such as antithesis, repetition and alliteration, which had the most influence upon Lyly. But none of the earlier works compares with the subtle shift in prose writing achieved by John Lyly.

The stylistic technique utilised by Lyly in *Euphues* and given the name 'Euphuism', has been the focus of extensive critical debate. Before exploring the manner in which it has been received, however, it is important to understand what the term means. One of the clearest descriptions is made by R. Warwick Bond in his comprehensive edition of Lyly's complete works, where he explains that:

> Lyly's famous Euphuism aims at writing prose, firstly with great fineness and precision of phrase, secondly with great display of classical learning and remote knowledge of all kinds. To these two desiderata correspond . . . the two characteristics; firstly, those concerned with the structure of his sentences, and secondly, those methods of ornament and illustration. (Lyly 1902, I, 120)

The 'fineness . . . precision . . . and remote knowledge' was partly drawn from North; while the sentence structure and ornamentation derive more from Pettie, but combined they produced an array of characteristics that were immediately recognised as innovative. Bond offers a useful list, so that structural devices may be summarised roughly as antithesis, rhetorical questions, and repetition (including alliteration, rhyme and puns). Ornamental devices are similarly denoted as historical allusion, references drawn from classical mythology, the display of recondite knowledge, and the use of proverbs. Examples of these techniques may be found throughout the two parts, but to explain the function and signification of the devices outlined by Bond I wish to look more closely at a single section.

Towards the close of *Euphues and his England*, Lyly introduces a smaller text within the whole, 'Euphues' Glass for Europe'. In this section Euphues addresses a letter to 'the Ladyes and gentlewomen of Italy' and describes how:

> I am come oute of Englande with a Glasse, wherein you shall behold the things which you never sawe, and marvel at the sightes when you have seen . . . not a Glasse to dress your haires but to redress your harmes. (Lyly 1902, II, 189)

There are several examples of Euphuistic style here, as for example the antithesis used in 'shall behold' and 'never sawe', and the repetition of 'dress' and 'redress'. Moreover, the whole tone is one of knowledge that may be categorised as ornamentation, particularly Lyly's use of the mirror trope. The text proper begins with a description of Britain that is replete with detailed information that Euphues has 'gathered by myne own studie and enquirie', although he states that he does not intend to write a 'Chronicle' since it 'seeme[s] tedious' (Lyly 1902, II, 191). There follows a description of the 26 cities in the country, the 120 churches in London, and a vignette upon London Bridge,

> And among al the straung and beautifull showes, mee thinketh there is none so notable, as the Bridge which crosseth the Theames, which is in manner of a continuall streete, well replenyshed with large and stately houses on both sides, and situate upon twentie Arches, whereof each one is made of excellent free stone squared, everye one of them being three-score foote in hight, and full twentie in distaunce one from another. (Lyly 1902, II, 192)

Of course, Lyly's Euphuistic style is apparent in the arcane knowledge of the bridge's construction, and the repetition of numbers, 'every' and 'each'. But the reader is also given a very definite picture of the bridge as it sweeps over the Thames like a 'continuall streete', which as Lyly later points out, 'seemeth so populous' (Lyly 1902, II, 192). The reader is made aware that the 'Glass' depicts the whole of Britain, like an image on a map, and that the purpose of contemplating the depiction is for moral self-improvement. But dispersed within the overall didactic theme, there are detailed material realisations, almost like a telescope zooming towards a particular physical feature so that we are able to see it in perfect detail. Thus Britain is described in distant terms as being 'in forme like unto a Triangle', while London Bridge is presented in close up so that we may see each of the 'free stones'. This division of perception is in itself an aspect of the antithesis expected in Euphuism, but it also opens up the text's inner contradictions.

Euphuistic style initially appears like a highly wrought exterior, the carefully fashioned phrases and terms catching the reader in a detailed analysis of the text's surface. And to a certain extent, Lyly's prose is constructed to produce just such a rhetorical self-awareness, for *Euphues* is a supremely self-referential work. Such reflective devices are particularly apparent in the passage addressed to 'fayre Ladies' as Lyly describes the idealised behaviour of English women:

The Ladyes [of England] spend the morning in devout prayer, not resembling the Gentlewoeman in *Greece* & *Italy*, who begin their morning at midnoone, and make their evening at midnight, using sonets for psalmes, & pastymes for prayers, reading ye Epistle of a Lover, when they should peruse the Gospell of our Lorde, drawing wanton lynes when death is before their face, as *Archimedes* did triangles & circles when the enimy was at his backe. Behold Ladies in this glasse, that the service of God is to be preferred before all things, imitat the Englysh Damoselles, who have theyr bookes tyed to theyr gyrdles, not fethers, who are as cunning in ye scriptures, as you are in *Ariosto* or *Petrarck* or any booke that lyketh you best, and becommeth you worst. (Lyly 1902, II, 198–9)

Structural and ornamental techniques are employed throughout the passage. For example, there are a series of antitheses, from 'sonets' and 'psalmes', to 'lyketh you best, and becommeth you worst'. Repetition occurs through the use of visual alliteration, as in '*p*salmes, & *p*astymes for *p*rayers' (italics mine). And the reference to Archimedes displays classical knowledge by alluding to Plutarch's description of how Archimedes was slain by the Romans during the capture of Syracuse (Lyly 1902, II, 530). Of course, Archimedes did not deliberately ignore the soldiers, turning his back on danger so that he could draw triangles, and Plutarch's account makes this clear. But by placing Archimedes' serious pursuit and violent death in the same sentence as the women 'drawing wanton lynes' (either with art materials or cosmetics), the mathematician's fate is mocked. The antithesis (scholar/wanton) hinges upon the fact that both perform the same activity (drawing lines). And this is precisely how Euphuism functions, for while the text seems to rely upon the delight of structure and ornament, it continually reveals a complex and often satiric signification beneath. Indeed, the final sentence of the passage quoted above allows us to understand the way in which Lyly used the 'Glass' to 'redresse . . . harmes'.

Euphues describes how English women have books tied to their girdles and we are given to understand that these are spiritual works since the women are 'cunning in ye scriptures'. To begin with, this is an accurate depiction of late-sixteenth-century English costume, although the books could have been for either spiritual contemplation or domestic assistance. As such, the first readers of *Euphues* would have recognised a detail from their own wardrobe. Euphues continues, however, with a condemnation of the reader – 'you' – who he claims prefers the immoral prose romances of Ariosto or the love sonnets of Petrarch, or indeed any book that 'lyketh you'. But rather than act as a stern warning to the romance-reading women of continental Europe, the moral warning shifts about the image of the glass, bifurcating possible significations. For, even though the didactic narrator Euphues might claim to address the women of Greece and Italy, the urbane author Lyly has in contrast dedicated the whole book to 'The Ladies and Gentlewoemen of England' (Lyly 1902, II, 8). As the female reader gazes into the mirror therefore, the image reflected back fragments. At first the mirror depicts an ideal woman with her pious text chained to her waist, while peering into the glass is a pleasure-seeking lady who holds a prose romance in her hand. Within the text Euphues delineates these women as pious Englishwomen who offer an example to their Italian counterparts. In the framework of the whole work, Lyly echoes the pious ideal of the woman pictured in the mirror, but this time she is viewed by the English ladies for whom the book was intended. Whatever nationality Euphues might prescribe to the onlooker, within the context of Lyly's fiction she is an English woman who enjoys reading romances and sonnets. And of course that is exactly what the reader is doing. The Elizabethan ladies who waited impatiently for the sequel to Lyly's first bestseller, were reading a romance or 'any booke that lyketh you best', in other words, *Euphues his England.* And that smaller text within text, 'Euphues' glass' suggests ironically that she shouldn't be reading the romance at all, but should instead be concentrating on the scriptures. The antithesis pivots on the mirror trope, at one moment revealing the pleasure of the romance, and at the other condemning the frivolity of fiction.

At first Lyly appears to aim his censure at a particular readership, but the reflection imaged in the text is not easily confined. The person reading *Euphues and his England* equates broadly with the reader who enjoys romances (Ariosto) and poetry (Petrarch). Thus, the reader is constructed, regardless of sex or age, as someone who enjoys literary works more than, or even as much as, the Bible. And given the very act of reading Lyly's own prose romance, such an estimate is a probable conclusion. Thus, if the satiric scope of *Euphues* was meant for the Elizabethan court, Lyly simultaneously ensured that the moral questions posed by the text had wider employment. The glass functions therefore on two levels, closing in upon the reading habits and personal belongings of an Elizabethan lady, while at the same time drawing back to an overview that reveals a moral chart that extends beyond the boundaries of time and place. Moreover, the literary techniques employed in Euphuism operate in a similar fashion, providing the reader with the ornate and often comic surface detail, as well as offering a span of moral and social commentary that is still accessible today. The two extremes, like the vaunted antitheses of Euphuism itself, flash alternately through the text's dextrous rhetoric, as well as through those personifications of difference, Euphues and Philautus. Transitions from one to the other are swift and seamless, yet difference remains entrenched until one final moment.

Before concluding my analysis of Lyly's *Euphues* and *Euphues and his England*, I should like to look briefly at the concluding passages of each work. In each instance Lyly addresses the reader directly, ending the first book with:

> I have finished the first part of *Euphues* whome now
> I lefte readye to crosse the Seas to *Englande,* if the
> winde sende him a shorte cutte you shall in the
> seconde part heare what newes he bringeth
> and I hope to have him retourned
> within one Summer. In the
> meane season I wil stay
> for him in the country
> and as soone as he ar-
> riveth you shall
> know of his
> coming.
> FINIS.
> (Lyly 1902, I, 323)

The first sentence begins the direct information that the author has finished writing the first part of his book, yet even this seemingly simple phrase breaks down as the split between the time of writing and the moment of reading becomes apparent. Moreover, the 'I' may be the author, but read at the close of the book, it also refers to the reader who has indeed 'finished [reading] the first part of *Euphues*'. In this way, the concepts of author/reader and writing/reading are recognised as dualities even at the moment of textual closure. And Lyly further complicates the work's internal relationships by imagining himself waiting in the country for Euphues, who as a real person, will soon arrive. Of course, what Lyly really means, and means us to know, is that he is going to retire to the quiet of the country in order to write his second book, and that the arrival of Euphues will be marked by the actual publication of the text. But the overall impact is the creation of a set of shifting dualities in which author, reader and character remain in play around the refracting devices of the text. There can be no conclusion and even the form of the words suggests an arrow pointing towards the new book.

In contrast, the conclusion to *Euphues and His England* runs directly on from the proceeding paragraph:

> . . . But were the trueth knowen, I am sure Gentle-
> women, it would be a hard question among Ladies, whe-
> ther *Philautus* were a better wooer, or a husband, whe-
> ther *Euphues* were a better lover, or a scholler. But
> let the one marke the other, I leave them both,
> to conferre at theyr next meeting, and
> committe you, to the Al-
> mightie.
> FINIS
> (Lyly 1902, II, 228)

The passage appears to carry the usual Euphuistic traits, such as the antithesis between Philautus and Euphues (in lines 3 and 4 of my quotation), but examined more closely the usual opposites fail to engage. The two lines are almost mirror images of one another. They begin with the second section of the hyphenated 'whe-ther', and replicate 'were a better' and 'or a'. This might well represent the ornamental repetition of Euphuism, but the distinctions of wooer, husband, lover and scholar, hardly offer oppositions either generally or with regard to the work's specific characterisations. The next line further blurs the distinction since 'one [will] marke the other'. The verb 'marke' might call the two characters to take notice or to heed the other, thereby suggesting that they might learn by studying other values, just as the ladies gained self-knowledge by looking in 'Euphues' glass'. Yet 'to mark' also means to make an impression or sign that offers evidence as to ownership or meaning. If Euphues and Philautus 'mark' one another in this sense, they claim an association with the other that breaks down difference. In present-day critical terminology we would say that the values represented by Euphues inhere within Philautus's signification, and vice versa, thus collapsing any single meaning. If the two characters mark one another they must, therefore, deconstruct their seeming oppositional value systems, so that the 'trueth' may never be 'knowen'. Or can it?

Euphues does not conclude with the characters, who are left 'to conferre'. Instead Lyly ends his work in prayer-like fashion committing the reader to God. The dialectic of spiritual and literary text has already been discussed, but here there is no suggestion of reading matter for by committing us to 'the Almightie', Lyly relinquishes the reader to God with a suggestion of the final passing of the soul into heaven. And indeed, the truth of such salvation cannot be known on earth, just as John Speed's map could never fully recapture the glory of God's creation. Yet, the trust is manifest. *Euphues* might traverse the convoluted paths of rhetoric, it might linger in contemplation of ornamental details along the way, but ultimately the journey's end is known even as the voyage begins. Lyly's literary route might well balance the virtues of delight and didacticism, of pleasure and virtue, but at the end the 'long reach' of *Euphues* was directed towards 'heaven'.

Thomas Nashe

If English Early Modern prose may be understood as a map, then the cartography of Thomas Nashe's *The Unfortunate Traveller* (1594) recalls purgatory rather than heaven. Nashe (1567–c.1601) was a professional writer whose steady production of satirical prose works earned him a reputation as a university wit, alongside others such as Lyly and Marlowe. But Nashe differs from both in terms of genre and style, particularly in his depiction of the dissolute exploits of Jack Wilton, the anti-hero of *The Unfortunate Traveller*. The book traces Wilton's travels around Europe during the time of Henry VIII, thereby invoking a historical setting for Nashe's Elizabethan contemporaries. The chronological distancing functioned, in common with other Early Modern satires, as a thin veil for harsh criticism of contemporary society. Nevertheless, Nashe represents with some accuracy, but little adherence to chronological fact, a series of events, which are witnessed by Wilton. For example, Wilton is present at Henry VIII's conquest of the French town Tournay in 1513, and shortly after (in narrative terms) sees the Anabaptist uprising at Münster of 1534. In addition, he meets a host of famous people from the period, from the humanists Erasmus and More, to the Earl of Surrey whose journey through Italy Nashe purports to recount. These English topical references are scattered through a text that almost seems to exemplify Maslen's definition of Early Modern English prose as 'slippery'. Indeed, in terms of genre and stylistic form *The Unfortunate Traveller* covers: jest books, a sermon, satire, travel literature, historical fiction, a revenge tale, tragedy and tragi-comedy. Moreover, there appear to be no underlying moral tenets, nor does virtue combine with pleasure, as in Lyly's *Euphues*. Wilton's final repentance is cursory to say the least. Yet for all its fragmentation and contrary impulses there is a sharp and muscular realism that drives the narrative forwards.

Until recently critics have categorised *The Unfortunate Traveller* as a picaresque novel. This term derives from the Spanish word *picaro*, meaning rogue, and the genre usually described the adventures of a character who lives up to the broader expectations of this designation. The Spanish picaresque novel was popular in England and several works had been translated into English. It is possible that one of these, *Lazarillo de Tormes*, which had been reworked in English in 1576 by David Rowland, influenced Nashe, although as Paul Salzman points out:

> Jack Wilton . . . is not a victim of poverty like Lazarillo; and he plays his tricks in the early part of his narrative for sheer enjoyment – he is not a rogue out of dire necessity, as is Lazarillo. (Salzman 1991, 89)

While the picaresque might, therefore, be a general influence upon Nashe, there are too many styles and genres vying within the text for any clear identification. Neil Rhodes has suggested with reason that *The Unfortunate Traveller* may be characterised as grotesque, drawing attention to the bodily concerns of the text and its sense of unrestrained misrule.[3] At the same time, this comic materialism is set alongside a pointed satirical evaluation of Elizabethan society that breaks through the timeless diachronicity of the grotesque. The various influences upon *The Unfortunate Traveller* are therefore as elusive and broken up as the multiple genres employed by Nashe within the text. Yet, the multiple discourses do function as a united whole, and in order to explore how such combinations succeed I intend to look at the separate generic components.

The correspondence between a map and Elizabethan prose is

particularly apt in describing the various literary styles and techniques employed by Nashe in *The Unfortunate Traveller*. As Jack Wilton begins his journey at the siege of Tournay in France, he employs a series of tricks that derive from contemporary jest books. Wilton enumerates his pranks against various members of the King's forces, from a foolish captain to a 'companie of coystrell Clearkes' who are afraid to meet the enemy (Nashe 1958, II, 225). And he similarly tricks a Swiss Captain who:

> . . . was farre gone for want of the wench, I lead [him] astray most notoriously, for he being a monstrous unthrift of battle-axes . . . and a notable emboweler of quart pots, I came disguised unto him in the forme of a halfe crowne wench . . . and I sympered with my countenance like a porredge pot on the fire when it first begins to seethe. The sobriety of the circumstance is, that after hee had courted mee and all, and given me the earnest penie of impietie, some sixe Crownes at the least for an antipast to iniquitie, I fained an impregnable excuse to be gone, and never came at him after. (Nashe 1958, II, 225).

The tale is based upon a common folk jest in which a man disguises himself as a woman in order to trick another out of his cash and goods, and the jest is replete with grotesque images. The Swiss Captain's greed encompasses food (the 'battle' refers to a meal allowance), alcohol (the 'quart pot' of ale) and sex (the 'halfe crown wench' being a prostitute). This merging of bodily desires continues throughout the passage as Jack describes his sexual allurement in terms of 'porredge' and as an 'antipast to iniquitie', which represents the prelude to sex as a culinary introduction to a full meal. But while the Captain remains fooled by Jack's tempting exterior with its allusions to food and drink, Wilton is aware of the 'sobriety' of the situation through his success at gulling the 'Switzer' out of 'sixe Crownes' before leaving with an 'impregnable' excuse – that is, having evaded sexual intercourse. The bodily excesses of the passage are emphasised further through an awareness of the possibility of Jack being unable to get away or of the repercussions should the Captain come 'at him after'. Indeed, the trick works precisely because of the rogue's clever escape from sexual assault or violent retribution. But at the same time, the passage uncovers a more complex awareness of textual practice.

The Captain is a caricature of bodily greed and an archetype of the grotesque, who is fooled in the narrative by Jack's jest-book impersonation of a woman. Moreover, the joke is elaborated through a series of food, drink and sex metaphors that disguise the immoral economic realities of the trick with a palatable comic exterior. Therefore, as the Captain desires the culinary/sexual delights offered by Jack, so the reader is constructed as enjoying the bawdy humour and grotesque comedy of both narrative and trope. At the same time, the outer form of prostitute and picaresque prose are exposed as superficial with, what appears to be, the knowledge of an underlying sobriety based on economic reality. But even this possible sense of meaning eludes us as Jack, the unfortunate traveller, remains sexually inviolate and the text, *The Unfortunate Traveller*, remains similarly 'impregnable'.

As Wilton continues on his journey across Europe the comedy's underlying reality becomes more starkly drawn. After the capture of Tournay, Wilton returns to England for a short time where he witnesses an outbreak of the sweating sickness, an epidemic of which occurred recurrently in Britain throughout the first half of the sixteenth century. Subsequently Wilton returns to Europe and fights at the battle of Marignano (1515) before travelling to '*Munster* in *Germanie*, which an Anabaptisticall Brother, named *John Leiden*, kept at that instant against the Emperor and the Duke of *Saxonie*' (Nashe 1958, II, 232). Beginning his description of the Anabaptists' spiritual words, Wilton condemns the 'violence of tedious investive Sermons without wit' (Nashe 1958, II, 234) and then proceeds with a four-page parody of just such a sermon. Wilton supposedly sets out to prove that sober and modest people are no more spiritual than anyone else, but his labyrinthine argument is itself burdened with rhetorical questions and spurious arguments loosely based upon biblical and classical authorities. Indeed, such confusion ensues that Wilton decides to 'use a more familiar example, since the heate of a great number outraged so excessively' (Nashe 1958, II, 235), although this argument proves even more convoluted than the one before. Despite the parody's elusiveness, however, the subsequent satire directed against the populist Anabaptists is observant and sharp. Leiden's followers are described generally as 'Verie devout Asses', as well as in individual detail as they prepare themselves for an unequal battle:

Another that had thrust a paire of drie olde bootes as a breast-plate before his belly of his dublet, because he would not be dangerously hurt. (Nashe 1958, II, 233)

Wilton might well ridicule the Anabaptists and parody their sermons, or plainly denounce them as 'villaines [and] . . . botchers', but 'compassion' for their suffering and final slaughter remains as he describes how the common men are 'too-too bloudily over-matcht', so that:

> At everie foot-step was the imbruement of yron in bloud, that one could hardly discern heads from bullets, or clotted haire from mangled flesh hung with goare. (Nashe 1958, II, 239–41)

The image presents an uncomfortable reality with its practical description of the soldiers' advancing footsteps and its detailed depiction of a head so smashed that 'haire', 'flesh' and 'goare' become indistinguishable. The conjunction of disturbing bodily images and ostentatious rhetorical features demands that, while satire and parody are recognised, they are similarly undercut with common compassion. The Anabaptists may be mocked, but they are also pitied.

After leaving Münster Jack Wilton meets Henry Howard, Earl of Surrey, and they travel together, first to Rotterdam where they meet Erasmus and More, and subsequently to Wittenberg where they encounter the magician Cornelius Agrippa. The two then journey south to Venice and Florence before Surrey returns home to England and Wilton continues to Rome. En route – both geographical and textual – Nashe, through the mocking narrative of Wilton, questions and debunks in turn the discourses of courtier, humanist and philosopher. Moreover, Nashe uses the distance of time and place from a contemporary English Elizabethan readership to veil, but not mute, these criticisms. Indeed, the attack is made more acute by the continued influence of Surrey and More's writings in England, and the fact that in Wittenberg Nashe represents the University of Cambridge. Satire and parody thus alternate in these sections until Nashe reaches Wilton's escapades in Rome, which he prefaces with an excerpt of travel literature. Paul Salzman points out that:

> An exuberant genre like the picaresque was naturally influenced by the expanding world pictured in travel narratives. Picaresque fiction

is episodic, and focuses on a wandering character, or group of characters, while travel narratives encapsulate the movement and energy
which may be created by the picaresque. (Salzman 1985, 218)

As a picaresque novel, therefore, *The Unfortunate Traveller* was suited
to the incorporation of travel writing, although rather than the more
common imaginary worlds, Jack Wilton offers a sightseeing tour of
sixteenth-century Rome, 'the Queen of the world & metropolitane
mistres of all other cities' (Nashe 1958, II, 279). The account covers a
number of sites, including 'the church of the seven *Sibyls*', 'a number
of other shrines and statues dedicated to the Emperours', 'the ruines
of *Pompies* theater, reputed one of the nine wonders of the world,
Gregory ye sixths tombe, [and] *Priscillas* grate' (Nashe 1958, II, 280–1).
In addition, Wilton notes with satisfaction that:

> I was at *Pontius Pilates* house and pist against it. The name of the
> place I remember not, but it is as one goes to Saint Paules Church not
> farre from the jemmes *Piazza*. (Nashe 1958, II, 280)

The text reads like a catalogue of famous buildings that have been
ticked off on a tourist's itinerary, with the added satisfaction of having
vented good Christian spleen – or in Wilton's case urine – on the
Roman who had ordered Christ's execution. The problem with such
an interpretation is, however, that the house had not belonged to
Pontius Pilate, even though it was called Casa di Pilato; rather it was
one of the stations of the cross in the local annual Passion play.
Wilton, therefore, chooses to deface a building associated only with
Pilate through its function as a backdrop in a play. Of course, Nashe
might have been unaware of the distinction, simply making an error
based upon the name of the house, but the problem with that interpretation is that none of the other sites he refers to are authentic
either. In the authoritative *The Works of Thomas Nashe*, edited by
Ronald B. McKerrow, the endnotes suggest a certain confusion; for
example, the 'church of the seven Sibels' is annotated with, 'I cannot
identify the church referred to' (Nashe 1958, IV, 283). Similarly,
'Sainte Paules Church' could refer to one of two in the city, but its
situation near 'jemmes *Piazza*' is described by McKerrow as 'I cannot
discover any place of that name, either in old or modern accounts of
Rome' (Nashe 1958, IV, 283). And so the list of errors continues.
Pompey's theatre did exist but it was not one of the nine wonders of

the world. Pope Gregory VI died in Germany and therefore was not buried in Rome. And of '*Priscillas* grate', McKerrow notes, 'I do not know what is referred to' (Nashe 1958, IV, 283). Apart from the statues of the emperors, nothing described by Wilton is genuine, and while Nashe might have made some errors, such wholesale inaccuracy could only have been deliberate.

Even if Nashe had not visited Rome himself, although McKerrow conjectures that he had, numerous details about Rome could have been found in travel writings, histories and cartographic books. John Speed's atlas, described at the beginning of this chapter, lists the most important sites as, 'The Church of Saint *Peter*, the Castle of Saint *Angelo*, the *Vaticane* Library, and the Pope's Pallace' (Speed 1627, 26). Thus, not only does Nashe create a travel account of errors and half-truths, but he also deliberately ignores the most well-known sights of the city. *The Unfortunate Traveller* incorporates the genre of travel writing in order to parody its superfluous list-like prose with a catalogue of fictional buildings and inaccurate histories. In addition, a satiric allusion to London through the reference to Saint Paul's in the English city, rather than the Roman Saint Peter's, is also likely given the condemnation of contemporary Elizabethan society in the text as a whole. But even this possible signification is undercut through the sequence of unrelated inaccuracies. The work is thus supremely self-referential, revealing the rhetorical array of style and form as fictional only in comparison with yet another literary allusion. When Wilton states, 'the name of the place I remember not' his tone seems direct and honest, but the phrase twists within the context of fake-travel writing, to warn that texts can never proffer a fixed name nor offer an accurate recollection.

The account of Wilton's exploits in Rome would have been expected by an Elizabethan readership, for the character reiterates tales of murder, theft, treachery and prostitution, all commonly believed to be prevalent in Italian cities. Indeed, Speed describes the Italians as 'most unnaturall in their lust' and much inclined to 'trechery and murther' (Speed 1627, 26). In addition to the narrative Nashe adds several parodies: of historical romance (Wilton's relationship with the courtesan, Juliana); of revenge tragedy (Cutwolfe's scaffold speech where he calls revenge 'the glorie of armes, & the highest performance of valure' [Nashe 1958, II, 326]); and finally of tragicomedy as Wilton escapes and marries Juliana. The concluding pages of *The Unfortunate Traveller* are, however, as shifting in meaning as any of the earlier passages. For example, after Cutwolfe has extolled the virtues of revenge he is subjected to a horrific execution that is described in gory detail by Wilton:

> Bravely did he [the executioner] drum on this *Cutwolfes* bones, not breaking them outright, but, like a sadler knocking in of tackes, jarring on them quaveringly with his hammer a great while together. No joint about him but with a hatchet he had for the nones he disjoynted halfe, and then with boyling lead souldered up the wounds from bleeding; his tongue he puld out, least he should blaspheme in his torment: venimous stinging wormes hee thrust into his eares, to keep his head ravingly occupied: with cankers scruzed to peeces hee rubd his mouth and his gums: no lim of his but was lingeringly splintered in shivers. (Nashe 1958, II, 327)

The description of Cutwolfe's torture needs little commentary and McKerrow notes only that 'quaveringly' means quickly and 'nones' means special purpose. The image of a man roaring with inarticulate pain, as he is slowly and methodically smashed to pieces is shocking, even to Nashe's contemporaries who would have been accustomed to the violence of the public scaffold. It comes as no surprise therefore that Wilton is so 'mortifiedly abjected and danted' that he decides to lead a 'straight life . . . thence forward' (Nashe 1958, II, 327). But what has interested critics is the sudden shift of tone from the disturbing torture of Cutwolfe to Jack Wilton's effortless repentance, spiritual salvation and social restoration. Roger Pooley comments that:

> Jack's repentance is as speedy as the end of any romance, and does not begin to match the indignation of his earlier satire. (Pooley 1992, 29)

Neil Rhodes and Paul Salzman similarly note the clash between the moral didacticism of Jack's penitence and the grotesque and 'sadistic pleasures of an execution' (Rhodes 1980, 37 and Salzman 1991, 93). Alternatively Margaret Ferguson reads the ending of the novel as the concluding moments of a spiritual allegory, as Wilton escapes damnation and hell (Ferguson 1981, 165–82). And, of course, each interpretation appears to be both an accurate understanding of the text's signification, as well as an inadequate response to the 'slipperiness' of this particular piece of English prose, because this is precisely the point of Nashe's shifting use of form and style. Moreover, if the description of Cutwolfe's torture is reread, it becomes possible to distinguish a linguistic warning of exactly such interpretative fragmentation.

To begin with, Wilton informs us that the executioner is good at cutting out hearts, 'as easily as a plum from the bottome of a porredge pot', at beheading 'as fast as a cooke cracks eggs', and racking, like a 'fidler turn[ing] his pin' (Nashe 1958, II, 327). These skills describe the common accomplishments of the Early Modern executioner and the first two at least would have been witnessed by Nashe's contemporaries. Moreover, as the comic allusions to cooking affirm, such bodily excesses lend themselves to the grimmer aspects of the grotesque. It is surprising therefore that none of these methods are chosen to torture Cutwolfe. Instead the executioner breaks the condemned man apart, leaving him 'on the wheele as in hell' (Nashe 1958, II, 327). The passage's vocabulary specifically depicts this disintegration in terms of 'breaking', 'jarring', 'disjoynted', 'scruzed to peeces', 'splintered' and 'shivers'. Furthermore, in almost Euphuistic fashion Nashe loads the phrases with irreconcilable opposites, so that wounds gape but are sealed, the tongue is pulled out as we are reminded of blasphemous language, and worms destroy the ears, not making Cutwolfe deaf, but so that his head will be 'ravingly occupied' with their gnawing sounds. Cutwolfe's torture therefore presents a compelling but distasteful voyeuristic episode alongside a fascinating play of rhetoric and grotesque humour. But more than that, it reveals through the form of torture chosen and its ensuing verbal description, that fragmentation and division undermine the possibility of a fixed signification, whether of character, narrative, allegory, genre or style. As Wilton aptly concludes: 'Unsearchable is the booke of our destinies' (Nashe 1958, II, 327). For as Jack Wilton travels across Europe in the episodic fashion of a picaro, so the reader traverses the text with its multiple genres and unstable meanings. And both are unfortunate travellers, for there is no happy homecoming for Wilton, who concludes his tale in France 'as my storie began', any more than there is a fitting moral conclusion to satisfy us. Ultimately, Nashe's traveller must remain 'unfortunate' because 'the booke of our destinies' is 'Unsearchable'. There is no map to direct us, simply a bleak awareness that signification is as 'lingeringly splintered in shivers' as Cutwolfe's bones.

Margaret Cavendish

In some ways Nashe's oeuvre proved surprisingly prescient, for during the seventeenth century the multiple genres, which the Elizabethan author had represented as fragments of a single text, proved too diverse to be constrained in a single form. Instead, history, religious writings, biography, travel literature, political diatribe, and philosophical argument, began to develop into quite distinct genres. The transition was inevitable as burgeoning knowledge and increased scholarly specialisation made the overarching prose works of the sixteenth century unmanageable and impractical. For example, the careful and independent historical researches of Edward Hyde, First Earl of Clarendon, provided authoritative accounts that left no room for the more fanciful narratives of Speed or Nashe. John Aubrey's biographical sketches, while often being more interested in salacious gossip than evidenced fact, remain overall witty and well-researched accounts of individuals, which are still valuable today. John Milton's studious prose treatises concentrate upon the religious questions of his time, and while they overlap with the concerns expressed in his poetry, his uses of the genres remain distinct. And the essays of Francis Bacon and Thomas Hobbes openly acknowledge the rational basis of their philosophical and scientific arguments, self-consciously evading the fictional excesses of their predecessors.[4] Stripped of a wide-ranging amalgamation of these multiple genres, seventeenth-century prose fiction may at first seem introverted and overly self-conscious. For example, Mary Wroth's *Urania* (1621) often appears like a stylised reconstruction of the Elizabethan age through which she retreats into her own Sidney inheritance. In parallel, Margaret Cavendish's *The Blazing World* (1666) has been criticised as 'tedious chaos' presenting the reader with a contradictory hodgepodge of ideas that supposedly reflect, as Virginia Woolf judged, the author's 'crack-brained and bird witted ideas' (Bowerbank 1984, 402 and Woolf 1925, 87). Finally, even John Bunyan's devotional allegory, *The Pilgrim's Progress* (1678), appears deeply immersed in its own particular, and often narrow, Christian understanding of the world. However, while the overt fictional setting for these works initially makes them look remote from material experience, seventeenth-century prose fiction was as deeply embedded in contemporary discourses as its sixteenth-century forebears. At the same time, however, the process of mapping the works themselves had changed. Although Speed had been able to extend the cartographic representation to a heavenly conclusion, which might be replicated, evaded or pushed beyond the limits of our knowledge, such certainties were no longer in place. By the mid-seventeenth century the world of prose fiction was no longer all-inclusive, nor could it claim to present a flawed reflection of God's glorious creation. But the challenge of the human journey through existence remained. In order to explore the way in which this transition developed I intend to look, in the next two sections of this chapter, at Cavendish's *The Blazing World* and Bunyan's *The Pilgrim's Progress*.[5]

English authors of the mid-seventeenth century were inevitably influenced by the Civil War (1642–6), the defeat of Charles I and the subsequent exile in France and the Netherlands of many of the nobility. For Margaret Cavendish (1623–73), therefore, any fictional accounts of travelling derived from personal and political necessity, rather than from a philosophical representation of a quest for knowledge, or of adventurous exploration. The young Margaret Lucas was a Maid of Honour to Charles I's consort, Henrietta Maria, and accompanied the Queen to Paris in 1644 when she was forced to flee the country. While in Paris, Margaret met William Cavendish, the Duke of Newcastle, who was similarly exiled, and despite the difference in their ages – she was in her twenties and he was a widower in his fifties – they appear to have fallen in love. The couple were married in 1645 and moved to Antwerp where they lived in relative poverty until the restoration of the monarchy in 1660, when they returned to England and retired to a secluded life at Welbeck Abbey on one of the Duke's estates. William Cavendish authored a number of poems and plays, and he certainly encouraged his daughters in their literary activities, so it is likely that it was he who first supported Margaret in her own attempts to write. She soon surpassed her husband's output, however, and in the space of 20 years (1653–73) produced a range of texts covering poetry, drama and prose, as well as focusing upon an array of topics from courtly wit to scientific research. However, a woman writing with serious intent and publishing her own works at considerable personal expense was uncommon, and Margaret Cavendish became an object of ridicule on the occasions she and her husband returned to London society. If Virginia Woolf's judgement of the Duchess as 'crack-brained and bird witted' seems harsh it was more than echoed by Cavendish's seventeenth-century contemporaries. Dorothy Osborne noted that, 'there are many soberer people in

Bedlam', and Samuel Pepys recorded in his diary that 'all the town-talk is nowadays of her extravagancies' (Lilley 1992, xiii, and Salzman 1985, 293). It is hardly surprising therefore that Paul Salzman prefaces his edition of her prose work with the hope that it 'will give readers the opportunity to judge for themselves whether *The Blazing World* is readable' (Salzman 1991, xviii). And of course Cavendish's work is negotiable, but only if you come prepared with the right map.

The prose fiction was first published as *The Description of a New World, Called the Blazing World* in 1666 and was appended to the quasi-scientific treatise, *Observations Upon Experimental Philosophy*. In the latter work Cavendish sets out to challenge Robert Hooke's *Micrographia* (1665), which promotes the use of a telescope, with an analysis of how the human eye is more suited to the study of moving objects. This explains why Cavendish's address to the reader of her fictional piece notes that 'I join a work of fancy to my serious philosophical contemplations', and is at pains to point out that, 'reason . . . [is] dividable, because material, cannot move in all parts alike' (Salzman 1991, 251). The conjunction of the two works also illuminates the narrative method employed in *The Blazing World* in which different 'parts' of the material whole are divided and their dissimilarities exaggerated. It is also important to realise that Margaret Cavendish used published works to expound her scientific theories because, as a woman, she was excluded from membership of the newly formed community of scientists and scholars, the Royal Society, which admitted only men. *The Blazing World* therefore offered her the opportunity to expunge her theories within a fictional realm that elevated women's position and created its own feminised version of the patriarchal discourses of her age.

The narrative outline of *The Blazing World* is, however, as tortuous as that of any Elizabethan romance. Therefore, in order to explicate the plot, in the subsequent analysis I intend to follow the text sequentially through its labyrinthine shifts.[6] To begin, an anonymous young lady is abducted by a foreign merchant while she 'gather[s] shells upon the shore' and carried away on his ship (Salzman 1991, 253). However, they are blown off course and travel to the North Pole where the merchant and his crew freeze to death and the ship itself is transported, via adjoining polar regions, to a new world. The Emperor of this 'Blazing World' falls in love with the lady and she is elevated to the position of Empress, from which she proceeds to make several improvements to her adopted land. In particular, she decides to found 'several societies' that are to be devoted to various scientific disciplines such as experimental philosophy, astronomy, natural philosophy and chemistry. In other words, the Empress installs her own Royal Society and she enrols as members the country's animal-like inhabitants, so that, 'the fox men [are] her politicians' and 'the spider and lice-men her mathematicians' (Salzman 1991, 261). Having thus mocked the patriarchal domination of the parallel institutions in seventeenth-century England, Cavendish goes on to castigate in particular the 'bird-men' astronomers for their use of the telescope. Indeed, in an open allusion to Cavendish's own disagreement with Hooke, the Empress judges that:

> I do plainly perceive that your glasses are false informers and instead of discovering truth, delude your senses. Wherefore I command you to break them, and let the bird-men trust only to their natural eyes. (Salzman 1991, 268)

To a certain extent, therefore, the Empress's views equate with the authorial voice, espousing Cavendish's own theories about vision, and exacting a literary revenge upon the male exclusivity of the Royal Society. At other times, however, the Empress's identity becomes separated from authorial concerns, so that her total domination seems overbearing and ill substantiated. For example, when she founds her own religion, the idea seems an experimental fancy rather than a critique of the contemporary Early Modern church. The Empress:

> considered by herself the manner of their religion, and finding it very defective, was troubled that so wise and knowing a people should have no more knowledge of the divine truth. Wherefore she consulted with her own thoughts whether it were possible to convert them all to her own religion, and to that end she resolved to build churches and make also up a congregation of women, whereof she intended to be the head herself, and to instruct them in the several points of her religion. (Salzman 1991, 288–9)

The precise nature of the 'divine truth' and the Empress's 'own religion' is unclear, and the tenets she 'instructs them in' are omitted from the passage. At first this new religion seems to lack both a narrative and a thematic foundation, but the Empress's determination to include women within the church hierarchy, with herself as head, does coincide with the overall feminisation of the Blazing World.

The Empress then decides to question the spirits of the Blazing World about the world she had originally come from and through their answers she gains sufficient information to write down her own cabbala, or system of philosophical knowledge. Realising that she will require a scribe for the project, she asks the spirits to provide her with one from, 'the souls of one of the most famous modern writers . . . Hobbes, H. More', but they reply that these men are:

> So self-conceited that they would scorn to be scribes to a woman. 'But,' said they, 'there's a lady, the Duchess of Newcastle, which although she is not one of the most learned, eloquent, witty and ingenious, yet she is a plain and rational writer.' (Salzman 1991, 306)

In a convoluted narrative stratagem, Cavendish the author is able to gesture towards the 'learned, eloquent . . . ' writing of contemporary male philosophers such as Thomas Hobbes and Henry More, while at the same time attacking their disparagement of female authorship, in other words her own work. Simultaneously, she introduces into that very same disparaged text, *The Blazing World*, a fictional second self, 'the Duchess of Newcastle' who will enable another Cavendish persona, the Empress, to write her own philosophical treatise, which will of course express the same hypotheses. To add to the confusion, the Empress determines that by choosing a female scribe the Emperor will have no cause for jealousy, to which the spirit replies:

> In truth . . . husbands have reason to be jealous of Platonic lovers, for they are very dangerous, as being not only very intimate and close, but subtle and insinuating. (Salzman 1991, 306)

Platonic female relationships are thus foregrounded in the text as 'dangerous' and the spirit's warning of a possible erotic attachment remains as the Empress salutes her scribe with 'a spiritual kiss' (Salzman 1991, 307). However, the possible eroticism of the female relationships further complicates the assemblage of authorial selves (Cavendish, the Empress, and the 'Duchess of Newcastle'), who must now represent the similitude of a single authorial identity, as well as the difference of sexually attracted individuals. Thus, *The Blazing World* depicts an identity, which may be whole, or divided within that

unity, but more importantly its focus also encompasses the movement endemic upon the relationships between those individual and
material parts. To a certain extent, therefore, Cavendish puts her own
identity under the telescope, enabling us to perceive the broad span
of her philosophical theories (her cabbala), while at the same time
allowing us to distinguish the various parts of her understanding
through the separate voices of the Empress and the Duchess. Yet the
static restraints of the scientific instrument, whether telescope or
rational treatise, are dismissed as incapable of reproducing the
complex relationships between those parts. The work argues that in
order to understand how that which is similar (the two women, and
the two worlds) may also be different (their erotic attraction to one
another, and the polar magnetism of the spheres), scientific discourse
has to be abandoned. As the fictional Duchess advises the Empress:

> Make a poetical or Romancical Cabala, wherein you may use
> metaphors, allegories, similitudes, etc. and interpret them as you
> please. (Salzman 1991, 308)

Moreover, the self-referential context of the Duchess's suggestion to
make a 'Romancical' text is underlined when the spirits point out that
it is easy to create 'a world within yourself' (Salzman 1991, 311). And
just as the Duchess and Empress begin to create their own worlds
through the subsequent passages, so they become a part of
Cavendish's own 'world within herself', the literary construction of
The Blazing World.

It is at this microscopic moment, however, when authors and texts
almost shrink to a single author in a single world, that Cavendish
alters the focus, drawing us back to a much wider perspective. In the
next section of the book the Duchess takes the Empress to visit her
own world, that is seventeenth-century England. The following
account of the 'majesty and affability' of the King and Queen and the
lamentable ruin and destruction of the Civil War (Salzman 1991,
317–18) are predictable, but brief. The two spirits then waft towards:

> Nottinghamshire (for that was the place the Duke [of Newcastle] did
> reside), passing through the forest of Sherwood, the Empress's soul
> was very much delighted with it, as being a dry, plain and woody
> place, very pleasant to travel in both in Winter and Summer, for it is
> neither much dirty nor dusty at no time. At last they arrived at

Wellbeck, a house where the Duke dwelled, surrounded all with a wood so close and full that the Empress took great pleasure and delight therein. (Salzburg 1991, 318)

The depiction of the forest is accurate and detailed, describing the roads that lead through the trees as 'pleasant to travel'. Yet these material journeys, either by coach or on horseback, are envisaged via the fanciful notion of the two ladies' souls, which are made 'of the purest and finest sort of air' (Salzman 1991, 318). At this stage a comprehensible narrative perspective is just possible if the reader imagines the souls looking down with telescopic vision upon the serviceable roads, but when the two women enter the body of the Duke of Cavendish even this quasi-rationale is relinquished. As the Empress and the Duchess watch William Cavendish riding and fencing, the latter expresses a commonsense concern about her husband's digestion and immediately enters his body. This astonishing merging of soul and flesh is further complicated when the Empress joins her friend, so that 'the Duke had three souls in one body' (Salzman, 1991, 319). William Cavendish, however, is so 'wise, honest, witty, complaisant and noble' that the Empress and he soon become 'enamoured of each other' (Salzman 1991, 319), making the Duchess, his wife, a little jealous. But she pacifies herself on realising that since they are all souls and Platonic lovers 'no adultery could be committed' (Salzman 1991, 319). Since the spirits have already warned of the dangers of Platonic love, however, the possibility of a dangerous erotic attachment remains, allowing Cavendish to explore a different perspective within this section of the text. For if the aerial view magnified the roads through Sherwood forest as if using a telescope, then the interior vision of the three souls within a single body suggests a metaphysical microscope. Thus, Cavendish through the action of the narrative, and the Empress and Duchess via the movement of their 'souls', inhabit a single material form with the uniting force of friendship set against the heterogeneity of erotic attraction. Moreover, it is only by accepting the possibilities of a Romancical world that such fluidity becomes realisable. The rational perspectives of telescope and microscope are invoked, therefore, precisely so that they may be undercut by the inner world of Cavendish's own creation.

The Blazing World, however, perpetuates a flux between 'Romancical' and rational discourses. Thus, before the Empress is called back to her own world she presides over a fantastical trial in which a personified Fortune is accused of being unjust to the Duke of Newcastle. While the setting itself is emblematic, with Fortune perched upon a 'golden globe' (Salzman 1991, 321), the Duchess's pleas suggest a heartfelt reality as she describes how her husband has been 'cast into banishment', had his estate ruined, and lost most of his friends (Slazman 1991, 322). An anguished petition that could have been made by any of the royalist exiles, and not just the Duke of Newcastle. A similar duality recurs in the short 'Second Part' of *The Blazing World* in which the Empress returns to her own world in a curious amalgam of fantasy – she carries a 'spear of one entire diamond' – and a practical knowledge of seventeenth-century diplomacy – she destroys the enemy's 'naval power, by which they were soon forced again to submit' (Salzman 1991, 335 and 337). And the whole episode ends with a description of the Empress's triumphant return to the Blazing World with her friend the Duchess, and the poetical and musical delights they enjoyed there. The final conclusion of the prose work is, however, an 'Epilogue to the Reader' in which Cavendish immediately categorises her text:

> By this poetical description you may perceive that my ambition is not only to be Empress but authoress of a whole world. (Salzman 1991, 347)

Thus, Cavendish initially presents herself as both 'authoress' of the textual *The Blazing World* and as 'Empress' of the fictional Blazing World in a formal and conventional parallel. But the text switches back upon itself yet again, for at the close of the Epilogue, Cavendish reworks the comparison:

> For concerning the philosophical world, I am Empress of it myself, and as for the Blazing World, it having an Empress already who rules it with great wisdom and conduct, which Empress is my dear Platonic friend. (Salzman 1991, 348)

It becomes clear that the Duchess of Newcastle is both the author of the 'philosophical world', that is the scientific *Observations Upon Experimental Philosophy*, and therefore the real Margaret Cavendish, while at the same time being the Empress's 'Platonic friend', in other words, a fictional character. The Epilogue makes perfect sense as an address to the reader by the actual author, who refers to the earlier scientific treatise, acknowledging the employment of a formal literary technique of parallel worlds. The Epilogue also makes sense as a continuum of the literary prose in which Cavendish retains the guise of a fictional second self. The rational view of the text may thus expand outwards to an overview of authorial presence and contemporary relevance caught within the telescopic frame of the text. Or, it may remain limited within a microscopic vision of the inner workings of the literary imagination. But of course, Margaret Cavendish did not accept such static and conventional identities, for *The Blazing World* sets out to prove through narrative and form that vision must encompass motion. Even the title suggests activity, for the blazon or emblem is not a noun to be decoded, but an adjective, resonating with the action of fire as much as with a formal understanding of meaning. Moreover, that this shifting world should be fraught with contradictory impulses, with material descriptions and extravagant fancies, with ideals of friendship and erotic disturbance, must be expected given the upheavals in English society in the mid-seventeenth century. *The Blazing World* has been described as a dystopia, and sometimes a feminised Utopia in which Cavendish represented her ideal world, and perhaps during some of the still emblematic moments of the text it is. But even as a single meaning blazons forth, it is divided and the perspective shifted, so that where unity once seemed possible only fragmentation actually appears. Early Modern prose fiction, despite an apparent removal from the rational and scientific genres it had once encompassed, continued to negotiate the material discourses of its time. And if the literary map appeared fragmented, it emerged as such precisely because the world could no longer be understood as a single entity, being in its post-Civil War frame as fractured and fragmented as the Blazing World itself.

John Bunyan

At first glance Margaret Cavendish's *The Blazing World* and John Bunyan's *The Pilgrim's Progress* seem to be utterly disparate works. The first was a dystopic fancy written by an eccentric noblewoman, who endeavoured to uphold the ideals of a discredited aristocracy while at the same time pioneering a radical new world in which a feminised scientific discourse was lauded. The latter was a deeply spiritual work written by a puritan preacher, which rehearsed a Christian message in terms simple enough for the common reader. Indeed, the image of the Duchess and Empress travelling in 'the purest and finest sort of air' offers a stark contrast to the vision of Christian 'solitary by himself' as 'he fell from running to going, and from going to clambering upon his hands and knees' (Bunyan 1966, 152 and 173). Yet within the context of Early Modern prose both Cavendish and Bunyan represent the way in which earlier discourses were changing to encompass both social and generic transformations.

Margaret Cavendish retreated into 'a world within [her]self' partly in an attempt to comprehend the social and philosophical fragmentation she had witnessed during the Civil War and its aftermath. And so John Bunyan created a spiritual world that represented his puritan beliefs in the face of religious persecution and the attempt to prevent a fracturing of the Protestant faith in England. In both cases personal enclosure – Cavendish retreated to her closet to write, while Bunyan composed *The Pilgrim's Progress* in prison – was coupled with an acute sense of historical, political and religious transformation in order to produce a literary commentary that was simultaneously private and public. Moreover, both works call upon the image of worlds, of maps and of journeys, and if Cavendish displays a broken vista, then Bunyan, even if he recognises Speed's spiritual rationale that 'Heaven was too long a reach for man to recover at one step', charts a path so beset with difficulties that heaven often seems unreachable. There is, however, an important distinction in the creation of such maps, for the Blazing World is a fantasy in which relationships shift and turn, whereas Christian's world is an allegory that openly invites a reading of hidden, but realisable, signification.

The Pilgrim's Progress has two parts. The first traces Christian's journey from the City of Destruction to the Holy City, in other words from a material existence to spiritual salvation (published in 1678). The second relates the history of how Christian's family follows him on their own pilgrimage (published in 1684). Spiritual allegory and symbolism dominate both books. For example, in this second part Bunyan presents a debate between Mathew, Christian's son, and the allegorical figure of Prudence:

> Mathew. *What should we learn by seeing the Flame of our Fire go*
> *upwards? and by seeing the Beams, and sweet Influences*
> *of the Sun strike downwards?*

Prudence. By the going up of the Fire, we are taught to ascend
to Heaven, by fervent and hot desires. And by the Sun
his sending his Heat, Beams, and sweet Influences
downwards; we are taught, that the Saviour of the
World, tho' high, reaches down with his Grace and
Love to us below. (Bunyan 1966, 329)

In this representation of fire and sun, which is described pictorially by
Mathew and decoded in spiritual terms by Prudence, Bunyan drew
upon an emblem in Francis Quarles's *Hieroglyphikes of the Life of
Man* (1639). Emblems linked a simplicity of image with weighty (often
religious) matters, offering the reader pleasure at their skill in decod-
ing, while simultaneously learning a moral message. By specifically
drawing upon an emblem book Bunyan highlighted this process in his
own text. The whole of the work may be read as a series of successive
images which Christian and the reader must decode, thereby uncovering true Christian signification. But before tracing the pattern of
these images, it is important to understand why Bunyan chose to use
static emblematic forms within the linear narrative structure of a spiritual journey.

John Bunyan (1628–88) was the son of a tinsmith who was educated
at the village school. He joined the Parliamentary forces during the
Civil War, but in 1648 had a religious crisis, which he describes in his
autobiography, *Grace Abounding to the Chief of Sinners* (1666).
Bunyan subsequently became a puritan preacher in a nonconformist
group in Bedford. In 1660 with the restoration of the monarchy puri-
tans were persecuted and Bunyan was banned from preaching and
imprisoned, off and on, for 12 years. It is likely that he wrote *The
Pilgrim's Progress* while in the small prison on Bedford Bridge. The
first part begins with an authorial second self:

As I walk'd through the wilderness of this world, I lighted on a certain
place, where was a Denn; And I laid me down in that place to sleep:
And as I slept I dreamed a Dream. (Bunyan 1966, 146)

In the 1679 edition Bunyan added a note explaining that 'Denn'
meant 'The Gaol'. Thus, while the literary device of the dream was
common to spiritual writing, Bunyan simultaneously located his work
in a personal and immediate context that commingles emblem
('Denn') with factual description ('Gaol'). After his release from prison

Bunyan became the pastor of a separist church in Bedford, although he continued to be a travelling preacher. Bunyan's evangelical dedi-cation is evidenced through his own life and in the considerable extent of his canon – he wrote 60 books of religious controversy and doctrine, as well as poetry, autobiography, and prose fiction. And his beliefs are apparent in the form and style of *The Pilgrim's Progress*, for while concerned with the weighty matters of religion and morality, he was determined to portray them with simplicity in order to make his works accessible to all. For Bunyan, therefore, the use of emblems and allegory was not so much a question of literary influence, although he had certainly read prose romances, but of offering uneducated readers and listeners a way to understand the complex questions of faith. Thus, as Cavendish challenged the patriarchal hegemony of the Royal Society with a radical feminisation of scientific discourse, so Bunyan confronted the established church with a text that undercut hierarchical elitism with its accessibility to common working-class people. Yet, as with *The Blazing World, The Pilgrim's Progress* has not always proved easy to understand.

The spiritual allegory of Christian's journey seems to have been readily accessible in the century following its first publication. Boswell comments that:

> [Samuel] Johnson praised John Bunyan highly. 'His *Pilgrim's Progress* has great merit, both for invention, imagination, and the conduct of the story; and it has had the best evidence of its merit, the general and continued approbation of mankind. Few books, I believe, have had a more extensive sale.' (Sharrock 1976, 51)

Such simplicity of reaction has not categorised subsequent criticism of the work, particularly in the latter part of the twentieth century. The debate may be roughly described as between those who continue to perceive Christian's journey as a linear form that accords with Early Modern Christian thought, and those who stress the way in which the allegorical structure of the text often impedes progress, suggesting doubts rather than certainty. For example, John R. Knott, Jr, argues that:

> In the terms of Bunyan's narrative one can gain entrance to heaven only by learning to understand the visible world of ordinary experi-ence in the metaphoric terms established by the Word: as an alien,

and ultimately insubstantial country through which God's people must journey until they attain the ultimate satisfaction of communion with God. To accept this mode of thought is to see in the Exodus a pattern explaining and assuring the deliverance of the faithful of all times. (Sharrock 1976, 240)

Knott perceives *The Pilgrim's Progress* as addressing Christian concerns about the human journey through existence, that have remained almost unchanged from Bunyan's time, and certainly Knott's argument accords with the way in which location is understood by John Speed in his atlas. However, other critics, in particular Stanley Fish, have pointed to the way in which the allegory does not equate with a universal truth, working rather in an 'antiprogressive' manner (Salzman 1976, 1985, 245). Unsurprisingly, this has led to an understanding of the text that comments upon precisely those heterogeneous features that characterise Early Modern prose, as Paul Salzman summarises:

> We do *The Pilgrim's Progress* an injustice by reading it only as didactic, or only as fable; only as a progress, or only as a stasis; only as realistic, or only as allegorical. All these oppositions combine to form Bunyan's masterpiece. (Salzman 1985, 249)

The term 'slippery' might seem at odds with the tone of Bunyan's work, yet the combination of genre, style and metaphor places *The Pilgrim's Progress* within the compass of Maslen's definition of Early Modern prose fiction as being 'the most slippery of literary mediums' (Maslen 1977, 11). In order to understand how these different discourses function simultaneously within the text I intend to trace the allegory from the City of Destruction to the Holy City.

In the first part of the work, Christian begins his journey as a pilgrim, leaving the earthly world (the City of Destruction and Worldly Wiseman) in order to attain spiritual salvation. He is aided by the Evangelist and stops briefly at the House of the Interpreter where he learns how to proceed. A number of emblematic sites follow, such as the Hill of Difficulty, House Beautiful, the Valley of Humiliation, the Valley of the Shadow of Death, and Vanity Fair. Christian is aided by two figures, Faithful and Hopeful, and although he also encounters Giant Despair and Doubting Castle, he finally attains the Delectable Mountains, the Enchanted Ground, and Beulah. And part one concludes as Christian and Hopeful cross the river and are taken into the Heavenly City. *Christian's* pilgrimage is clearly presented as an allegory of the life of a *Christian* man (my italics), and the places he visits and the people he meets are symbols of ideas important to spiritual enlightenment and psychological conversion. But this analysis of the narrative fails to take account the fact that the whole journey has been framed by the device of a dream. Indeed, the first part of the work has a final episode in which the dreamer perceives Ignorance approach the gates of heaven, where entry is refused, and the two angels:

> Took him up, and carried him through the air to the door that I saw in the side of the Hill, and put him in there. Then I saw that there was a way to Hell, even from the Gates of Heaven, as well as from the City of *Destruction*. So I awoke, and behold it was a Dream. (Bunyan 1966, 271)

While the overall narrative moves the pilgrim forwards to a state of grace, the images recall the dream-state of the text, reminding us that, even if Christian has attained heaven, the dreamer in his 'Denn' remains perilously close to hell. The same image – the Holy City – thus functions on two levels simultaneously: representing salvation, grace, and completion for Christian within the dream, while also denoting unconsummated desire, continued danger and a return to reality for the Dreamer. Even as the first part of *The Pilgrim's Progress* concludes the text remains caught between the forward movement of the allegory and the retrograde action of a persistent spiritual quest. Appropriately, therefore, the second part of *The Pilgrim's Progress* covers exactly the same ground as the first part, only this time describing the journey of Christian's wife, Christiana, his children, and Mercy, Christiana's friend. They too begin at the City of Destruction, visit the House of the Interpreter, climb the Hill of Difficulty, and rest in the town of Vanity before finally encountering the Delectable Mountains, the Enchanted Ground, and Beulah. And lastly Christiana enters the 'Gate with all the Ceremonies of Joy that her husband *Christian* had done before her' (Bunyan 1966, 395). Yet there are distinct differences between the two narratives.

The most noticeable distinction between the two parts of *The Pilgrim's Progress* is the contrast between an individual quest (part one) and a social understanding of faith expressed through the context of family and friends (part two). Consequently, Bunyan alters the perspective in order to include concerns relevant to this group of pilgrims, so that marriage, medicine and children become the focus of Christiana's mission. And the whole tone of the second pilgrimage is more forgiving, suggesting support and comfort rather than the hardships encountered by Christian. This is particularly evident in the parallel description of the town of Vanity. In part one the Dreamer describes Vanity Fair as '*lighter then* Vanity' and depicts the activities of that place as 'Thefts, Murders, Adulteries, [and] False-swearers' (Bunyan 1966, 210–11). The townsfolk unjustly arrest Christian and Faithful and 'beat them pitifully, and hanged Irons upon them, and led them in Chaines up and down the *fair*' (Bunyan 1966, 213). Moreover, it is in Vanity that Faithful is martyred:

> First they Scourged him, then they Buffetted him, then they Lanced his flesh with Knives; after that they Stoned him with Stones, then prickt him with their Swords, and last of all they burned him to Ashes at the Stake. (Bunyan 1966, 218)

After witnessing the cruel execution of his companion, Christian is thrown into prison from whence he escapes and resumes his pilgrimage. Not surprisingly, when Christiana and her children approach Vanity they are unsure whether or not to pass through the town, but they are reassured that the house of Mr Mnason will offer security, and while there they are informed by Mr Contrite that:

> They [the people of Vanity] are much more moderate now then formerly. You know how *Christian* and *Faithful* were used at our Town; but of late, I say, they have been far more moderate. I think the Blood of *Faithful* lieth with load upon them till now; for since they burned him, they have been ashamed to burn any more: In *those* days we were afraid to walk the Streets, but *now* we can shew our Heads . . . [and] Religion is counted Honourable. (Bunyan 1966, 367)

The differences are immediately apparent. Vanity is now seen to house a character from the Bible, since Mr Mnason is the old disciple in Acts (xxi:16). Moreover, the people are 'far more moderate'; they feel guilty about executing Faithful; they have stopped persecuting those who follow a nonconformist faith; and 'Religion is counted Honourable'. Christiana and her companions are safely lodged within the town and two of the children wed local inhabitants while staying in Mnason's house. 'Contrition' and forgiveness are thus united to a sense of renewal through the motif of marriage with its promise of new life. Vanity Fair cannot therefore be contained within a single emblematic understanding, for it is both damned and redeemed, both a site of danger and safety, and while being a spiritual test for Christian, offers support and succour for Christiana and the children. But Vanity Fair evades static representation in yet another manner, because it is also the actual fair that was held every year on Stourbridge common to the north of Cambridge.

In order to appreciate the full implications of the contemporary allusion to Stourbridge, it is essential to retrace the road from the City of Destruction to the Holy City once more. However, the sites identified in the subsequent analysis present only a small number of geographical allusions often identified by Bunyan scholars. At the same time, a general contemporary allusiveness is apparent, although it is important to note that specific referents are not made here. *The Pilgrim's Progress* begins with the Dreamer in his 'Denn', which we know from Bunyan's own annotation refers to the gaol in Bedford, possibly the County Gaol, or the Town Gaol which stood on Bedford Bridge. Given that Christian begins his journey at the same point the dream begins, a tentative correspondence between Bedford and the City of Destruction might be made, yet the overall sense of material excess and the neglect of faith is kept sufficiently open. Still, as Christian proceeds more specific places become identifiable and here a map is useful in understanding the way in which Bunyan incorporated regional sites into his spiritual allegory (see Figure 5). On leaving the City of Destruction Christian falls into 'a very *Miry Slow* that was in the midst of the Plain . . . The name of the Slow was *Dispond*' (Bunyan 1966, 150). The Slough of Despond is commonly identified with a boggy road that used to connect Bedford with Hockliffe and was known to be virtually impassable in the winter (Harper 1928, 72–3). Subsequently Christian visits the House of the Interpreter, in whom Bunyan represents William Gifford, the first pastor of the dissenting church in Bedford who lived in the rectory of St John Baptist's Church. This church is discernible on a map produced by none other than the cartographer John Speed in 1610, and it is easy to see the bridge over the Ouse with its town gaol as well as the church lying to the south of the river (Brown 1969, 97). The Hill of Difficulty, which Christian climbs on his way to House Beautiful, alludes to

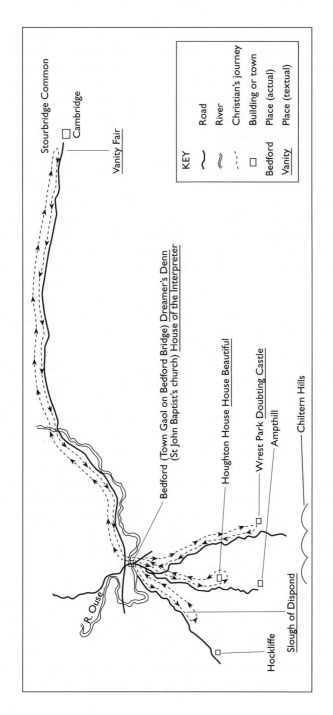

Figure 5 Map of *The Pilgrim's Progress*

Ampthill, which must be traversed on the road from Bedford to Houghton House, the most probable original for House Beautiful. Consequently, the Delectable Mountains Christian sees when he looks south from the roof of the house may be linked with the Chiltern Hills that are visible from Ampthill. Christian's pilgrimage continues until he reaches Vanity Fair that has already been noted as representing the large annual fair at Stourbridge. Critics generally note the mixture of stalls and amusements that prevailed at this month-long fair, but it is important to remember that Vanity is also where Faithful is martyred. Faithful is, of course, more than a moral symbol for all Christians, although he has come to mean that in the centuries after the publication of *The Pilgrim's Progress*. Rather, Faithful's martyrdom must also be seen in the context of the persecution of the nonconformists after the Act of Uniformity in 1662, which aimed to ensure conformity with the Episcopacy and the consequential suppression of nonconformist ministers and congregations. Nonconformist preachers were attacked and imprisoned; Bunyan himself remained in gaol for 12 years. Still, the violence of Faithful's death is not drawn from contemporary accounts, invoking rather a wider discourse of Early Modern martyrdom.

Returning to the pilgrimage, the narrative moves to Doubting Castle in which Christian and Hopeful are imprisoned and beaten by Giant Despair, before they escape using the key of Promise. The moral allegory is evident, and the material basis for the castle has been identified with Cainhoe Castle near Wrest Park to the east of Ampthill, although it might also refer to Bedford nonconformist church, two of whose members committed suicide. But the idea of despair and the image of the castle and giant are also very close to Book I of Spenser's *The Faerie Queene* in which the giant Orgoglio imprisons the despairing Red Cross Knight in the dungeons of his castle (Spenser 1977, 95–107). Thus, while geographical situations remain plausible within the context of the text, as the pilgrimage progresses Bunyan's locational discourse gradually gives way to that of Christian textual allegory. Indeed, the final site of the pilgrimage, the Holy City, is described in biblical terms – the source being the Geneva Bible – thereby returning Christian firmly to the linear narrative. Simultaneously, however, the Dreamer reminds us of the City of Destruction before awaking in his cell, presumably in Bedford gaol.

At no point does the text insist upon close geographical allegory, yet a sense of place permeates the work. Moreover, Bunyan seems to locate the text in the immediate environment of his home Bedford, just as he uses simple images and common language to make the work accessible to the lower-class readers of his day. The books are therefore grounded in the realities of everyday seventeenth-century life, linguistically, imagaically and in terms of location, and as such succeed in imbuing Christian's pilgrimage with a muscular realism that could easily have been lost if Bunyan had relied upon moral allegory and textual allusions alone. Nevertheless, if the map of Early Modern Bedfordshire as depicted in *The Pilgrim's Progress* is set alongside the moral chart with its linear structure, either progressive or antiprogressive, a disparity becomes visible. If we place the Dreamer (Bunyan's authorial second self) in the prison at Bedford itself, the imagined journey takes us along the boggy road south to Hockliffe, back to Bedford and the rectory at St John's church, south again to Ampthill and Houghton House, east to Stourbridge fair near Cambridge, and then back south to Cainhoe Castle. The geographical allusions of the text make no sense in terms of a linear pilgrimage, but they do offer a good sense of the area around Bedford as if viewing the map from above. The roads, valleys, towns and country houses that Bunyan knew well are presented on a horizontal plain, which may be viewed in its entirety by the dreamer, even as it is travelled through by Christian. It is perfectly possible from this perspective to understand how the Dreamer is able to perceive the City of Destruction alongside the Holy City at the end of part one, and this overview is sustained in part two.

At the beginning of the second section the Dreamer admits that he has been:

> kept back from my wonted Travels into those Parts . . . but having had some concerns that way of late, I went down again thitherward. Now, having taken up my Lodgings in a Wood about a mile off the Place, as I slept I dreamed again. (Bunyan 1966, 281)

The framework constructs a dream vision again, but the setting becomes more important since Christian's home ('Parts') are identified as a material presence both within and outside the dream itself. But the second book introduces yet another framing device, this time in the form of the guide, Mr Sagacity. Dream visions conventionally introduced another character to guide or inform the dreamer, and here Mr Sagacity takes over the role of narrator, recounting the story of Christiana's pilgrimage to the Dreamer. Moreover, the Dreamer and his guide walk together 'as Travellers usually do', while the Dreamer asks Mr Sagacity about the City of Destruction *'that lieth on the left hand of our way'*, and what happened to Christian, *'a man sometime ago in this Town'* (Bunyan 1966, 281–2). Subsequently, the Dreamer is left alone, 'to Dream out my Dream' (Bunyan 1966, 293), once Christiana has left the confines of the town, again allowing an overview of the journey. Yet, for the first 12 pages of the book the Dreamer has entered physically into Christian's realm, bridging the divide between the material external and allegorical internal worlds. Moreover, this sense of unity is reintroduced at the end of the whole work as the Dreamer concludes:

> As for *Christian's* Children . . . I did not stay where I was, till they were gone over. Also since I came away I heard one say, that they were yet alive, and so would be for the Increase of the Church in that Place where they were for a time.
>
> Shall it be my Lot to go that way again, I may give those that desire it, an Account of what I am here silent about; mean time I bid my Reader *Adieu*. (Bunyan 1966, 399)

What is perhaps most startling about this conclusion is that the Dreamer does not wake up, for the vision device has been abandoned for a more direct address to the 'Reader'. Thus, if the Dreamer is not commensurate with Bunyan at this point, he certainly assumes an external, self-aware, authorial voice. But at precisely the same moment, the Dreamer moves more deeply into the text, claiming that he 'came away' from 'that Place', although he might 'go that way again', presenting himself as another character within the moral allegory. The Dreamer thus conflates the exterior place of the author into the interior world of the text. The linear narrative of moral allegory must therefore be displaced onto the flat cartographic surface of the Bedford area, just as the diachronic line of the allegory must be bisected by the synchronic plane of material relevance. In other words, the text is simultaneously spiritual and worldly, just as Bunyan explains at the very beginning in 'The Author's Apology for his Book', where he elucidates his 'stile':

> *Dark Clouds bring Waters, when the bright bring none;*
> *Yea, dark, or bright, if they their silver drops*

Cause to descend, the Earth, by yielding Crops,
Gives praise to both, and carpeth not at either,
But treasures up the Fruit they yield together:
(Bunyan 1966, 140)

In expected emblematic style Bunyan represents the heavenly spirit as rain dropping down upon the earth with its crops, which represent the growth of the faithful in this world. The intersection of the two is, moreover, presented as a meeting of the vertical lines from heaven and the horizontal plane of the earth, at which point of uniting 'together' the spiritual 'Fruit' may be yielded. For Bunyan, therefore, different discourses were an essential part of his 'stile', since it was only by working 'together' that the spiritual informed the worldly, so that the worldly might return to the spiritual. In *The Pilgrim's Progress* the synchronic map of Bedford must act upon and with the spiritual map of heaven, so that without St John's church in Bedford to shelter the young John Bunyan, there could have been no House Beautiful for Christian to rest in on his way to the Holy City. If John Speed's atlas demonstrated to his readers that 'Heaven was too long a reach for man to recover at one step', Bunyan argues through a uniting of allegorical and geographical descriptions that the steps taken on earth were commensurate with those taken on the road to heaven.

Conclusion

This chapter began with a description of the first world atlas to be compiled by an Englishman, John Speed's *A Prospect of the Most Famous Parts of the World*. Originally published in 1627 the plates were augmented and reproduced for nearly a century before the diverse and all-encompassing nature of the work finally made it appear outdated. Today, *A Prospect* is regarded merely as a curiosity and hardly as a serious work of cartography. The expectations of accurate mapping had already changed by the close of the seventeenth century, making Early Modern compilations redundant. Correspondingly, the prose works of the sixteenth and seventeenth centuries with their all-embracing structure and multifaceted contents were replaced with the more formal patterns of the eighteenth-century novel. Indeed, it is important to realise that Early Modern prose fiction was not a forerunner for the novel but a distinct form in its own right. Reading the works discussed in this chapter has been a process in which thematic overview is as important as linear narrative, in which the end may be known even as the journey begins, and in which fragmentation is endemic to textual meaning. Like reading a map, Early Modern prose demands a philosophical, moral or spiritual diachronic line to be recognised alongside the material synchronic plane of time and place. The worldly discourses of the court, European travel, the Civil War, the role of women, and the persecution of nonconformists, must be read in the context of moral certainties, spiritual doubts, Utopias, and religious pilgrimages. It is precisely this comprehensive yet shifting vision that unites Early Modern prose as a genre. Sixteenth-century works were certainly more at ease with the all-encompassing and fractured nature of the genre still perceiving, even in its unattainability, the link between the spiritual and material worlds. Yet, even in the seventeenth century multiple discourses were engaged in recognition of social and religious fragmentation, although the fictional worlds represented withdrew to the closeted and private spheres of authorial invention. While Early Modern fiction evolved in itself, however, it does not offer a transition to a similar, developing aspect of the same genre, as was the case with poetry and drama. Like Speed's *A Prospect*, the prose fiction of the sixteenth and seventeenth centuries became quickly outmoded and has mostly been discounted as a quaint precursor to the novel. Yet, read within their own context and with a recognition of their own literary techniques, the works of Lyly, Nashe, Cavendish and Bunyan present an intriguing insight into the dominant concerns of Early Modern Europe. They offer not so much a transition in genre, but a way in which readers of today may identify and trace the textual maps of sixteenth- and seventeenth-century England, rereading the process of transition – of being in transit – through the cartographic axes of signification.

Notes

1. John Speed's dates are c.1552–1629.
2. A full account of the compilations and individual translations may be found in J. J. Jusserand's comprehensive *The English Novel in the Time of Shakespeare* (1890), and Paul Salzman's excellent *English Prose Fiction 1558–1700* (1985).

3. See Neil Rhodes, *Elizabethan Grotesque*, London: Routledge, 1980, for a thorough and compelling account of the grotesque fictions of the sixteenth century.

4. A single chapter cannot do justice to the fulsome array of seventeenth-century prose writing. In my brief references to Clarendon, Aubrey, Milton, Bacon and Hobbes I am indebted to the comprehensive analyses of Roger Pooley in his *English Prose of the Seventeenth Century, 1590–1700* (1992).

5. Although Wroth's *Urania* is an important work of seventeenth-century prose fiction, I do not intend to analyse it in detail in this chapter, since Wroth's canon is dealt with in detail in chapter 2. For an analysis of the work and its Sidneian influences see, Salzman 1991, 138–44.

6. While editions of *The Blazing World* are now readily available for study, a systematic analysis of the whole with students in mind has not been undertaken. While the section in this chapter cannot be comprehensive, by tracing the narrative of Cavendish's prose alongside thematic concerns I hope to make the text more accessible.

Conclusion

> 'I thought best not to suppress what I had written'
> (John Milton)

The quotation at the beginning of this Conclusion is taken from John Milton's *The readie and easie way to establish a free Commonwealth* which was published in a second edition in April 1660. Milton's desire to sustain the Commonwealth and prevent the restoration of the monarchy was openly declared. And in the first paragraph he defends his honesty:

> I thought best not to suppress what I had written, hoping that it may now be of much more use and concernment to be freely published, in the midst of our Elections to a free Parliament . . . I never read of any State, scarce of any tyrant grown so incurable, as to refuse counsel from any in a time of public deliberation; much less to be offended. (Milton 1980, 408)

But two months later Parliament was 'offended'. On 16 June 1660 the Commons ordered the immediate arrest of John Milton and requested that the newly restored King Charles II issue a proclamation calling for two of Milton's books, *A Defence* and *Eikonoklastes*, to be 'publickly burnt by the hand of the Common hangman' (Wolfe 1971, 100). Milton, however, had foreseen the possibility of personal danger and had gone into hiding when Charles arrived in England in May. Indeed, he can hardly have hoped to escape punishment since he had, as Christopher Hill points out:

> publicly advocated the accountability of kings immediately after Charles I's trial, and had defended regicide in the face of all Europe . . . Short of actually signing the death warrant Milton could hardly have done more [and] . . . when so many of the King's former enemies lay low, Milton proclaimed his republicanism from the house-tops. (Hill 1977, 207)

It seemed likely that Milton's name would be added to the list of those who were exempted from the Act of Indemnity, which would have meant public execution. Indeed, Milton's name was proposed for exemption, although he seems to have been defended by a number of friends in the Commons, and his name was left off the list, thereby evading the hanging, drawing and quartering suffered by some of his Parliamentary associates. Nevertheless, he was arrested, imprisoned, and risked hanging again in November 1660, before being finally pardoned and released before Christmas of that year. When reading Milton's epic poems, *Paradise Lost* and *Paradise Regained*, it is often easy to forget that their author barely escaped execution and might never have lived to compose these hugely influential works. And it is important to remember that Milton turned to poetry partly as a way to evade the harsh censure laws that had been passed with the Licensing Act of 1662, since polemical prose treaties would once again have put his life in danger. Indeed, he would never again be able to claim that he 'thought best not to suppress what I had written'.

The persecution of the puritan poet and the destruction of his books in 1660 might at first appear to be remote from the carefully preserved manuscript verses of a lauded nobleman, yet in some ways the former proved to be a valid precursor of the latter. In Chapter 1 of this book the analysis of Philip Sidney's sonnets, together with Elizabeth I's verse, revealed the way in which art was being relocated within the powerful arena of materiality. In addition, the conjunction of discourses was seen to destabilise political authority and question the fixed signification of dominant cultural ideologies, and if Sidney evaded imprisonment he certainly suffered exile. Moreover, the fragmentation evinced by the works of Philip Sidney and John Milton was replicated throughout the various genres of Early Modern literary production.

In Chapter 2 the sonnet form was explored in relation to the momentous and rapid changes that were occurring throughout the Early Modern world. During the sixteenth and seventeenth centuries fundamental transformations occurred in the presentation of text (manuscript/press), in the understanding of the universe and the world itself, through divisions of faith, in challenges to the heirarchies of class and gender, and in the triumph of individualism. And these crucial changes were traced through a tradition of Petrarchanism and in the poetry of Thomas Wyatt, Henry Howard, Earl of Surrey, Edmund Spenser, George Herbert, John Milton, John Donne, Walter

Ralegh, Michael Drayton, Rachel Speght, Mary Wroth, William Drummond and Anne Bradstreet. Yet even as the poems discussed evince commonality of discourse and form, at the same time Early Modern poetry proclaimed startling shifts of individual and political identities.

Of the genres considered in this book, Early Modern drama is the most succinct and contained in terms of its chronological production, while at the same time being the most radically mutating of all the forms discussed here. The late-sixteenth century saw an eruption of dramatic activity that was produced and facilitated by the expansion of new and exciting theatres. From the huge open-air auditoriums, such as the Rose and the Globe, through the marginal performance spaces as at the Inns of Court, to the small covered theatres, like Blackfriars, productions transformed the texts' meanings on a nightly basis. The enormous popularity of the theatres and the considerable repertory of plays employed by dramatists and their companies, cannot be unquestioned. In Chapter 3 the impact of these works was examined in relation both to performance space and to four plays: Shakespeare's *The Taming of the Shrew* and *Twelfth Night*, Christopher Marlowe's *Tamburlaine*, and Thomas Middleton's *The Changeling*. While, therefore, the period of dramatic productivity considered here is necessarily narrow, at the same time it incorporated an acute and powerful transition of ideological and generic formulations.

The Early Modern prose discussed in Chapter 4 has often proved the most inaccessible genre for present-day readers. Its wide-ranging and amorphous style diverges from the more familiar linear structure of the novel, and its rag-bag of literary techniques and figures confuses our critical appreciation of form. In order to understand Early Modern prose it is necessary to develop a different strategy of reading, one that encompasses a static overview definition alongside continual and materially located movement, rather as in reading a map. In the process of exploring this different technique the chapter focused on John Lyly's *Euphues*, Thomas Nashe's *The Unfortunate Traveller*, Margaret Cavendish's *The Blazing World* and John Bunyan's *The Pilgrim's Progress*. In each instance, a movement between the diachronic and synchronic axes of the text proved essential to an understanding of the way in which social and cultural fragmentation could be both represented and undermined within the same discourse.

The diachronic and synchronic axes necessary to the understanding of Early Modern prose return us to the Introduction to this volume and Matthew Arnold's description of the alternating 'central current(s]' and 'cross stream[s]' of the Renaissance. Throughout this book the dominant ideologies or 'central current[s]' of Early Modern Britain have been explored, uncovering numerous 'cross stream[s]' through the poetry, drama and prose of the period. Nor have the dominant discourses been sustained, rather suggesting a wave-like pattern in which political authority mutates and cultural certainties shift against one another in an ongoing process of transformation. Yet such a developmental representation almost lulls our understanding of Early Modern literature into reflecting upon a gradually progressing continuity. It is therefore essential that we recall the 'common hangman['s]' fires of 1660 when the burning of Milton's books revealed, through its need to silence the poet, the potent political force of the texts themselves. And so too we must recall: those who could 'gape' at a Queen; Walter Ralegh's recklessly self-fashioning scaffold speech; Anne Bradstreet's invocation of a new world intimacy; Marlowe's indomitable Tamburlaine played by Edward Alleyn strutting across the public stage; Feste's sly misrule challenge to class boundaries; Nashe's inexorable vision of a dark and fractured world; and finally the persecution of another puritan, John Bunyan, in his 'denne' on Bedford bridge. Therefore, although it is important to note the continuing transformations of literary discourses through the sixteenth and seventeenth centuries it is also essential to recall those individual literary transitions that shattered and revolutionised the dominant discourses of their day.

Chronology 1476–1685

Dates	Literary events	Historical events	Cultural and religious events
			Francesco Petrarch 1304–1374
1476			Establishment of Caxton's printing press in England Thomas More 1477–1535
1483		Edward V	
1483		Richard III	
1485		Henry VII	
1492			Columbus in the Americas
1500		England annexes Ireland	
1503			Thomas Wyatt 1503–42
1509		Accession of Henry VIII	
1513	Machiavelli, *The Prince*		
1516	Thomas More's *Utopia* Ariosto, *Orlando Furioso* (first edition)		
1517			Luther's 95 'Theses'; start of the Reformation Henry Howard, Earl of Surrey c.1517–47

Dates	Literary events	Historical events	Cultural and religious events
1520		Meeting between Henry VIII and Francis I on the Field of Cloth of Gold	
1524			Pierre de Ronsard 1524–85
1528	Castiglione, *The Courtier*		
1533	Thomas Wyatt, *Satires* written	Henry VIII divorces Catherine and secretly marries Anne Boleyn Birth of Princess Elizabeth	Elizabeth I 1533–1603
1534		Act of Supremacy	England's final break with Rome More's refusal to take the Oath of Supremacy The Pope's powers taken over in England by Henry VIII
1535		Union of England and Wales	Henry VIII named Supreme Head of Church Trial and execution of Thomas More
1542		Henry assumes title of King of Ireland	
1545			The Council of Trent: beginning of the Counter-reformation
1547		Henry VIII dies; Edward VI succeeds to throne	Surrey executed for treason
1549	Thomas Wyatt, *Certaine Psalmes* published		
1552			Walter Ralegh c.1552 –1618

Dates	Literary events	Historical events	Cultural and religious events
1552			Edmund Spenser 1552–99
1553		Death of Edward VI Lady Jane Grey proclaimed Queen, later executed Mary I proclaimed Queen	
1554	Elizabeth I, 'Woodstock' poems	Roman Catholicism re-established in England by Parliament	Princess Elizabeth imprisoned in Woodstock John Lyly 1554–1606
1557	Earl of Surrey's translation of Virgil's *Aeneid* (Books II and IV) Publication of *Tottel's Miscellany*, including poems by Wyatt and Surrey		
1558		Mary I dies, Elizabeth I succeeds to throne	
1559		Act of Supremacy and Act of Uniformity; Protestant faith re-established	
1560			Geneva Bible translated
1561	Thomas Hoby translates *The Courtier*		Mary Sidney 1561–1621
1562			Philip Sidney 1562–86
1563	John Foxe's *Acts and Monuments* (Foxe's Book of Martyrs)		The plague in London kills many thousands Michael Drayton 1563–1631 Robert Sidney 1563–1626
1564			Christopher Marlowe 1564–93

Dates	Literary events	Historical events	Cultural and religious events
1564			William Shakespeare 1564–1616
1565	Arthur Golding translates Ovid's *Metamorphoses* (Books I–IV)		
1566	William Painter, *The Palace of Pleasure*		James VI of Scotland and I of England 1566–1625
1567	Red Lion playhouse built Geoffrey Fenton, *Tragicall Discourses*	Abdication of Mary Queen of Scots	Thomas Nashe 1567– c.1601
1569			John Davies 1569–1626
1570	Roger Ascham, *The Scholemaster*		
1572		St Bartholomew's Day massacre of the Protestants in Paris	John Donne c.1572– 1631
1574			Joseph Hall 1574–1656
1576	The Theatre playhouse built George Pettie, *Petite Pallace* David Rowland translates *Lazarillo*		
1577	Blackfriars and Curtain playhouses built		Francis Drake begins his circumnavigation of the globe
1578	John Lyly, *Euphues: the Anatomy of Wit* Philip Sidney, *The Lady of May*	James VI takes over the government of Scotland	
1579	Thomas North translates Plutarch's *Lives* Edmund Spenser, *Shepherd's Calendar*		

Dates	Literary events	Historical events	Cultural and religious events
1580	John Lyly, *Euphues and his England* Philip Sidney, completes manuscript of *Apologie for Poetrie* and *The Old Arcadia*		Performance of plays on Sunday forbidden Francis Drake returns to England William Herbert, 1580–1630 Thomas Middleton 1580–1627
1581	Joseph Hall, *Ten Books of Homer's Iliads* Philip Sidney begins work on *Astrophil and Stella*		Harsh laws against Roman Catholics passed
1583		Discovery of the Catholic Somerville Plot to assassinate Elizabeth I Discovery of the Throgmorton Plot for the Spanish invasion of England	
1584	Philip Sidney begins to revise the *Arcadia*		
1585			William Drummond 1585–1649 Walter Ralegh establishes a colony in Roanoke, Virginia
1586	Christopher Marlowe's *Doctor Faustus* (acted; published in 1604)	The Star Chamber court condemns Mary Queen of Scots to death	
1587	Abraham Fraunce translates Tasso's *Amyntas*	Execution of Mary Queen of Scots	Philip Sidney's funeral Mary Wroth c. 1587–c.1651
1588		Defeat of the Spanish Armada	
1589	George Puttenham, *The Art of English Poesie*		

Dates	Literary events	Historical events	Cultural and religious events
1590	Christopher Marlowe, *Tamburlaine* Parts I and II published Philip Sidney's *The New Arcadia* published Edmund Spenser, *The Faerie Queene*, I–III		
1591	John Harington translates Ariosto's *Orlando Furioso* William Shakespeare, *Henry VI* Parts I and II acted; *The Two Gentleman of Verona* acted Philip Sidney posthumous publication of *Astrophil and Stella* Edmund Spenser, *Complaints*		
1592	William Shakespeare, *Henry VI* Part I acted John Lyly, *Galatea* Christopher Marlowe, *Edward II* acted Rose theatre opens		Establishment of the Presbyterian Church in Scotland
1593	Mary Sidney begins translating the Psalms William Shakespeare, *Comedy of Errors,* and *Richard III* acted; *Venus and Adonis*		George Herbert 1593–1633
1594	William Shakespeare, *Titus Andonicus* acted; *Lucrece* Michael Drayton, *Ideas Mirrour* John Davies, *Gullinge Sonnets* Thomas Nashe, *The Unfortunate Traveller*		

Dates	Literary events	Historical events	Cultural and religious events
1595	Mary Sidney, *The Tragedy of Antonie* William Shakespeare, *Love's Labour's Lost, Midsummer Night's Dream, Richard II* and *Romeo and Juliet* acted Edmund Spenser, *Amoretti, Epithalamion, Colin Clout's Come Home Again*		Death of Francis Drake
1596	Ben Jonson, *Everyman in his Humour* acted William Shakespeare, *Merchant of Venice*, and *King John* acted Edmund Spenser, *The Faerie Queene* IV–VI and *Four Hymnes*		
1597	Francis Bacon, *Essays* Joseph Hall, *Virgidemiarum* I–III		Rachel Speght 1597-c.1630
1598	George Chapman translates Homer's *Iliad* I–II and VII–XI; Chapman also completes Christopher Marlowe's poem, *Hero and Leander* William Shakespeare, *Henry IV* Parts I and II acted Batholomew Young translates Montemayor's *Diana*		
1599	Ben Jonson, *Every Man Out of his Humour* acted		

Dates	Literary events	Historical events	Cultural and religious events
1599	William Shakespeare, *Julius Caesar, Henry V* and *Much Ado About Nothing* acted Joseph Hall, *Virgidemiarum* completed		
1600	Mary Sidney translates Petrarch's *Triumph of Death* and competes the Psalms William Shakespeare, *The Merry Wives of Windsor, As You Like It* acted		
1601	William Shakespeare, *Hamlet* and *Twelfth Night* acted	Essex Rebellion and execution of the Earl of Essex	
1602	John Marston, *Antonio's Revenge* acted William Shakespeare, *Troilus and Cressida* acted	Reconquest of Ireland commences	Bodleian Library founded
1603	Ben Jonson, *Sejanus* acted William Shakespeare, *All's Well That Ends Well* acted; *Hamlet* first Quarto Michael Drayton, *The Barons Warres*	Queen Elizabeth I dies and is succeeded by James VI of Scotland as James I	
1604	Christopher Marlowe, *Doctor Faustus* earliest surviving edition William Shakespeare, *Othello* acted; *Hamlet* second quarto	James I proclaimed King of 'Great Britain, France and Ireland'	
1605	Michael Drayton, *Poems* Ben Jonson, *Volpone* acted	The Gunpowder Plot	

Dates	Literary events	Historical events	Cultural and religious events
1606	William Shakespeare, *King Lear* and *Macbeth* (c.1605–6) acted		Suppression of Roman Catholics by English Parliament
1607	William Shakespeare, *Antony and Cleopatra* written		English colony founded in Virginia
1608	Thomas Heywood, *Rape of Lucrece* William Shakespeare, *Coriolanus* and *Timon of Athens* written, and *King Lear* two quartos published		John Milton 1608–74
1609	Ben Jonson, *Epicoene or the Silent Woman* acted William Shakespeare, *Pericles* acted; *Troilus and Cressida* two quartos published; *Sonnets* published		
1610	George Chapman continues *Iliad* Ben Jonson, *The Alchemist* acted William Shakespeare, *Cymbeline* and *The Winter's Tale* possibly written John Donne, *Pseudo-Martyr*		Thomas Gates publishes an account of the Bermuda shipwreck
1611	Complete translation of *Iliad* by George Chapman published Thomas Dekker and Thomas Middleton, *The Roaring Girl* published William Shakespeare, *Macbeth* first recorded performance; *The Tempest* probably written	The colonisation of Ulster	

Dates	Literary events	Historical events	Cultural and religious events
1612	Michael Drayton, *Poly-Olbion* I John Webster, *The White Devil* published		Anne Bradstreet 1612–72
1613	William Shakespeare, *Henry VIII* acted		Globe theatre burns down Poisoning of Sir Thomas Overbury
1614	George Chapman translates the *Odyssey* I–XII Ben Jonson, *Bartholomew Fair* acted Walter Ralegh, *The History of the World*		
1615	George Chapman, translates the *Odyssey* XIII–XXIV		
1616	Ben Jonson, *The Devil is an Ass* acted, and *Underwoods* John Webster, *The Duchess of Malfi* acted William Drummond, *Poems* II		
1617	Rachel Speght, *A Mouzell for Melastomus* Joseph Swetnam, *Arraignment of Women*		
1618	Ben Jonson visits William Drummond, who records their conversations (manuscript)	Start of the Thirty Years War	Execution of Walter Ralegh

Dates	Literary events	Historical events	Cultural and religious events
1620	Mary Wroth, *Love's Victory* (possibly completed)		Freedom of worship granted to Roman Catholics in England in terms of marriage treaty between England and Spain Pilgrim Fathers depart from Plymouth, England, on the *Mayflower*
1621	Robert Burton, *Anatomy of Melancholy* Mary Wroth, *Pamphila to Amphilanthus* published; *Urania* I published; *Urania* II completed in manuscript Rachel Speght, *Mortality's Memorandum*		
1622	Michael Drayton, *Poly-Olbion* Part II Thomas Middleton and William Rowley, *The Changeling* acted		
1623	William Shakespeare, *Comedies Histories and Tragedies* (the First Folio) published John Webster, *The Duchess of Malfi* acted		Margaret Cavendish 1623–73
1624	Thomas Middleton, *A Game at Chess* acted		
1625		Accession of Charles I Marriage of Charles I and Henrietta Maria	
1627			First atlas compiled by an Englishman, John Speed

Dates	Literary events	Historical events	Cultural and religious events
1628			John Bunyan 1628–88
1631	Ben Jonson, *The Devil is an Ass* and *The Staple of News* published		
1633	John Donne, *Poems* (published posthumously) John Ford, *'Tis Pity She's a Whore* published George Herbert, *The Temple* published		
1634	John Milton, *Comus* acted		
1637	John Milton, *Lycidas*		
1641	John Milton, *Of Reformation*		
1642	Thomas Browne, *Religio Medici* John Milton, *Apology for Smectymnuus*	Civil War begins Battle of Edgehill	
1644	John Milton, *Areopagitica* Jane and Elizabeth Cavendish, *The Concealed Fancies* and *Poems* completed in manuscript		
1645			Prohibition of the Prayer Book by Parliament Execution of Archbishop Laud
1648	Robert Herrick, *Hesperides*		
1649		Execution of Charles I Abolition of the monarchy Declaration of the Commonwealth	

Dates	Literary events	Historical events	Cultural and religious events
1650	Anne Bradstreet, *The Tenth Muse*		
1651	John Cleveland, *Poems* William Davenant, *Leviathan*	Battle of Worcester	
1653	Izzak Walton, *The Compleat Angler* Margaret Cavendish, *Poems and Fancies*	Long Parliament expelled by Cromwell Establishment of Protectorate: Oliver Cromwell made Lord High Protector	
1654		Union of England, Scotland and Ireland	
1656	Margaret Cavendish, *A True Relation*		
1658		Death of Oliver Cromwell; succeeded by Richard Cromwell, his son, as Lord Protector	
1659	Samuel Pepys begins diaries	Long Parliament restored	John Bunyan imprisoned
1660	John Milton, *The Readie and Easy Way*	Restoration of the monarchy; Charles II succeeds to the throne	
1662		Act of Uniformity Licensing Act Royal Society founded	
1664		Conventicle Act outlaws meetings of nonconformists	
1665	John Bunyan, *The Holy City*		Great Plague
1666	Margaret Cavendish, *The Blazing World* John Bunyan, *Grace Abounding*		The Great Fire of London

Dates	Literary events	Historical events	Cultural and religious events
1667	John Milton, *Paradise Lost*		
1671	John Milton, *Paradise Regained* and *Samson Agonistes*		
1674			Rebuilding of Theatre Royal, Drury Lane
1678	John Bunyan, *The Pilgrim's Progress*, Part I Anne Bradstreet, *Several Poems* (published posthumously)		
1681	Andrew Marvell, *Miscellaneous Poems* (published posthumously)		
1684	John Bunyan, *The Pilgrim's Progress* Part II		
1685		Death of Charles II, succeeded by James II	

Annotated Bibliography

Bakhtin, Mikhail *Rabelais and His World*, translated by Helene Iswolsky. Bloomington, IN: Indiana University Press, 1984.

An important and influential theoretical treatment of Early Modern European literature. The name 'Bakhtin' has been adopted to describe the work of a group of Russian critics who looked at the way in which social and cultural inversions were negotiated by literary texts. The concepts of carnivalesque and the grotesque have been particularly useful for understanding the radical texts of the Early Modern period.

Dollimore, Jonathan and Alan Sinfield (eds) *Political Shakespeare. New Essays in Cultural Materialism.* Manchester: Manchester University Press, 1985.

The *Foreword* to this volume provided British critics of the Early Modern period with a politicised version of the American New Historicism. The book combines this new form of theory with historical enquiry and close readings of Shakespeare's plays. It is useful both in terms of describing a new methodology as well as giving examples of how that theory works in practice.

Dutton, Richard and Richard Wilson (eds) *New Historicism and Renaissance Drama.* London: Longman, 1992.

An informed and scholarly collection of essays which serve to introduce readers to a range of Early Modern drama. The work also provides key analyses and examples of new historicist and cultural materialist methodologies.

Foucault, Michel *Madness and Civilization. A History of Insanity and the Practice of Social Ornament.* Chicago: Chicago University Press, 1961; repr. 1980.

Foucault's theoretical texts have provided important insights into literatures in English generally. *Madness and Civilisation* has, however, been applied more in the field of Early Modern studies. The book traces the change in approach to madness, from the Medieval idea of demonic possession through to a sense of insanity as illness. The processes described prove invaluable for readings of Early Modern literature that focus upon the role of the insane, the outsider and any marginal figure in society.

Greenblatt, Stephen *Renaissance Self-Fashioning. From More to Shakespeare.* Chicago: Chicago University Press, 1980.

Greenblatt's polemical work altered the face of criticism on the Early Modern period. It heralded a period of chronological, cultural and political contextualisation of texts that became identified as New Historicism. Even now it is essential reading for an understanding of sixteenth- and seventeenth-century English literature.

Gurr, Andrew *The Shakespearean Stage 1574–1642.* Cambridge: Cambridge University Press, 1992.

In its third edition, Andrew Gurr's book describes the acting companies, theatres, stagings and audiences of Early Modern London. An invaluable account for understanding the way in which dramatic space interacted with text.

Hawkes, Terence *That Shakespeherian Rag.* London: Metheun, 1986.

This collection of essays on Shakespeare's plays contextualises the works in terms of the way in which different societies process dramatic meaning and cultural production. Hawkes excavates the way in which Shakespeare has been used as an ideological tool, but he points out in successive readings of the text, that no authoritative or final reading of the plays can exist.

Howard, Jean E. *The Stage and Social Struggle in Early Modern England.* London: Routledge, 1994.

A path-breaking work that explores the role of theatre in the social transitions of the period. Jean Howard incorporates contemporary materialist and feminist criticism to investigate the way in which gender, class, and sexual conflict were represented on stage.

Maslen, R. W. *Elizabethan Fictions.* Oxford: Clarendon Press, 1997.

A thorough and scholarly treatment of an often neglected topic. Maslen analyses the prose fictions of the sixteenth century chronologically, providing detailed textual analyses alongside a sense of the developing genre. Complex material is dealt with sensitively, doing full justice to the fascinating works of the period.

Pooley, Roger *English Prose of the Seventeenth Century, 1590–1700*. London: Longman, 1992.

One of the Longman Literature in English Series, Pooley's work is a comprehensive and invaluable account of a huge and diverse field of literature. This study offers a clear and careful categorisation of a neglected area, allowing us to appreciate the excitement and variety of seventeenth-century prose.

Waller, Gary *English Poetry of the Sixteenth Century*. London: Longman, 1993.

This work also belongs to the Longman Literature in English Series and so offers a comprehensive coverage of sixteenth-century poetry, from the lyric, through Ralegh, Donne, Sidney and Spenser. However, it also offers radical rereadings of canonical texts in terms of gender, race and class, in which Waller uncovers the acute ideological struggles of the age.

Wilcox, Helen *Women and Literature in Britain, 1500–1700*. Cambridge: Cambridge University Press, 1996.

This was the first introduction to the writings and social contexts of early Modern English women. The essays included deal with an array of genres, concepts, and histories. It also has an invaluable chronology that details important events from a female perspective.

Bibliography

Note: editions may appear in both Primary and Secondary bibliographies if texts and editorial material are referred to.

Primary texts

Ascham, Roger. *The Scholemaster*, ed. John E. B. Mayor. London: Bell and Daldy, 1863.

Bradstreet, Anne. *The Works of Anne Bradstreet*, ed. Jeannine Hensley. Cambridge, MA: Harvard University Press, 1967.

Brooks-Davies, Douglas (ed.). *Silver Poets of the Sixteenth Century*. London: J. M. Dent, 1992.

Bunyan, John. *Grace Abounding to the Chief of Sinners and The Pilgrim's Progress*, ed. Roger Sharrock. London: Oxford University Press, 1966.

Castiglione, B. *The Book of the Courtier*, trans. C. S. Singleton. New York: Doubleday, 1959.

Cavendish, Margaret. *The Blazing World* in *An Anthology of Seventeenth-Century Fiction*, ed. Paul Salzman. Oxford: Oxford University Press, 1991.

Cerasano, S. P. and Marion Wynne-Davies (eds). *Renaissance Drama by Women: Texts and Documents*. London: Routledge, 1996.

Davies, Sir John. *The Poems of Sir John Davies*, ed. Robert Krueger. Oxford: Clarendon Press, 1975.

Donne, John. *John Donne*, ed. John Carey. Oxford: Oxford University Press, 1990.

——. *John Donne. The Complete English Poems*, ed. A. J. Smith. Harmondsworth, England: Penguin Books, 1971.

Drayton, Michael. *The Works of Michael Drayton*, ed. J. William Hebel. Oxford: Basil Blackwell, 1941.

Drummond, William. *The Poetical Works of William Drummond of Hawthornden*, ed. L. E. Kastner. Manchester: Manchester University Press, 1913, Vol. I.

Evans, M. (ed.). *Elizabethan Sonnets*. London: J. M. Dent, 1977.

Fenton, Geoffrey. *Certaine Tragicall Discourses* (1567). Published as *Bandello: Tragicall Tales*, ed. H. Harris. London: Routledge, 1924.

Greville, F. *Sir Fulke Greville's Life of Sir Philip Sidney (1652)*. Oxford: Clarendon Press, 1907.

Hall, Joseph. *The Collected Poems of Joseph Hall*, ed. A. Davenport. Liverpool: Liverpool University Press, 1949.

Herbert, George. *The English Poems of George Herbert*, ed. C. A. Patrides. London: J. M. Dent, 1974.

Herbert, William, Earl of Pembroke. *Poems Written by the Right Honourable William Earl of Pembroke, Lord Steward of his Majesties Household. Whereof Many of which are answered by way of Repartee, by Sr Benjamin Ruddier, Knight.* London: Mathew Inman, 1660.

James I. *New Poems by James I of England*, ed. Allan F. Westcott. New York: Columbia University Press, 1911.

Jonson, Ben. *The Alchemist*, ed. Peter Bennett. London: Methuen, 1987.

Lant, T. *Sequitur celebritas & pompa funeris quemadmodum a Clarencio Armorum et Insignium rege institut est.* London: 1587 (STC 15224).

Latham, Agnes (ed.). *The Poems of Sir Walter Ralegh*. London: Routledge and Kegan Paul, 1951.

Lyly, J. *The Complete Works of John Lyly*, ed. R.Warwick Bond. Oxford: The Clarendon Press, 1902.

——. *Euphues: The Anatomy of Wit (1578)* in *An Anthology of Elizabethan Prose Fiction*, ed. P. Salzman. Oxford: Oxford University Press, 1987.

Marlowe, Christopher. *The Complete Plays*, ed. Mark Thornton Burnett. London: Everyman, 1999.

Middleton, Thomas. *Thomas Middleton. Three Plays*, ed. Kenneth Muir. London: Everyman, 1975.

Milton, John. *Complete Shorter Poems*, ed. John Carey. London: Longman, 1971.

——. *Complete Prose Works of John Milton*, Vol. VII, ed. Robert W. Ayers. New Haven, CT: Yale University Press, 1980.

Nashe, Thomas. *The Works of Thomas Nashe*, ed. Ronald B. McKerrow. Oxford: Basil Blackwell, 1958.

Painter, William. *The Palace of Pleasure* (1566), ed. J. Jacobs. London: David Nutt, 1890.

Pettie, George. *A Petite Palace of Pettie his Pleasure* (1576), ed. H. Hartman. London: Oxford University Press, 1938.

Petrarch, Francesco. *Rime Sparse*. Milano: Murisia, 1979.

Ralegh, Sir Walter. *The Works of Sir Walter Ralegh*. Oxford: Oxford University Press, 1829.

Ronsard, Pierre de. *Les Amours*, ed. Henri Weber and Catherine Weber. Paris: Editions Garnier, 1963.

Salzman, Paul (ed.). *An Anthology of Seventeenth-Century Prose Fiction.* Oxford: Oxford University Press, 1991.

Shakespeare, William. *As You Like It,* ed. Agnes Latham. London: Routledge, rpt. 1987.

——. *Richard II,* ed. Peter Ure. London: Routledge, 1966.

——. *The Taming of the Shrew,* ed. Ann Thompson. Cambridge: Cambridge University Press, 1984.

——. *Twelfth Night,* ed. J. M. Lothian and T. W. Craik. London: Routledge, 1975.

Sidney, Mary. *The Collected Works of Mary Sidney Herbert Countess of Pembroke,* ed. Margaret P. Hannay, Noel J. Kinnamon and Michael G. Brennan. Oxford: Clarendon Press, 1998.

——. *The Psalms of Philip Sidney and the Countess of Pembroke,* ed. J. C. A. Rathmell. New York: New York University Press, 1963.

Sidney, Philip. *An Apology for Poetry or The Defence of Poesy,* ed. G. Shepherd. Manchester: Manchester University Press, 1973.

——. *The Poems of Philip Sidney,* ed. William A. Ringler Jr. Oxford: Clarendon Press, 1962.

——. *Selected Poems,* ed. Katherine Duncan-Jones. Oxford: Clarendon Press, 1973.

——. *The Countess of Pembroke's Arcadia (The Old Arcadia),* ed. Katherine Duncan-Jones. Oxford: Oxford University Press, 1985.

——. *The Countess of Pembroke's Arcadia,* ed. M. Evans (The New Arcadia). Harmondsworth: Penguin Books, 1977.

Sidney, Robert. *The Poems of Robert Sidney,* ed. P. J. Croft. Oxford: Clarendon Press, 1984.

Speed, John. *A Prospect of the Most Famous Parts of the World.* London: John Dawson and George Humble, 1627.

Speght, Rachel. *Mortalities Memorandum.* London: Edward Griffin, 1621.

——. *A Mouzell fo Melatomus.* London: Nicholas Okes, 1617.

Spenser, E. *The Works of Edmund Spenser,* ed. Edwin Greenlaw, Charles Grosvenor Osgood, Frederick Morgan Padelford and Ray Heffner. Baltimore, MD: The Johns Hopkins Press, 1943.

——. *Poetical Works,* ed. J. C. Smith and E. de Selincourt. Oxford: Oxford University Press, 1970.

——. *The Faerie Queene,* ed. A. C. Hamilton. London: Longman, 1977.

Strachey, William. 'A True Reportory of the Wreck', in *The English Literatures of America,* ed. M. Jehlen and M. Warner. London: Routledge, 1997.

Surrey, Henry Howard Earl of. *Poems,* ed. Emrys Jones. Oxford: Clarendon Press, 1964.

Wyatt, Sir Thomas. *Collected Poems of Sir Thomas Wyatt*, ed. Kenneth Muir and Patricia Thomson. Liverpool: Liverpool University Press, 1969.

——. *Sir Thomas Wyatt. Collected Poems*, ed. Joost Daalder. Oxford: Oxford University Press, 1975.

Wynne-Davies, M. (ed.). *Women Poets of the Renaissance*. London: J. M. Dent, 1998.

Secondary texts

Arnold, Matthew. *Culture and Anarchy*, ed. R. H. Super. Ann Arbor, MI: University of Michigan Press, 1965.

Bakhtin, Mikhail. *Rabelais and His World*, trans. Helene Iswolsky. Bloomington, IN: Indiana University Press, 1984.

Bos, S., Lamge-Meyer, M. and Six, J. 'Sidney's Funeral Portrayed' in Jan Van Dorsten, Dominic Baker-Smith, and Arthur Kinney (eds), *Sir Philip Sidney. 1586 and the Creation of a Legend*. Leiden: Leiden University Press, 1986.

Bowerbank, Sylvia. 'The Spider's Delight: Margaret Cavendish and the Female Imagination', *English Literary Renaissance*, 14 (1984), 392–408.

Brooks-Davies, Douglas (ed.). *Silver Poets of the Sixteenth Century*. London: J. M. Dent, 1992.

Brown, John. *John Bunyan*, revised by Frank Mott Harrison. Hamden, CT: Archon Books, 1969.

Cerasano, S.P. 'Edward Alleyn: 1566–1626', in Aileen Reid and Robert Maniura (eds), *Edward Alleyn. Elizabethan Actor, Jacobean Gentleman*. London: Dulwich Picture Gallery, 1994.

—— and Marion Wynne-Davies (eds). *Renaissance Drama by Women: Texts and Documents*. London: Routledge, 1996.

Dollimore, Jonathan and Alan Sinfield (eds). *Political Shakespeares*. Manchester: Manchester University Press, 1985.

Dutton, Richard and Richard Wilson (eds). *New Historicism and Renaissance Drama*. London: Longman, 1992.

Evans, M. (ed.). *Elizabethan Sonnets*. London: J. M. Dent, 1977.

Ferguson, Margaret. 'Nashe's *The Unfortunate Traveller*. The "Newes of the Maker" Game', *English Literary Renaissance*, 11 (1981), 165–82.

Fish, Stanley Eugene. *Surprised by Sin: the Reader in Paradise Lost*. Berkeley, CA: University of California Press, 1967.

Foucault, Michel. *Madness and Civilisation. A History of Insanity in the Age of Reason* (1961), trans. Richard Howard. London: Tavistock Publications, 1967.

Fumerton, P. *Cultural Aesthetics. Renaissance Literature and the Practice of Social Ornament.* Chicago: University of Chicago Press, 1991.

Greenblatt, Stephen. *Sir Walter Ralegh.* New Haven, CT: Yale University Press, 1973.

——. *Renaissance Self-Fashioning. From More to Shakespeare.* Chicago: University of Chicago Press, 1980.

Gurr, Andrew (ed.). *King Richard II.* Cambridge: Cambridge University Press, 1984.

——. *The Shakespearean Stage 1574–1642.* Cambridge: Cambridge University Press, 1992 (third edition).

Hager, A. 'The Exemplary Mirage: Fabrication of Sir Philip Sidney's Biographical Image and the Sidney Reader', in *Sir Philip Sidney. An Anthology of Modern Criticism*, ed. D. Kay. Oxford: Clarendon Press, 1987, pp. 45–60.

Harper, Charles G. *The Bunyan Country.* Oxford: Kemp Hall Press, 1928.

Hawkes, Terence. *That Shakespeherian Rag.* London: Methuen, 1986.

Hill, Christopher. *Milton and the English Revolution.* London: Faber and Faber, 1977.

Howard, Jean. *Stage and Social Struggle in Early Modern England.* London: Routledge, 1994.

Jones, A. R. and Stallybrass, P. 'The Politics of *Astrophil and Stella*', *Studies in English Literature*, 24 (1984), 53–68.

Jusserand, J. J. *The English Novel in the Time of Shakespeare.* London: Ernest Benn, 1890.

Kastan, David Scott (ed.). *A Companion to Shakespeare.* Oxford: Blackwell, 1999.

Kay, D. *Melodious Tears. The English Funeral Elegy from Spenser to Milton.* Oxford: Clarendon Press, 1990.

Kirkpatrick, Robin. *English and Italian Literature from Dante to Shakespeare. A Study of Source, Analogue and Divergence.* London: Longman, 1995.

Korda, Natasha. 'Household Kates: Domesticating Commodities in *The Taming of the Shrew*', in M. Wynne-Davies (ed.), *'Much Ado About Nothing' and 'The Taming of the Shrew'*. New Casebook, London: Palgrave – now Palgrave Macmillan, 2001, pp. 192–25.

Latham, Agnes (ed.). *The Poems of Sir Walter Ralegh.* London: Constable, 1929.

Lilley, Kate (ed.), Margaret Cavendish, *The description of a new world called the blazing world and other writings.* London: Pickering and Chatto, 1992.

Lindley, David. *The Trials of Frances Howard.* London: Routledge, 1993.

Maslen, R. W. *Elizabethan Fictions.* Oxford: Clarendon Press, 1997.

Minta, Stephen. *Petrarch and Petrarchanism.* Manchester: Manchester University Press, 1980.

Nicholl, Charles. *The Reckoning. The Murder of Christopher Marlowe.* London: Cape, 1992.

Osborn, J. *Young Philip Sidney.* New Haven, CT: Yale University Press, 1972.

Pooley, Roger. *English Prose of the Seventeenth Century, 1590–1700.* London: Longman, 1992.

Rhodes, Neil. *Elizabethan Grotesque.* London: Routledge, 1980.

Royal Shakespeare Company. *Twelfth Night Programme.* Stratford: RSC, 1991.

Salzman, Paul. *English Prose Fiction 1558–1700. A Critical History.* Oxford: Clarendon Press, 1985.

——. (ed.). *An Anthology of Seventeenth-Century Prose Fiction.* Oxford: Oxford University Press, 1991.

Sharrock, Roger (ed.). *Bunyan. The Pilgrim's Progress.* London: Macmillan – now Palgrave Macmillan, 1976.

Shepard, Simon (ed.). *The Women's Sharp Revenge: Five Women's Pamphlets from the Renaissance.* London: Fourth Estate, 1985.

Sinfield, A. *Faultlines. Cultural Materialism and the Politics of Dissident Reading.* Oxford: Clarendon Press, 1992.

Waller, G. *English Poetry of the Sixteenth Century.* London: Longman, 1986.

Wilcox, Helen (ed.). *Women and Literature in Britain, 1500–1700.* Cambridge: Cambridge University Press, 1996.

Wolfe, Don M. *Milton and His England.* Princeton, NJ: Princeton University Press, 1971.

Woolf, Virginia, 'The Duchess of Newcastle', in *The Common Reader. First Series.* London: Hogarth Press, 1925.

Wynne-Davies, M. (ed.). *Women Poets of the Renaissance.* London: J. M. Dent, 1998.

Index